WAR VIRGIN

My Journey of Repression, Temptation and Liberation

A Memoir by

Laura Westley

ISBN: 0692766936
ISBN 13: 9780692766934
Library of Congress Control Number: 2016913416
War Virgin, Inc., Dunedin, FL

Edited by
Niva Dorell

Niva Dorell is a freelance writer, ghostwriter and editor with a background in film directing and screenwriting. She is a member of the American Society of Journalists and Authors (ASJA), Gotham Ghostwriters, Women in Film-Los Angeles, The Director's List and Film Fatales. Niva has a master's degree in filmmaking from University of Southern California and a bachelor's degree in communication from Temple University. She is currently writing a memoir based on her experiences as a wife, caregiver and widow, along with recovering from devastating loss. Niva blogs about her journey at RidingBitchblog.com, and she also co-founded WriteUP New York, a collective of professional writers and authors in upstate New York. Follow Niva on Twitter (@nivaladiva) and Instagram (@NivaDorell), and read more about her work at NivaDorell.com.

To My West Point Sisters,

Stop beating yourselves up for not being perfect. So many of you torture yourselves to be the perfect officer, leader, scholar, jock, wife, mother and daughter. You're human. Super human at that. You are the strongest, most intelligent, capable, generous and beautiful women I know. Revel in your amazingness. Delight in your power. Embrace your uniqueness. The world needs you. I need you. I'm so proud of you. I dedicate this book to you, my fellow warriors—my Sisterhood of the Traveling Trou.

Love,
War Virgin

DISCLAIMER

The events in this book are true as depicted. However, with the exception of certain individuals who agreed to be identified, all names and some identifying characteristics have been changed. Some events appear out of sequence and have been composited for the sake of clarity and brevity.

Map of Journey from Kuwait to Baghdad

20 March to 10 April 2003

Presented to 1LT Laura Westley on 10 April 2004 as a farewell gift from

Aviation Brigade, 3d Infantry Division (one year post combat operations)

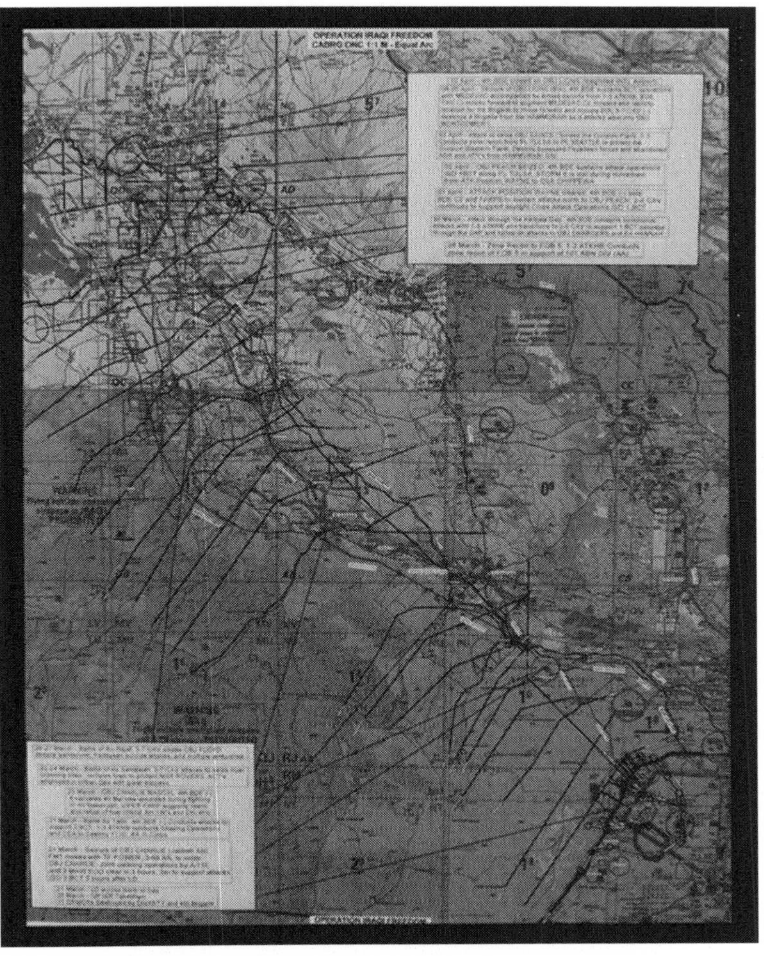

Map issued to 1LT Laura Westley for Journey from Kuwait to Baghdad

<Page intentionally left blank, just like my chain of command's intent to send me off to war with no map.>

PART 1

Repression

CHAPTER ONE

"I want you to put your hand on it," my boyfriend Connor whispered into my ear.

"You mean, on your… *cock*?"

"Yeah, I want you to touch it."

"Really?" I asked, surprised. Connor knew I had never touched a penis, despite being twenty years old. As leaders in the West Point Christian community, we were supposed to be as chaste and pure as possible. Penis touching, despite not being specifically mentioned in the Bible, was off-limits in my book.

"Yeah, go ahead."

"OK."

I nervously reached inside of Connor's pajama pants and gently ran my fingers over his penis. *I hope God isn't mad at me for doing this,* I thought.

"Can you start stroking it?"

I suppressed images of my West Point church mentors looking down on me in disgust.

"Can you squeeze it harder and stroke faster?"

"You mean you want me to give you a *hand job*?"

"Yes. I want a hand job."

I wrapped my entire hand firmly around his penis and stroked vigorously. Despite this being my first hand job, the mechanics felt natural, as if I were an old pro. Pushing aside heavy waves of guilt, I tried to enjoy bringing this form of pleasure to Connor.

He was pleased, because only three minutes later he finished, his semen squirting out on his stomach and into my hand. I marveled at the way it released in three fast sequential pumps, nothing like I had imagined after watching science documentaries about procreation. Its consistency also surprised me, as I had always assumed it to be thicker and stickier. Part of me wanted to hurry up and wipe the sin away. But a bigger part of me wanted to let it linger in my hand so I could study what it felt like, now that it was literally in my grasp and no longer a conceptual phenomenon I was supposed to avoid until marriage.

I was proud of this feat, proud of my accomplishment, proud that I could make my boyfriend feel so good. But I also felt like I no longer belonged to the club of pure and holy couples. I doubted any of the other girls in my Bible study group were giving their boyfriends hand jobs. *Oh well, nobody's perfect,* I thought, mildly annoyed at my lack of willpower. Before I could dwell more deeply on the sinful nature of my actions, Connor interrupted my thoughts.

"Now it's your turn."

"What do you mean?"

"I want to touch you."

"I don't know. Aren't we going a little too far?"

"I'll touch you through your panties, that way I'm not directly touching it."

"I guess that sounds all right." *He's supposed to be the leader in our relationship anyway.*

I held up my pajama pants so Connor could slip his hand inside. I had to admit, what he was doing felt good. Like, really good. I closed my eyes. *At least we're not sinning that badly... and when it's over, I'll still have my sparkle.*

⟿ ⟾

Back in high school, my father created home church. Every Sunday, he, my mother and I sat at the kitchen table for a Bible lecture and family prayer time. My father, who ordained himself the family pastor, always began home church by reading a Bible passage. Usually he read from the Book of Job, the infamous story of suffering and faith. My father thought he was like Job since he too was a dutiful Christian, despite having lost all of his money—after being sued for violating a noncompete agreement)—and having yet to find another source of employment. My mother worked as a teacher's assistant and spent what little money she earned mostly at the pharmacy on my father's prescription painkillers. We were broke, but we still loved Jesus. Daddy explained that our poverty was a direct result of Satan attacking our family. And Satan had launched his attack by targeting the weakest member.

Daddy never specified what criteria he used to designate the weakest family member, but it was usually whoever was most upset with him at the time. Sometimes I was the weakest member. Other times it was my mother. It was never my father. During family prayer time Daddy gave extra attention to the weakest family member by laying hands on us and chanting a rebuke to Satan.

Home church time also gave Daddy the perfect opportunity to launch into one of his infamous lectures about the dangers of my burgeoning hormones, and how they would ruin my chances of getting into a good college if I gave into them. "Boys are the devil," he told me.

I always performed well in school and had enough self-discipline, work ethic and ambition to set and achieve lofty goals, so no boy was ever going to derail me from being the top math student in my grade or graduating from a prestigious university. I wanted a good job that paid a lot of money, so I could buy a big, fancy house and drive something far nicer than my mom's '82 Chevy Caprice Classic. And I certainly didn't want to have to rely on a man to help me afford these things. But I guess Daddy didn't think that my 4.0 GPA in the ninth grade was enough proof that I was already well on my way down the straight and narrow path. Especially because that GPA was earned at a Florida school, while "Jewish kids in New York are training to kick your ass in college," as he constantly reminded me. So he sat me down at the kitchen table and began yet another lecture.

"Laura, if you lose your virginity, I will be able to tell."

"What?" I blurted out, my cheeks hot.

"Yes, if you ever have sex, I will be able to tell right away."

My father had been claiming mind-reading abilities for as long as I could remember, so any doubts were overcome with blind faith in his declaration. But the skeptic in me still needed a thorough explanation.

"Daddy, how can you do that?"

"Well, there's something special about a virgin. You can literally see her happiness and purity in her eyes. It's like a beautiful sparkle. But when that virgin has sex, you can tell because that sparkle disappears and gets replaced with a deep sadness. She becomes damaged goods."

I wanted to believe my infallible father, but needed more convincing. Was he insinuating that only nuns remain happy for life?

"But what about Mommy?" I inquired, pointing at my mom who was putting dirty dishes into the dishwasher, pretending not to play close attention, but hanging on to every word. She looked up at us when I called her out. "Mommy's obviously not a virgin. Are you saying that she's sad and that she's damaged goods?"

With only the slightest hesitation, my father answered, "If you wait to have sex until you're married, which is what you're supposed to do, that loss of innocence and purity is still a very unfortunate change in a woman's life."

I looked at my mother. Now that I thought about it, she did look rather sad. Needless to say, it was imperative that I did whatever it took to keep my sparkle intact. The idea that I had a special sparkle fascinated me. I wondered if other girls were aware of their sparkle, or was I privy to some special secret knowledge that their unfortunate souls would never know? If they did know about their sparkle, what were their sparkle preservation techniques? And how did my sparkle compare to theirs?

I began looking for sparkles everywhere, especially at the mall.

Guess the Slut became my new favorite game. I would inspect all of the lady shoppers, paying close attention to their eyes, trying to determine if they were still virgins or if they were slutty damaged goods. I determined that the sluts were more inclined to shop at stores like Wet Seal and The Body Shop, and the virgins preferred to build their wardrobes at Montgomery Ward. But even this focused approach still didn't yield a sparkle discovery. As a last resort, I conducted a comparative analysis between the eyes of my fellow Sunday school classmates with those of the "naughty girls" at my public school. But the only conclusion I was able to derive is that the naughty public school girls were far prettier than the church girls, and I secretly yearned to be more like the public school girls.

Regardless of never actually being able to see my sparkle, I was determined to keep it until marriage, and I knew I had the willpower to achieve my goal. When my youth group went away to a church camp in Tennessee, and we were all presented with virginity promise cards, I knew my signature was as good as gold. I questioned if the signatures from friends like Alyssa and Aaron were as valid, sensing a conflict in them wanting to do right by Jesus, but also experiencing powerful attractions to the opposite sex—but never did I doubt my own commitment. Boys, and especially sex with boys, didn't appeal to me in the least.

I learned about the birds and the bees when my Aunt Irene bought me the book, *How Babies Are Made*, for my third birthday (probably to piss off my parents since they were always torturing her about her hippie, free-loving ways). By the time I was four, I knew all about the mechanics of my reproductive system, courtesy of the colorful diagrams of a woman's ovaries, fallopian tubes and uterus. Other pages outlined the same body parts in cartoon drawings of flowers, chickens and dogs, complete with a cartoon dog sporting a giant erection.

Pages 65 and 66 explained how all of these body parts fit together in order to make a baby: "The sperm, which come from the father's testicles, are sent into the mother through his penis. To do this, the father and mother lie down facing each other and the father places his penis in the mother's vagina. Unlike plants and animals, when human mothers and fathers create a new baby, they are sharing a very personal and special relationship."

Up until I was fourteen, I assumed that sex merely involved a man sticking his penis inside of a woman's vagina and leaving it in there all night as they slept. Ironically, it was the movie *Schindler's List* that taught me differently, specifically the scene when a beautiful blond woman was running around a room, naked and screaming, being chased by a naked Liam Neeson.

I turned to my friend Alyssa and asked, "Why doesn't she run away?"

Alyssa giggled quietly and whispered in my ear, "Because they're having sex, silly."

"But he's raping her."

"No, he isn't."

"Then why is she screaming?"

"Because she's enjoying it!" Alyssa blurted out.

A couple of nearby moviegoers turned around to shush her.

"But they're bouncing around all over the place," I whispered.

"Laura, that's how people have sex."

I looked back at the screen, appalled. If that was how people had sex, I definitely wanted no part in it. I decided I would remain a virgin at least until marriage, and perhaps for life. Maybe my future husband would be OK with celibacy.

⁂

"I want to touch you without your underwear," Connor said.

"Really? I don't know," I replied. This went way beyond good Christian boundaries. I only agreed to let him touch me *outside* of my underwear.

"You should let me do it. I really want to touch you," he whispered in a sexy tone.

"I guess, if you think it's OK." To be honest, I was enjoying the sensation of him touching my most intimate parts. I lay there in pure ecstasy, enjoying his technique, when he said, "I want to try something I've never done to you before. Just relax."

"You don't mean sex, right?" That was out of the question, no matter how bad he wanted me.

"No, don't worry. Just relax," he promised and then scooted toward the foot of the bed, bringing his face up to my privates. I glanced down at him, he smiled and then starting licking. It was the most unbelievable feeling I had ever experienced, and I didn't want guilt to ruin the moment. I focused solely on the pleasure instead. Within two minutes, I exploded into an intense orgasm.

"Oh my God, that was unbelievable!" I screamed. I was quite vocal at expressing my sexual pleasure.

"I'm glad you liked it."

"Thank you so much."

"Of course." Connor lay next to me for a moment, proud of himself. Then he sat up. "Well, we should probably get ready for 500th Night."

"Yeah, time to put on our uniforms and act like soldiers," I sighed.

Connor and I got ready for my West Point class formal, celebrating 500 days until graduation, and drove back onto the campus. I walked around among my classmates and their dates feeling exhilarated, my heart racing. I gave a hand job and received oral sex for the first time, all without losing my sparkle or getting kicked out of West Point. I was walking on cloud nine.

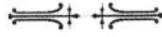

Little did I know that just three years later, I would be heading off to war, still a virgin, and encountering even more tempting situations in a far more dangerous, even life-threatening environment.

CHAPTER TWO

I arrived at West Point—The United States Military Academy—on June 30, 1997, to begin New Cadet Basic Training, a.k.a., "Beast." This was just three weeks after graduating from high school in New Port Richey, Florida (and two and a half years prior to celebrating 500th night with Connor). I was an eighteen-year-old virgin. My parents couldn't afford the airfare to New York, so my high school boyfriend's mother paid for the flight. Uncle Dominick (my mother's brother) picked me up from LaGuardia Airport and treated me to my last dinner as a civilian. The next morning, as we drove the hour-long trip from his home to West Point's upstate New York campus, through the majestic mountains that line each side of the Hudson River, I couldn't help but feel a tiny pang of regret. *Why do I always have to choose such uncomfortable, difficult life endeavors?*

I knew there would be a special ceremony at West Point for parents to say goodbye to their children. I'd read about it and seen pictures in the material included in the acceptance package, which showed proud parents tearfully wishing their soon-to-be-adult children well as they embarked on their new journey of becoming warriors. I dreaded it then, and I dreaded it now. My parents weren't sad to see me go, or at least they seemed happy to be rid of me. If they really wanted the best for me, they wouldn't have "borrowed" behind my back $3,000 worth of life savings, my gifts from relatives over the years, leaving me with only $42 to start my new life.

Uncle Dominick and I weren't that close. My parents badmouthed him when I was growing up and didn't allow me to have a relationship with him. They only reached out to him when they needed his help. He was gracious and hospitable, and I loved him, but hugging him goodbye in the midst of heartbroken families bidding their farewells was awkward and only reminded me of what I didn't have. As I watched him leave with all of the other families, I resisted the urge to run after his car and beg him to take me out of there. Instead, I turned around and faced the academy's foreboding campus. *Might as well get this over with.*

Basic training began with the infamous ritual of reporting to the Cadet in the Red Sash. Traditionally, this is such a nerve-racking, intimidating experience that I was warned about it in high school, two years in advance. So I'd spent months in front of my bedroom mirror practicing a crisp salute and shouting: "SIR NEW CADET

WESTLEY REPORTS TO THE CADET IN THE RED SASH FOR THE FIRST TIME AS ORDERED!"

Once I felt satisfied with that, I moved on to the only four phrases I would be allowed to utter in the presence of upperclassmen: "Yes Sir;" "No Sir;" "No excuse Sir;" "Sir, I do not understand." I practiced these responses so much that by the time I arrived at West Point, I could execute them perfectly in my sleep.

When it was my turn to approach the Cadet in the Red Sash, I saluted him just as rehearsed, "SIR NEW CADET WESTLEY REPORTS TO THE CADET IN THE RED SASH FOR THE FIRST TIME AS ORDERED!" He returned my salute according to proper military protocol. Then I dropped my salute and waited for further instructions.

I stood there feeling great. I fucking nailed it! I figured that the rest of our interaction would go smoothly. But the one thing I hadn't anticipated was that the Cadet in the Red Sash would be a drop-dead gorgeous hunk.

As his crystal blue eyes stared into my green eyes for what seemed like an eternity, I started imagining him unbuttoning his crisp white uniform shirt, revealing his bulging muscles, taking me into his arms and...

"New Cadet, are you wearing contact lenses?" he yelled, interrupting my fantasy.

"Yes Sir!" I responded, trying not to blush. *So he was staring at my eyes!*

"You're dismissed," he said curtly. Then he looked past me to the next new cadet.

My heart sank with disappointment. *What the fuck?* All of that hype, and it was over just like that. I was confused by the contact lenses question, but there was no one to ask, so I simply marched on, following the other new cadets to a room with a long row of chairs. Behind each chair stood a West Point official holding a pair of scissors. My stomach tightened.

⁂

"Laura, look at your hair. It's disgusting." My father glanced at me sitting on the toilet cover in his bathroom. Since I was a little girl, it had always been our morning ritual that I would watch him shave.

My nine-year-old hand immediately shot up to touch my hair. "What's wrong with it?" I asked. I was already plagued with insecurity that I wasn't as pretty as a lot of the popular girls at elementary school, like the two Kristis with their matching permed hair, designer clothes and bright white smiles.

"It's too long," my father said, pulling the razor slowly down his cheek.

"It is?" I was surprised. My hair only went an inch past my shoulders.

"Yes, you need a simple pixie cut."

"I don't want my hair that short, Daddy. I'll look like a boy." Then I winced with the sudden realization that I'd fallen right into his trap.

Daddy openly lamented that I wasn't born a boy and that he didn't have a son. He often said, "I wish you'd been born a boy. Then I'd have a son instead of a lousy daughter."

To compensate for this missed opportunity, he used to dress me like a boy when I was a toddler and insist that my hair be kept short. I quickly learned that acting like a boy garnered positive attention, especially when I belched out loud or engaged in a back and forth game of pull-my-finger. Farts made Daddy laugh the hardest. His bellowing laugh let me temporarily forget his temper, which was just as explosive as his laughter. I never knew what would set him off. Sometimes me just looking like a girl pissed him off.

"You should look like a boy." He suddenly grabbed the scissors that were laying on the counter and with one movement chopped off a chunk of my hair.

"What did you do that for?" I cried.

"It's for your own good."

"But I didn't want a haircut!" I stood up to stare in the mirror at my lopsided head.

"Just let me finish it," he assured me, still holding the scissors, his face half-covered with shaving cream.

I reluctantly turned myself over to his scissors and imagination. He seemed so happy and content, chopping away. When he finished, he stepped back, smiling.

"That's more like it," he declared.

"I look too young." I frowned at my reflection. My hair was now just above my ears in an awkward-looking, bowl-like bob. I wanted to cry.

"You look cute," he pinched my cheeks and returned to shaving the rest of his face.

I sat in the chair and held back my emotions as my hair was chopped to an inch below my ears.

A few hours after meeting the Cadet in the Red Sash, I finally understood why he asked if I wore contact lenses. Another upperclassman handed me the most hideous pair of glasses ever manufactured in world history.

"New Cadet, contact lenses and civilian glasses are prohibited during basic training. We acquired these glasses for you; they're your prescription. Do you have any questions?"

"No Sir!"

When I got to my new barracks room, I removed my contacts, donned the brown, thick plastic rimmed contraption and stared at my reflection in the mirror. Between the glasses, my new ill-fitting uniform and my hair that now barely brushed past the bottom of my ears, I didn't recognize myself. *Holy shit? I'm really fucking ugly!*

So much for the 7:1 male to female ratio. The only way I would ever attract a guy in this condition was if I were the last woman on the face of the planet, and the future of the human race required my ovaries to continue existing. As I would learn later, these glasses were unofficially dubbed "birth-control goggles."

Not that I needed birth control or was even trying to get laid. I had Tim, my high school boyfriend, waiting for me in Florida, and I was determined to keep my sparkle until marriage. When I had thumbed through West Point's thick orientation package, I realized that, in this respect at least, I definitely picked the right school. West Point had thousands of rules that governed every facet of human conduct imaginable, including absolutely no sex in the dorm rooms, a.k.a. barracks.

Lucky for me, and in contrast to many of my fellow healthy, red-blooded young cadets, getting laid was my lowest priority. The ban on sex and the accountability infrastructure reminiscent of the Vatican didn't bother me at all. But even a virgin wants to look pretty.

CHAPTER THREE

New Cadet Basic Training lasted seven weeks. Each day started at 0500 hours (5:00 a.m.) with the upperclassmen (who were responsible for running basic training) banging on our doors, screaming at us to wake up. Their authority made them seem decades older, when in reality, they'd gone through the same training themselves only two or three years prior.

Upon wakeup, we had just a few minutes to throw on our gym clothes, run outside and form up for reveille. During reveille, we stood at full attention and saluted as bugles played, cannons fired and the American flag rose above our heads in what was literally dawn's early light. I wasn't moved. Instead of focusing on the magnitude of this ritual, which thousands of troops around the globe were practicing at the same time (or in their respective time zones), I cursed my existence and fantasized about going back to bed.

After reveille, we followed the upperclassmen to the outdoor training field for physical training (PT), where they led us in group exercises and thankfully refrained from hazing us. They demonstrated each exercise and did every repetition with us, teaching us that, "Good leaders never ask their people to do anything that they're not capable of doing"—a lesson I would adopt and apply for the rest of life. They motivated us to try our best and push beyond our limits. Building morale was an important aspect of PT and West Point in general. It was supposed to keep us cohesive, loyal and less likely to surrender or give up in the face of opposition or hardship.

After forty-five minutes of group exercise, we left the field for a formation run around West Point's campus. One person ran at the head of our formation carrying a small flag, a.k.a. guidon, that represented our unit's designation. Another person ran at the back of our formation calling out phrases, a.k.a. cadences, which we responded to as a group. The upperclassmen let us take turns carrying the guidon, and sometimes they even let us call cadence. Depending on what run group placed into after an initial qualification test (green, blue, gray and gold), we would run anywhere from two to five miles.

To qualify for the elite green group, one had to run two miles under thirteen minutes. Only the lightning fast cadets qualified for the green group, including a few women who ended up being our cross-country track stars. The blue group consisted of cadets who could run two miles in under fourteen minutes. I placed in the gray group after running my two miles in under sixteen minutes. The gold group was for all of the cadets who needed more than sixteen minutes for their two-mile runs. While the fastest cadets received a lot of affirmation, no one seemed judgmental about our run times.

Not everyone at West Point is a strong runner. If we fell out of formation and had a difficult time keeping up, an upperclassman would hang back and cheer us on until the end. I didn't mind running, as long as I didn't have to call cadence up the steep hills, which never failed to make me out of breath and fall behind. At first, I was surprised by how nice the upperclassmen were during run time. Then I realized some of them were also struggling to keep up.

After the run, we had about fifteen minutes to go back to our rooms, shower, dress and be in breakfast formation with our rooms in inspection-ready condition. Cleaning our rooms wasn't too difficult—they were already Spartan-like, furnished with metal-framed twin-sized beds, scuffed desks, vinyl chairs circa 1960 and our personal storage trunks. But making our bed according to SOP (standard operating procedure) was challenging.

Both our sheets and wool gray blankets needed to be taut and have crisp hospital corners. The easiest way around this was to sleep on top of our blankets and not "break sheets." But at TAPS each evening, when the upperclassmen did accountability checks, if we weren't tucked under the sheets, they would mess up our beds, so we would have to remake them. Needless to say, making beds took away from ample shower time. Not that I wanted to linger in the shower rooms any longer than necessary.

While the barracks were co-ed, we were only allowed to have roommates of the same gender. Luckily, West Point had separate bathrooms for men and women. But that still didn't prevent my embarrassment at having to shower in front of all of the women in my unit. There were only about five showerheads for twenty women, so from day one, we were ordered to buddy up. This was shortly after our first urinalysis drug screening, where a female upperclassman had to chaperone me going to the bathroom, and I got stage fright. Eventually I overcame my public-nudity shyness, which included being able to piss on command, but not without one of the most humiliating life experiences I could possibly imagine.

About three weeks into basic training, I had the rare opportunity to take a long shower on a Sunday afternoon. My roommate accompanied me and because there were no upperclassmen around, she started chatting—a stark violation. New cadets weren't allowed to talk outside of their rooms unless approached by an upperclassman. I barely responded and quietly warned her about breaking the rules, but she just kept chatting. Soon enough, Cadet Karen Stonato walked in and heard us.

Standing at four feet nine inches, Cadet Stonato had a mouth to compensate for her tiny stature. She was mean, especially to other women, and she never broke her stern demeanor, not for a second. Eventually a lot of the upperclassmen allowed their personalities to show through, but Cadet Stonato always portrayed herself as a pissed off woman who was going to make everyone in her path suffer.

"NEW CADETS, FREEZE!" Cadet Stonato shouted.

Oh shit. I hoped she would simply tell us to shut up and then allow us to finish showering, but Cadet Stonato always brought discipline to a new level.

"Turn around and face me!" she commanded.

I could tell my roommate had the same slight hesitation I did before locking up to Cadet Stonato, i.e. standing with perfect posture and hands cupped at our sides. Our two showerheads kept running behind us, and soapsuds adorned our naked bodies. Cadet Stonato began a tirade, reminding us about the rules, chastising us for being bad new cadets. The longer she carried on, the more I began to wonder if she was really into discipline, or if she was secretly perverted, not in a sexual sense, but more in delighting at our complete humiliation.

In the middle of her lecture, she kept asking us if we understood.

"Yes Ma'am!" we responded in naked robotic fashion. Finally, she had enough and released us. Cadet Stonato left, and my roommate and I finished our showers in silence. Later I learned that naked shower hazes weren't all that uncommon at West Point.

Every meal took place in the grand mess hall. Unfortunately, the same attention given to its grandeur was not paid to the quality of our food, which included Grade D meat delivered in a truck that said "For Institutional Use Only." The mess hall was a fascinating display of organization and attention to detail at its finest.

We sat at assigned tables of ten people, with our squad leader, dubbed the Table Commandant, at the head of the table. Before being allowed to eat, we had to perform a ritual of table duties, like opening the new jar of peanut butter and removing its foil. If an upperclassman happened to open it and discover that a new cadet failed at this duty, they would begin a lecture about attention to detail, and how failing to open the peanut butter was a foreshadowing of killing our platoon in battle, due to our gross negligence. I hated these analogies and refrained from rolling my eyes at this logic.

Once our Table Commandant allowed us to eat, we commenced a ritualized charade: cut meat, place knife back in its proper place on the side of the plate, use fork to place meat inside of mouth, place fork back in its proper place on the side of the plate, place hands on lap, stare directly at crest on plate, chew-chew-chew-chew-chew (only three to five chews per bite), swallow. Repeat.

Table commandants could make us stop eating at any time for a number of reasons: if they thought someone was chewing too much, if someone wasn't stoic enough or if they just felt the urge to tell a joke. Sometimes it was nice seeing their more human side when they wanted to joke around, but it interfered with eating time, which we barely had enough of to complete a meal. Soon I started to overcompensate by eating well past the point of fullness when a Table Commandant left us in peace. We weren't allowed to have any food back in our rooms, so this was our only opportunity to eat. I needed to make the most of it.

It only took a few weeks for me to gain the Freshman 15—ironically, the one element that united me with new collegiates across America, minus all of the fun debauchery and underage beer guzzling. One might wonder how a West Point new cadet could rapidly gain so much weight, especially during basic training, when half of the day is spent doing some form of athletic activity. The culprit: Mess Hall food!

I showed up to West Point a lean and muscular 124 pounds due to my rigorous preparation and self-imposed strict diet. But when you have no say in your nutrition plan, and are subject to meals of greasy meatloaf and Doritos, it can turn any hot little bod into the Stay Puft Marshmallow Man. That and my new habit of food guzzling during meals.

To add insult to injury, we were forced to weigh in publicly every week, so all of the guys could keep tabs on my hip and thigh expansion: 124 pounds… 128 pounds… 133 pounds… 136 pounds… 139 pounds.

"New Cadet, how the hell are you gaining so much weight?" an upperclassman yelled at me.

"No excuse Sir!"

Soon I embodied the urban legend about the Hudson Theta—the name of the angle between a female West Point cadet's thigh and the shaft of the saber she wears for parades. Every year that angle gets bigger and bigger…

It was heart-wrenching enough to feel ugly, but then I felt fat on top of it. Just when I lamented the loss of my femininity altogether, we were forced to chant a new battle cry: "WE ARE NOT MEN, WE ARE BEASTS, FOR YOU HAVE MADE US BEASTS!" I wondered what would happen if I tried to use that as a pickup line in a bar. In any case, it would only take me 14 years to shed my extra West Point tire and resume my pre-Army weight.

I never bought into the theory that eating in this rigid manner or folding my panties into thirds for inspection (an actual rule in the SOP) instilled the kind of discipline that would make me a better leader. We were young but technically adults, and smart ones at that. Even in my West Point infancy, I could distinguish the importance between policing up my peanut butter and panties versus ensuring my troops were ready for battle. *And what exactly did battle mean in this day and age?* Most of these so-called rituals seemed like hazing for the sake of hazing, an opportunity for bragging rights. I wanted to be left alone so I had more bandwidth to focus on more important things—like my actual education. But strangely, that didn't seem to be the top priority.

The rest of basic training was spent either in the classroom or outside, learning how to parade. Classes taught us about West Point's history and way of doing things. I enjoyed being able to sit down in an air-conditioned room (the barracks had no AC), but sleep always threatened to consume me, and if we couldn't stay awake, we were ordered to stand in the back of the classroom. My favorite time in the classroom was when we departed from our typical West Point knowledge sessions and took academic placement exams. I delighted at working my brain in this familiar manner and ended up acing all of them, not surprising since most of the exams were similar to my high school AP exams.

West Point told me that I could skip a whole year of freshman chemistry (I opted to take it anyway, because this would be my major) and the first semester of English. I was also placed in advanced classes for economics, world history and computer science (huge mistake, as I had never studied computer programming before).

My least favorite activity was learning to drill. I loathed marching around like toy soldiers, carrying a heavy M14 rifle, learning to coordinate our steps and movements. Being short made it nearly impossible to stay in step, and all of the petite cadets were scolded to stop bouncing, something that naturally happens when trying to keep up with the guys in front who were ten inches taller. It was obvious that drill was more about impressing the general public than teaching us good order and discipline, especially the rich older grads who would attend the parades. Whether the administration admits it or not, West Point relies heavily on hefty private donations, and sucking up to wealthy alumni is a big part of its mission. The only way I got around participating in this farce was by eventually becoming a parade announcer.

Our days finally ended at 2200 hours (10:00 p.m.). My roommates immediately collapsed into bed, but I seemed to always have a pile of clothes to fold and put away, or some other chore that had to be finished before morning. Instead of offering to help, my roommates criticized me for being too slow. After a few weeks of listening to their shit, I scolded them for not embodying West Point's value of teamwork. But this only made things worse. I had falsely assumed that West Point cadets would share a deep bond with one another and step in if someone was struggling. But these ladies were clearly out to fend for themselves.

In a way, their attitude made sense. As much as West Point prides itself on teaching values like duty, selfless service and teamwork, it also forced us to compete with each other... in EVERYTHING. It wasn't just about who earned the highest grades, but who was the strongest and fastest, who shined their shoes the brightest, and so on. We were constantly compared to and graded against one another, especially as women. This extra pressure made it tough to form bonds with the other women, because the competition among our gender felt even more fierce.

Teams competed against each other for certain accolades, but individuals were highlighted and then evaluated for a military grade. Our smallest unit of division was the squad, consisting of about seven to eight cadets. For the military grade, only one cadet in the squad was allowed to earn the A. Two cadets could earn Bs, and then everyone else had to earn Cs. Naturally, I earned Cs. So did my roommates.

Some of the guys in my squad had gone to the Military Academy Prep School (USMAPS) in New Jersey, so they knew everything cold. But I was starting from ground zero. As soon as I learned about the cadet ranking structure and realized I was being judged in every facet of my character, demeanor and personality, I uncharacteristically gave up trying to get As. I would never stand a chance to do well militarily, especially when the grades were subjective and determined by my squad leader. I wasn't going to change who I was for some college kid who was barely older than me. *There's just no point,* I thought. *I have zero control over this.* That realization ended up being the biggest takeaway from basic training and pervading theme as I formally began my West Point education as a freshman.

CHAPTER FOUR

"The Imperial March" from *The Empire Strikes Back* played forebodingly as new cadet basic training ended and we migrated to our academic year companies. All of the upperclassmen who had been away on other summer assignments (not just the ones who ran our basic training) waited for our arrival. They were clad in long, gray raincoats, which made me imagine Darth Vader emerging from the barracks, blending right in as one of the upperclassmen. Instead of feeling frightened or nervous, I had to stop myself from laughing. This welcome was entirely too cliché. Not long after, I became known as a laugher, someone who easily broke military decorum, because any cadet's attempt to haze was just so damn funny.

As a member of company F-1, I delved into "normal" cadet life. Freshman, a.k.a., plebes, have no say in their course curriculum, as most classes are mandatory in accordance with a rigid syllabus, and majors aren't declared until sophomore year. But I knew that I wanted to major in chemistry and minor in nuclear engineering. (All cadets are required to select one of seven engineering sequences, the equivalent of a minor.) My days were consumed with classes like Discrete Dynamic Systems, an absurd math class that even being the president of my high school math club couldn't have prepared me for, World History, Literature, PE and Advanced Computer Science. For some reason the academic gods thought it made sense to put me in an advanced computer science class because I had placed out of so many other classes, but the best grade I could muster while learning the programming language C++ was a C+. Unfortunately, my instructor awarded no extra credit for the irony.

Time management was a skill I had yet to master. I tried to do all of my homework, just like I did in high school, but military duties and parade practice prevented me from starting my homework until around 7 or 8 p.m. Even though TAPS was at 11:30 p.m., and lights out was at midnight, I often stayed up until 3 a.m. With breakfast formation just before 0700 hours, I was constantly in a state of narcolepsy due to sleeping for only three to four hours every night. If the whole West Point experience was about transforming us from young men and women into warriors, no one warned us just how tough it would be on our bodies. Mine had an especially hard time adjusting. Sometimes, though, I thought the men had it even worse.

When the guys discovered the loss of their morning wood during basic training, panic quickly spread that our mess hall food was contaminated with saltpeter, a potassium nitrate compound the military has long been rumored to secretly put in its food to suppress new recruits' sexual urges. But the upperclassmen reassured them that their boner disappearance was due entirely to stress, and they admitted that it had happened to all of them during basic training too. They promised that as soon as the new cadets completed basic training, their phantom erections would return.

And return they did—often at the most inopportune times, like when asked to "take boards" and write out math homework on the chalkboard. I thought our polyester uniform pants did a horrible job of camouflaging my bubble butt; apparently, they were completely incapable of concealing spontaneous arousal. None of the guys could explain why this happened. It's not like my pudgy presence did anything to turn them on. But they made do. Seeing a guy holding a textbook—or his hands—in front of his crotch became a regular occurrence. Concealing my propensity for sleeping in class (and drooling all over my desk) proved to be more challenging.

Sleep deprivation seemed to serve as a kind of weeding out mechanism. The students who eventually rose to the top of the class weren't necessarily the smartest—they were the ones who could handle little to no sleep better than everyone else. For me, it was a genuine struggle to keep up, regardless of my skills and natural discipline. My personal life also unraveled. Trying to keep a long distance relationship alive (at eighteen years old) with weekly phone calls that lasted no more than ten minutes proved too much to bear. (Ironically West Point and my father both enforced ten-minute phone call limits.) Tim and I agreed to break up in the middle of my first semester. No hard feelings.

I unexpectedly enjoyed my PE classes, especially swimming and gymnastics, even though the gymnastics course seemed like it was designed to torture women. We were graded on skills like "ankles to the bar," which required us to hang from a monkey bar and lift our asses up to our heads. (Note: While a comprehensive study has yet to be conducted, it's safe to assume that no soldier has ever needed this skill in combat.) Then there was the infamous asbestos-laden, vomit-inducing IOCT—the Indoor Obstacle Course Test—replete with using the heel of your foot to thrust your body over a six-foot-high shelf and leaping over a high wall, which I couldn't execute without smashing my boobs into it. I think my A cups, small stature and pretending to be Nadia Comaneci as a child enabled me to not only pass this test, but actually earn a coveted "tab." Many of my other classmates, not just the women, didn't fare so well, and the IOCT was known as the ultimate haze. (Another note: Studies have yet to be conducted to determine the correlation between running the IOCT and developing lung cancer.)

Every physical fitness test had separate grading scales for men and women—which sparked a lot of debate. I didn't think much of it at the time and accepted that women were perceived as weaker than men, because this made it easier to get a higher grade, and I was all about trying to achieve the highest GPA possible. Sure, according to biology, men are supposed to be stronger and faster, but at West Point, this wasn't necessarily the case. Being surrounded by some super human women showed me it really depends on the individual and specific physical task. I tried to block out whenever I heard a male cadet complain that the women were getting over. Sometimes I wanted to yell, "You have no idea how hard it is to be a woman here!" but instead, I just made sure I kicked their asses by training extra hard.

I quickly rose to the top 10 percent of my class in the physical category. It felt weird but cool to be rewarded more for my "jock" skills instead of my "nerd" skills. Unfortunately for me, though, the physical grade only accounted for 10 percent of our overall GPA. My first semester I earned a 3.25 academic GPA, substantially lower than high school, but for West Point, pretty damn good—and good enough for the dean's list.

I came home to Florida that first Christmas and promptly fell asleep for fifteen hours the first night. When I woke up the next day, my father was sitting in the living room holding my report card, which was mailed to my parents at the end of each term. His eyes rose from the piece of paper to my tired face. "I'm disappointed in you, Laura," he said. "You're not trying hard enough." Too tired to defend myself, I simply turned around and went back to bed. He continued to berate me for "half-assing West Point" for the rest of my vacation, which frustrated me to no end. I was sure that my fellow classmates' families were applauding them just for *surviving* the first term, let alone if any of them had made the dean's list. The thought of dropping out and running away from home momentarily flashed in my mind. *Why was I even trying to go to this godforsaken school?*

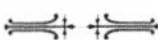

I was studying at the kitchen table when my father came home with the *U.S. News & World Report* issue that ranked all of the colleges in the United States. He called me over to his La-Z-Boy recliner chair in the living room and proceeded to read out loud about the top ten schools. At fourteen years old, I was already starting to think about college. I stood by his chair, trying to picture myself at schools like Harvard, Princeton and Stanford. I knew they were good schools, but the descriptions didn't do anything for me. Then my father read the feature for the United States Military Academy at West Point. Whether it was the narrative itself or the palatable enthusiasm in his voice, something resonated with me:

"The U.S. Military Academy is a four-year co-educational federal undergraduate liberal arts college located 50 miles north of New York City. The world's pre-eminent leader development institution, it was founded in 1802 as America's first college of engineering. Its mission remains constant—to educate, train, and inspire the Corps of Cadets so that each graduate is a commissioned leader of character committed to the values of Duty, Honor, Country and prepared for a career of professional excellence and service to the Nation as an officer in the United States Army."

Beside the picture was a photo of the graduating cadets throwing their hats into the air.

"Could you imagine yourself belonging to this elite group of people?" my father asked. I didn't answer right away. Challenges didn't scare me, but West Point was at a completely different level.

My father tapped the picture with his finger, "That's the epitome of short-term sacrifice and long-term happiness." This was his infamous mantra for me.

I stared at the picture and tried to imagine myself as one of those cadets in uniform… marching with hundreds of my fellow cadets, proudly carrying the American flag, my father sitting in the bleachers looking down on me proudly. *Maybe the sacrifices would be well worth it.*

The following day at school, I started telling my classmates, "I'm going to go to West Point." They laughed. When I told my teachers, some of them also seemed to hold back laughter. I was a scrawny, awkward fourteen-year-old girl with ugly red plastic-framed glasses and low self-esteem. Smart, yes. But Army material I was not. How would I ever get into West Point?

My father and I researched the application process. West Point ranked its applicants in three key areas: academics, physical fitness and leadership (the same categories it uses to rank its own cadets). It also required each applicant to obtain a congressional nomination. If I wanted to ensure acceptance into this esteemed institution, I was going to have to spend my entire time in high school carefully selecting activities that would impress both the admissions officers and my Florida congressional staff.

Academics were a given. From the time I was little, academics had been paramount in my household, even trumping family time and religion. Daddy was an anomaly at Calvary Temple because his number one passion was science. He had won the New York City science fair as a teenager and was very proud of this accomplishment. He blamed the fact that he didn't have a college degree on growing up in the Bronx without a father. Since I had a father and didn't live in the Bronx, there was absolutely no excuse for not getting straight As in every AP and honors class offered in my school. Any time I came up short, he reminded me that he had won the New York City science fair at the same age.

Often, it seemed like homework was more important than God. While a lot of my Christian friends believed the Bible's creation story literally, I knew that seven days was just a metaphor. When debating creationism with my friends, I used carbon-14 dating as proof, something I learned back in elementary school. Daddy used to say things like, "Jesus didn't use computers, but just because they're not mentioned in the Bible doesn't mean that they're bad," to teach me how science and religion could coexist. And the one thing that was drummed into my brain as early as I could remember was that I would one day attend a prestigious university.

After the ninth grade, my father convinced the school board to allow him to take me out of high school for a year so he could homeschool me. I had skipped kindergarten at the recommendation of my teachers (because my parents already taught me the entire curriculum), so I was already a year younger than the rest of my classmates. Despite skipping kindergarten being a good move for my academic acceleration, my father later told me that he regretted this decision because of my social awkwardness and immaturity. I think Daddy especially freaked out at the stories I shared with him about my fellow ninth graders dating seniors, drinking and smoking pot—and this was at a Catholic school!

I spent my homeschooling year under his tutelage, watching educational videos, reading textbooks and completing homework he assigned. I enjoyed learning this way and had a lot of self-motivation. Daddy was happy with my progress and proud of eliminating bad social influences.

I also spent this homeschool year accompanying my father to the gym and kicking my fitness into high gear. He taught me how to use all of the Nautilus machines and encouraged me to use them regularly, which caused me to quickly gain fifteen pounds of muscle. Being strong and muscular garnered a lot of positive attention from Daddy, but I still felt conflicted with my new body. My clothes didn't fit anymore. I didn't like having big thighs, and I felt less pretty. One day, while gazing at my new frame in my bedroom mirror, a wave of anger overtook me, and I suddenly kicked the wall (to my surprise), creating a big hole. My father was furious about the damage, but I could tell that a part of him was secretly proud of my newfound strength.

After my year of homeschooling, I started tenth grade at the local public school, because my parents couldn't afford the Catholic school tuition anymore. Plus, the Catholic school was over an hour away, and it didn't have enough clubs and organizations that I needed to join in order to satisfy West Point's leadership requirements.

As soon as the school year started, I joined the National Honor Society, Math Club, French Club,

Community Service Club and Student Council (as a class representative). I also made the junior varsity basketball team—motivated by my father's promise that I could start wearing contact lenses if I secured a spot—and I made the golf team, which was completely expected.

My father had encouraged me to start playing golf when I was thirteen. Initially, it was a time for us to enjoy each other's company and relax in the great outdoors. But as my game improved, and it became apparent that I was going to be the top female golfer in my school district, my father would become furious if I didn't play perfectly. Ironically, he always claimed to be too busy or sick to attend any of my high school matches, but after I got home, he made me give him a play-by-play recap of my match. He didn't accept fatigue and stress from academic pressures as a valid excuse for a poor performance.

The summers in between school years, he entered me into a golf league and attended those Saturday matches religiously. His presence on the sidelines, yellow legal pad in hand to document every swing I took, made me nervous. I botched almost every tournament. On the long drive home, he forced me to analyze everything I did wrong and discuss how to avoid it in the future. One day I finally told him, "I'd do better if you weren't there."

"You need to know how to handle pressure," he responded. "I'm doing you a favor."

Berating me for getting a bad grade was also doing me a favor, like the time I got a 96 (out of 100) on a chemistry quiz.

"Why did you only get a 96?" he asked.

"Oh come on, Daddy, I missed one silly question. A 96 is good. You should be happy for me."

"How dare you talk to me that way!" he yelled as he jumped up to hit me. I ran to my room and locked the door. He started beating and kicking the door so hard that the wood started to split. Fearing that it would break apart, I unlocked the door and accepted my fate. He whipped me with a belt until my arms, back and legs were red and swollen. At that moment I wished him dead. *How does someone get an A on a quiz and get their ass beat for it?*

My razor sharp focus in high school left barely any time to socialize. My weekdays consisted of waking up at 5:30 a.m. for a five-mile run, school and golf practice. I lifted weights on days that I didn't have practice. Taking all AP and honors classes left me with several hours' worth of homework in the evenings. Strangely, the better I did in school, the more demanding my father became. It wasn't enough that I had a perfect GPA. I had to be the top student in every single one of my classes. If someone else beat me on a test, my father blamed it on my desire to have some semblance of a social life.

"Wanting friends and needing people is a huge weakness," he told me.

"Daddy, I'm sorry, but I don't like being all by myself. I deserve to have some fun. I work so hard."

He had few friends of his own and spent his free time reading, watching TV and keeping tabs on my achievements, so having my way was next to impossible.

"It's a shame I couldn't raise you on a deserted island," he said, shaking his head. "Then you wouldn't be influenced by your worthless friends, and I would have complete control over everything."

He's disgusting, I thought. *And West Point might just end up being easier than this hellhole.*

Despite my father's obsession with my West Point candidacy, we never actually spoke about the military. No one in the family had ever served, and my father was medically discharged from Marine Corps basic training due to a pre-existing condition that should have prevented him from joining in the first place. I knew I would have a five-year active duty Army obligation upon graduating from West Point, but we just pushed that fact aside and focused on getting there. Whenever anyone asked why I wanted to go to West Point, I simply said, "I want to be a military doctor." My father coached me to say, "I want to serve my country" during all of my interviews, but I didn't really understand what that meant. I must have done a great job acting because everyone bought it.

CHAPTER FIVE

Despite catching up on sleep during Christmas vacation, I returned to West Point feeling even worse. Having unsupportive parents, irritable roommates and no boyfriend undermined my usually upbeat demeanor. I also didn't realize my susceptibility to seasonal affective disorder, as this was my first bout with a bitter cold, gray winter in the Northeast. But what stung the most is that I knew I didn't fit it, and it was going to be a long three and a half years until the finish line.

Everyone else seemed to love West Point a lot more than I did. Sure, we were all stressed and exhausted and loved to complain about it, but other cadets acted like they wouldn't have chosen any other path for their lives, and I often fantasized about being anywhere *but* West Point. Their love for West Point came pouring out of their hearts, for one reason or another. For a lot of the guys (and a few women), it had been New Cadet Basic Training, where running through the woods like Rambo, drilling with rifles and parading in a fancy uniform seemed like an extension of their childhoods. For others, it was being part of the Long Gray Line and embracing an esteemed institution with a rich history and traditions.

I wished I could be more like my classmates who beamed with pride and sometimes cried when we stood in unison to patriotic music, like "God Bless the USA." I wanted to feel something deep in these moments. In theory I understood what all of my training and indoctrination were about, but on a practical level, it still didn't make much sense to me. I certainly wanted to serve something higher, but nothing about West Point clicked.

I had to accept that I would probably never fit in, that I would never drink the Kool-Aid, and, therefore, would need to fake a lot of enthusiasm to get by. One day, an upperclassman actually ordered us to display "false motivation" if we weren't happy… and that became my new motto. But false motivation was both draining and easier said than done, especially with no nurturing from my family or instructors, who were mostly active duty Army officers (i.e. nice, but still formal and professional). Desperate to find people with whom I could connect, I turned to the one thing that felt familiar to me amidst this inhospitable, grueling, essentially foreign environment. Soon all of my extracurricular time was devoted to the one person who'd always had my back… Jesus.

Like with any man, my relationship with Jesus was complicated. In the beginning, I idolized him. As a little Catholic girl, I would stare up at him on the cross during services and think, *He's actually kind of cute, except for the blood oozing down his body.* I believed he was watching my every move, and that I would definitely see him in heaven as long as I obeyed my parents, cleaned my room and stopped chopping the hair off of my neighbor's favorite Barbie dolls. If I slipped up, all I needed to do was go to confession and say a few Hail Marys and Our Fathers, which I knew by heart by the time I was five, and Jesus would forgive me.

I genuinely loved going to my Catholic church. The priests and nuns were friendly and had the most adorable Irish accents. And it seemed like they were always hosting social events.

"B-Y-O-B," I spelled out loud as my mother and I perused the church bulletin board one Sunday. "What does that mean?" I looked up at her.

"It means bring your own booze," she said under her breath, grabbing my arm and pulling me away from the bulletin board.

From then on, I naturally assumed all churches encouraged alcoholic consumption of your own personal preference. I loved my church community and had many friends at Sunday school. At the end of weekly services, we routinely congregated at McDonalds and gorged ourselves on pancakes.

When I turned eleven, however, my father learned about becoming a born-again Christian. Soon thereafter, our beloved priests, nuns and friends couldn't satisfy his new religious fervor. Daddy complained when they couldn't answer his combative questions about the Bible verses he'd learned from his new born-again friends, and he mocked Father Earner for deflecting those questions with a polite, "We're not actually answering these questions today."

It seemed like my father had become a biblical scholar overnight, and it was imperative that he find a church worthy of his new knowledge. So he ripped us out of St. Thomas Aquinas Catholic Church and threw us into Calvary Temple Pentecostal Church. It happened so fast that I didn't even have time to react or know what to think, other than Daddy knew what was best.

The first time my father brought us to Calvary Temple Church of God, an old man with a missing eye and no teeth jolted from his seat to greet me with a hug. He totally freaked me out, but I didn't want to offend him or embarrass my father, so instead of flinching and fleeing, I let this one-eyed, toothless old man grab my arm and lead me into the center aisle so we could start square dancing with each other. I almost had a panic attack at eleven years old.

This was nothing like the reserved Catholic rituals I'd been practicing all of my life and grew to love. When I frantically looked around for the pastor, I saw him smiling, enjoying this raucous behavior, especially when other parishioners flocked to the center, singing boldly and waving their hands in the air. I felt like I'd suddenly landed on the set of American Bandstand. I tried to navigate a path to the nearest seat, so I could observe this charade from a safe distance, but I was trapped. Then I tried to make eye contact with my father, hoping he would come rescue me and yell at the old man for being an inappropriate pervert. But when I finally caught his gaze, my father nodded in approval, as if do-si-doing with Quasimodo was the right thing to do.

Later my father explained that this old man was simply "filled with the Holy Spirit." I didn't get it. In the Catholic Church, the Holy Spirit was the third station of the sign of the cross. Here in Pentecostal land, it made people act like rabid dogs bit them while walking into church. I didn't want to get infected with rabies. Church was serious, and Jesus deserved more respect. This wasn't an elementary school playground. But instead of anyone appreciating these sentiments (not that I dared to express them), I learned that my bad attitude stemmed from me being a good-for-nothing Catholic, who was doomed to eternity in hell because I wasn't saved.

I couldn't believe it. All of my beloved Catholic friends were heading straight for hell, and they didn't even know it. And I was going to burn right alongside them, with the devil laughing in our faces. This sucked. How unfair! We were good people, upstanding citizens and loved our priests and nuns. We didn't deserve to go to hell. I was sad, not just for me, but for everyone I had ever loved, especially my Nana, the nicest Catholic lady in the entire world. But before I had a chance to panic, much like I had a few years prior when I studied the Cold War in school and asked my parents if nuclear missiles were going to strike our neighborhood, the pastor told us how to fix the situation. All we had to do was ask Jesus to come into our hearts and save us.

That's it? I thought. *No way. You can't just change your eternal fate by asking Jesus a question in your mind.* But every Sunday, the pastor kept urging us to do just that.

My father was the first one in our family to get saved. At the end of service, about a month after attending Calvary Temple, when the pastor invited all unsaved souls up to the front of the church, my father walked forward, repenting in a tearful chant, hands raised in the air. I felt embarrassed for him. He was acting like a two-year-old. Then the pastor laid a hand on him and started to pray, and my father fell to the ground in a trance, all 260 pounds of him. I froze in shock and started bawling my eyes out. The Holy Spirit scared the shit out of me. There was no way I was going to let this happen to me. But then my father got up, wiped the tears out of his eyes, embraced our family—and implored us to also get saved.

I hated seeing my father so vulnerable, especially to something that I still didn't understand. I was mad at Jesus for taking all of my father's power and strength away, and I was afraid of what this meant for our family's future. But still, I needed to make sure I was never going to burn in hell. The next week, at the end of the church service, I quietly asked Jesus into my heart, from the safety of my inner dialogue, with my butt planted firmly in my seat.

I was sick of all of the tearful public displays of repentance and healing around me every Sunday. I figured that as long as I declared my devotion to Jesus privately, I was good to go, even if it didn't feel entirely genuine. For some reason, confessing my sins to Father Earner and reciting Catholic prayers felt more like I was working toward Jesus's forgiveness. At least Father Earner assured me I was a good girl, something no one assured me of at Calvary Temple. Now I not only felt incredibly insecure about what Jesus really thought of me, but also deep sorrow for my Catholic community and their faithful devotion, which apparently meant nothing and was all a waste of time. *I guess I'm one of the lucky ones who got chosen to learn about salvation,* I thought. But a part of me wished I could have remained blissfully ignorant.

Once I was privately saved, I didn't feel any special spiritual transformation or joy that compelled me to dance in the church aisles or raise my hands in the air. I just became increasingly scared of burning in hell and needed more assurance that I was safe. But after attending Calvary Temple for a few months, even its peculiar rituals started feeling more routine. I began to feel more comfortable in my role as a silent observer and to enjoy my private conversations with Jesus. That is, until shit just got wild.

Upon becoming born again, my father started listening to Christian music and, unfortunately, made us listen to it too. To my eleven-year-old ears it sounded like nails on a chalkboard compared to what I liked: Debbie Gibson, Tiffany, Miami Sound Machine, Madonna and Paula Abdul. As fate would have it, one of my father's favorite Christian singers was Janet Paschal, a pretty, bubbly blonde who often sang with Bill Gaither, another Jesus performer, at his popular homecoming events. Basically, I felt 70 years too young to appreciate her. But my father loved her, and she was coming to our town for a revival, where she would actually be singing in the flesh, with cassette tapes of her music on sale at the back of the church.

I walked around the revival thinking a compilation of fart noises would have been a better investment. Once Janet was done wailing away, they turned things over to a special guest pastor who delivered a fire and brimstone sermon that concluded with an altar call. This is where everyone in the entire congregation goes up to the front of the church to get a special blessing in the form of a smack on the head.

I was perfectly content to stay in my seat and watch everyone else get blessed, but my father made us go up. When I stood in line, I hoped nothing more than for the electricity to go out, so the service would come to an abrupt end. But even then the congregation probably would have taken that as a sign from God, like the end times were here.

When the first wave of people started dropping like flies, I felt a wave of panic. First the pastor asked them their names and what they wanted him to pray for. Then he raised his hand in the air and said something like, "Shoma -longa-ding-dong-M-Knight-Shyamalan-may the Lord heal you!" Then he smacked them on the head, and they fell to the ground like a sack of potatoes and started convulsing. If this was a Wal-Mart parking lot, I'd call 9-1-1 instantly, but in a Pentecostal church, this was normal. They were "slain with the spirit."

I knew Daddy had long renounced his half-Italian, part Jewish, Bronx-born roots and would go through the whole theatrical ordeal, but I expected better from my mother—a Bronx native, full blooded Italian Roman Catholic and first generation American. I hoped she wouldn't fall to the ground and would instead politely thank the pastor for his blessing—just like she taught me to do in the Catholic Church when the priest handed me my communion wafer. Then I could follow suit and not have to fall.

Holy shit my mom fell!—*Goddamnit, now I'm really screwed!*

When I walked up to the pastor to receive my special blessing, I tried to psych myself up to feel something spiritual, something supernatural, something that would help me fall like everyone else. But I still felt nothing... so I faked it.

The pastor laid his hand on my head, and I slowly forced myself backwards, bending my knees so I could break my fall without hurting myself. (I couldn't use my hands; that would have been too obvious.) I sat on the ground in an "L" shape for about thirty seconds, figuring this was an appropriate duration to be slain with the spirit. Then I got up and walked back to my seat, relieved it was over. Thankfully no one detected my fraudulent blessing because they were all consumed in their own slayings. I figured Jesus would forgive me. After all, I was only eleven.

The minute I walked into West Point's grand chapel, I felt a sense of both joy and calm. A massive granite building, sitting high on a cliff overlooking West Point, it looked like a cross between a Gothic cathedral and a battleship. The inside was lined with checkered floors, red velvet seats, beautiful stained-glass windows, American flags from various periods in history and US Army regimental flags. Walking into this large, majestic and hushed building immediately put my frayed nerves at ease. I sat down in one of the red velvet chairs and bowed my head. In a very real way, I felt a sense of home.

I couldn't really settle into the church community right away because I was just too tired to do anything outside of classes and duties. In the second half of freshman year, all I could manage were a few Bible study meetings and choir rehearsals, for which I had auditioned during basic training. Though I was still getting my bearings, it was good to know there were places where I could go to get the attention and nurturing I so desperately wanted and wasn't getting from my own family. Soon all of my extracurricular time was devoted to Jesus. Luckily, it was cool to love Jesus at West Point.

CHAPTER SIX

Between freshman and sophomore year, my classmates and I attended Cadet Field Training at Camp Buckner, or what we dubbed Bucknam. For six weeks we marched around the woods surrounding West Point, carrying rifles and learning infantry ground tactics in order to understand the role of an infantry platoon leader—something many West Point graduates go on to do (but only if they have a penis). There was no academic focus this summer—just grunt soldier work—which was a huge reprieve for many who loved being away from the stressful classroom.

We also went to Fort Knox, Kentucky, via a torturous fifteen-hour bus ride, to learn all about being a tanker, as Fort Knox was home to the Armor school. My favorite part of this week's long adventure was learning how to drive a Bradley Fighting Vehicle, which is a mechanized infantry vehicle much like a tank. (Talk about driving a giant truck to compensate for something else—I felt like I had a big penis just taking it around the practice course.) We also learned a lot about artillery, especially the howitzer cannon. While all of this training gave us an appreciation for what transpires on the battlefield in the mechanized infantry, armor and artillery fields, it was not actually relevant to any possible career I could have in the military. (No vaginas allowed.)

Still, it was more fun than the academic year, especially for the boys. Many of the exercises were reminiscent of games like Capture the Flag, paintball, and G.I. Joe. They were so happy to be in the woods, in their element. I tried to have fun too. I carried the heavier weapons to prove my manhood and toughness. More importantly, I remained cheerful, despite knowing that I would never use any of this stuff in my life.

One day we were tasked with completing a water confidence exercise called the Slide for Life. It was set up like a circus trapeze over a big lake. Cadets have to climb an eighty-foot tower, grab a bar and swing out over the lake for a really far distance. Then they have to drop into the water from about twelve feet in the air. It was terrifying.

"I'll go first," I volunteered, trying to prove I wasn't scared. The boys cheered me on as I climbed the tower and grabbed ahold of the bar. Standing at the top, I was so nervous I could hardly breathe. Then the buzzer sounded, indicating it was time to go. I pushed out over the water, the wind in my face, and at what I thought was twelve feet above the water, let go. We'd been instructed to enter the water at a certain angle, which I tried to do.

But I miscalculated how fast I'd be going and ended up hitting the water face first.

The impact was so painful I froze in the water. A couple of upperclassmen jumped in to drag me out of the water, even though I was wearing a life vest. Afterward, I had a headache and everything was blurry. But we were in the middle of a big competition. I rested for about thirty minutes, and then I went back into the competition, which involved crossing a big lake in full combat gear while one of my male classmates clung to my neck, since I was considered an advanced swimmer and he was only a "rock" swimmer. When that was over, it was time for land navigation, which included climbing the side of a mountain to find one of the locations. At the end I received the Recondo badge, along with about half of my class. (Most of us mocked this badge as a dorky award, but it was also humiliating to not receive it.) The next day a doctor confirmed that I had a concussion.

I didn't think much of it at the time—this was before the head injury awareness became popular. I thought it was just par for the course at West Point. I attributed my soreness and fatigue to the very grueling military challenge I'd just completed. After a few days, those feelings went away. But every now and then I'd experience a headache in moments of exertion.

After Camp Buckner, my sophomore, a.k.a. "yearling" or "yuk," year began. Theoretically yuk year still sucks, although not as bad as being a plebe with no privileges, because while cadets can finally act normal, they still can't leave the academy grounds as often as the other upperclassmen. The most notorious haze about yuk year is mandatory physics, although this paled in comparison to my first real chemistry major class: Organic Chemistry. Still, I felt more at ease being familiar with cadet life, enjoying an incredible roommate and having more bandwidth for church activities.

Spending more time with the Christian community allowed me to cultivate a stronger friendship with Anna, my first real friend at West Point. We met the year prior. It was a particularly stressful day, and I had struggled to carry a heavy bag and arm full of textbooks across the cadet area, my head pounding with a headache, when someone behind me suddenly grabbed my heavy bag. I was surprised to see a young woman just shy of five-feet tall walking next to me. Because we couldn't talk, she moved her head, indicating she would follow me wherever I was going. She carried my bag the entire way to my room.

"Hi, I'm Anna," she said in a mousy voice when we were finally allowed to talk.

"I'm Laura. Thanks for your help."

"No problem," she smiled.

We became fast friends. Anna hailed from Indiana and was an all-around star in high school—excelling in leadership activities, academics and sports, especially soccer. Her parents were teachers and, despite being churchgoers, a lot more liberal than Anna. She was also a fellow chemistry student.

"Are you finally coming to ECF?" she asked at the beginning of yuk year.

"I think I should be able to swing it."

"Come with me this Tuesday. I'll introduce you to everyone." That was Anna—sweet and nurturing.

True to her word, Anna showed up at my dorm on Tuesday night to take me to my first official Bible study with the Elite Christian Fellowship (ECF), whose mission was to "glorify God by uniting devout, upstanding Christians for biblical fellowship and outreach, empowering them to minister effectively in the military society."

We entered a lecture hall in one of the academic buildings, joining about 250 other people for a series of praise and worship songs and an introductory speech by a man who appeared to be in his mid-fifties. The speaker explained that after prayer, we would break up into smaller groups of ten for Bible study lessons led by either active duty or retired officers. The purpose of ECF was to give us an opportunity to socialize, go on retreats and be around mentoring faculty members. Many of them had graduated from West Point and knew what we were going through. They would be available to listen to our woes and provide us with applicable advice.

"We're here to show you there is a light at the end of the tunnel," the man said with a smile. Everyone sighed with relief. "And to teach you valuable lessons that will help you deal with not only West Point, but also situations that you'll face as real officers," he continued. "Finally, we'll teach you how to uphold your Christian values and principles in a tough environment."

After prayer, I followed Anna to her group. We sat in a small classroom with the leader, Captain Devon Smith, a tactical officer and West Point graduate twelve years our senior, and his wife, Cathy, who passed around a plate of cookies she had baked.

Captain Smith told us he was there to look out for our spiritual welfare and development. He used passages from the Bible to teach us how we could apply scripture to being a better leader to our future soldiers, and a better person overall. It was imperative to be a disciple of Christ, and Captain Smith taught us that we should use our authority in the military to preach the gospel of Christ to our soldiers. I felt embarrassed when I heard this, knowing that officially we're not supposed to do that. But Captain Smith and the other Bible study leaders openly encouraged us to evangelize to our soldiers. The more time I spent in the military, the more I realized that the separation of church and state is a concept many ignore, much like our nation's Republican leaders who push their Christian agenda, with the Republican Party being the party of choice for a majority of West Pointers and Army officers.

As Captain Smith preached, his wife, Cathy, smiled, nodded in agreement and occasionally added her commentary—emphasizing her husband's valuable role in this Christ-centered mission.

Cathy was a tall, athletic woman with a bubbly, sweet personality. To look at her, you would never have guessed she was once a Marine Corps Officer and Dartmouth Marine Corps ROTC graduate. Now she was a staunch homeroom mom volunteer at her daughters' school. I would soon learn that all of our Christian leaders' wives were stay-at-home moms, no matter what their academic or military background happened to be.

"When a woman becomes a mother," Cathy told us, "she needs to stay home full time in order to properly care for her children. If she doesn't, and chooses to work instead, then her children will become attention-deprived and seek affection from outside sources like teachers and their friends' mothers."

Wow, I thought. *My mother was a working mom and a terrible role model. I don't know anything about raising kids, having a family, getting married…*

⟜ ⟝

"Mommy, you're not listening to me," I cried as my mother hovered over the stove, stirring the marinara sauce.

"Yes I am," she said flatly.

I knew she wasn't really paying attention to my fifth-grade angst and that my words fell on closed ears. But I tried anyway. I had to get her to stop being so mean to me in front of my friends, publicly embarrassing me.

"I want you to stop yelling at me when you come to my school. Kristi's mom has a sweet and gentle voice, and everyone likes her."

"I don't yell at you!" my mother ironically yelled.

"You're doing it right now," I explained, "and I don't deserve it. I'm a good girl."

"Your mother can't help herself," my father interrupted as he walked into the kitchen. "She's not a good listener. And she can't help her yelling. She's a product of growing up in the Bronx."

My mother offered no response and kept stirring the sauce.

In high school, before I had my driver's license, I needed a ride to our school's culture fair kickoff event in the evening. My mother hated driving, especially at night, but I would earn extra credit for attending.

"I don't want to take you!" she screamed.

"But Mommy, I need to go. It's important for my class."

"You're such a pain in my ass, Laura! You make my life so difficult!"

She used to say the same things to me when I needed a ride to gymnastics class in the sixth grade. I was used to her complaining about these basic motherly tasks, but on this particular evening, she was angrier than ever. (My father wasn't around to witness our conversation.)

"Please stop yelling at me, Mommy," I cried.

She called a taxi, but one wasn't available.

"Get in the fucking car!" she reluctantly conceded to driving me.

For the rest of the ride she berated me for being a difficult daughter and ruining her life.

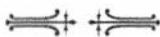

Cathy claimed that she could instantly single out the children of working mothers in the classroom, because they would always run to her, starving for affection. "They're not getting what they need at home, and it's very sad. That's why you must commit your lives to raising your children properly."

I tried to not feel self-conscious, as if she was talking about me, and instead focused on feeling grateful that

Cathy and the other wives were here to support me and teach me how to handle adulthood.

I was fascinated by the fact that every male leader in ECF told us that a woman was supposed to submit to her husband's leadership, frequently offering examples from his own marriage, and every wife sat beside her man, nodding in agreement. I couldn't tell if the wives were genuinely content and happy, or if they were just going along with the program.

Both out of curiosity and a desire for pleasant company, occasionally I would go to the Smiths' house to do laundry and have a home-cooked meal. They lived on West Point's campus because Devon was assigned to oversee one of the cadet companies.

Their house was like every officer's house at West Point—old fashioned, historic, and decorated in a typical Americana theme, with lots of red, white and blue knickknacks and hand-stitched signs like "God Bless My Home" and "God Bless America." In Devon and Cathy's home, there were also toys strewn about because they had two young children. Every time I went over there, the house smelled like home-cooked food and felt warm and inviting.

Captain Smith was a typical dorky officer: medium height, glasses, thinning hair. He was clearly a hard worker, dedicated dad and would do anything for his soldiers. His personality was very military, making him socially awkward, especially when he said things like "HOOAH" instead of "Yeah." Cathy was the glue of his Bible study class, especially for us women. And we hung on her every word.

One day, she explained that when encountering a conflict, issue or major crossroad in their family, she and Captain Smith would discuss it in a respectful manner and devise different solutions. I completely agreed with this approach—at first. Cathy continued that if they couldn't come to an agreement, then she would automatically submit to her husband's wishes, even if she knew deep in her heart that he was wrong.

At this point, I had to pipe up with a question. "What if you know that his decision is wrong and could bring harm to your family?"

"That's between Devon and God," she answered with a smile. "It's his responsibility for hurting our family. Devon is the one in our marriage who is accountable to God. If we face this situation, then I am supposed to pray that God reveals the right answer to him and that he follows God's guidance."

I looked around at the other students like *do you believe this bullshit?* By the expressions on their faces, apparently they did. I wanted to shout, "But that's so stupid!" but I held my tongue. Then in an eerily Stepford wife manner, Cathy exclaimed, "And it's just such a relief that I'm not the one accountable. The burden is on Devon. I just feel this amazing freedom that he's the one responsible for our family."

I couldn't believe it. Here was an intelligent, formerly ambitious military officer, averting responsibility in her adulthood merely because she had a vagina. Even worse was that she acted like a biblical authority figure, imparting her values on our Bible study group like they were the gospel. People were buying it and would eventually apply this logic to their own marriages.

I left that particular Bible study session incensed by the idea that God would want me to blindly agree to do something that could hurt me, or my family, just because my husband was the only one accountable to God. *That's bullshit!* I thought, stomping all of the way back to the barracks. Wanting a second opinion, I decided to seek out the advice from another ECF wife I had befriended.

Charlene "Colonel Mom" McKinney was the wife of Steve McKinney, the retired Colonel in charge of ECF and whom we all called "Colonel Dad." Steve was a decorated Vietnam war hero and fellow alum. Now he led the entire ECF organization at West Point (and was the one who gave the introductory speech when I first attended). Colonel Dad was gruffer than the other Bible study leaders, but he also felt more authentic, loving and nurturing, especially compared to Captain Smith. He was also open about not always having been a Christian, as he became "saved" later on in life.

Once I had driving privileges, I enjoyed treating Charlene to dinner. Unlike the other wives, I sensed an underlying misery. She essentially ran a bed and breakfast in her home, always cooking, cleaning and doing laundry. She never had any privacy because her home was technically the ECF home, and it existed as a sanctuary for cadets to enjoy a respite. It didn't help that Colonel Dad seemed to make the cadets more of a priority than his own wife.

Although they, too, had a very traditional marriage, I didn't hold it against them, because they were from an older generation. A part of me scoffed at the younger wives who I felt had fallen into a traditional homemaker role without ever trying to have a career or anything else outside of their marriage and children. By contrast, my heart went out to the women of previous generations, who didn't have the same opportunities and had been pressured by society to rush into marriages and motherhood. I felt exactly this way about Charlene.

Charlene and I grew very close and starting spending a lot of quality time together away from official organization meetings. She was very open with me about her everyday struggles, especially her battle with depression, and I cherished her experiences, vulnerability and wisdom. I also felt that she didn't inflict the same judgments that a lot of the younger Bible study leaders did, so I could candidly ask tough questions and offer my opinions on critical issues.

"Charlene, I don't understand something," I said at one of our dinners.

"What is it, Love?"

"In Bible studies, I keep hearing that only the husband is accountable to God, not the wife. I don't get it. I'm accountable to God now, so why wouldn't I be if I were married? What do you believe?"

"Well, in a marriage, I do believe that the man is the one responsible for the leadership. Even if it pains me, I submit to Steve. Even when he makes decisions that I don't agree with, that's the way it is. I'm not accountable to God for these things, so it's not my fault."

"But don't you want to be accountable to God? Don't you want that responsibility?"

"No, it's a very freeing feeling. Steve is the authority figure in our marriage, and I am relieved that he's the one burdened for making sure that we are following God in a righteous path."

I didn't understand why Charlene and the other ECF women associated responsibilities with burdens. I delighted in the fact that I was on the path to becoming a powerful and independent woman, responsible for my own decisions and capable of becoming anything I desired—basically the opposite of my mother! I mean, isn't that why women like me flock to West Point to begin with? To challenge our already talented selves into becoming the best version of ourselves, grab life by the balls and own our power It was certainly not to relinquish all of that simply because we were born without a penis.

I completely disagreed with Charlene, but I didn't want to hurt her feelings, so I politely told her that I was struggling with comprehending and accepting that concept, and then quickly changed the subject.

Even after I graduated from West Point, I made every effort to visit Steve and Charlene at least once a year. During these visits we would discuss the same spiritual topics that we typically did in the past, only this time, I was more eager to argue my point of view. Steve and I also had a special relationship in that we both shared similar personality characteristics and believed in being stubborn and blunt in order to foster improvements and get things done. On one of these visits, I treated Charlene and Steve to a fancy Mother's Day lunch, during which I stated that I disagreed with the Christian stance on a woman's role in a marriage.

"I just don't see it. Because a man is a man, because of his parts, that means the man is in charge? It makes no sense. I'm a woman, and I'm in charge of myself. Why would I want to get married, just to have a man be in charge of me?"

"Laura, the way you're describing it is so crude, said Steve. "That's not the way we see it at all. Let's compare a marriage to a ship. On a ship, you can only have one person in charge; otherwise, there would be too much dissention and chaos, and the ship won't function properly. The ship's captain is the ultimate authority and has the final say. But that doesn't mean he operates the ship on his own. He has people to rely on to help him make crucial decisions, people like the first mate. On every ship, that first mate is always right next to the captain, weighing in on important matters."

"So you're saying that the husband is the captain and the wife is the first mate?" I asked.

"Exactly," said Steve.

"But why does the husband get to be the captain? Just because he's a man? And why can't a marriage just have two co-captains who share a 50-50 relationship?"

"It doesn't work that way. Life doesn't work that way. Ultimately they would butt heads and have a dysfunctional relationship. Someone always has to be in charge."

"See, that's where I disagree," I said. "I don't think someone has to be in charge. Ideally I think a husband and wife should both be in charge and that authority shouldn't automatically go to one just because of their gender. I just can't accept the fact that gender dictates authority. And I hate the concept of authority. Why can't it just be mutual respect and a looking out for one another?"

"Of course there's mutual respect and prioritizing your spouse over yourself. I'm not saying that the husband does whatever he wants to. But in disagreements, someone has to make a decision."

"And why can't that be me? Because I'm a woman?"

"God commands the husband as the spiritual authority. God says it. It's His intent."

"Well if that's the case, then I'm never going to get married. My life functions just fine the way it is, and I wouldn't want to change that, just because I'm not a man."

Steve and Charlene smiled at me, and we came to an agreement that we respectfully disagreed with each other's perspectives. I didn't want to carry on further, at fear of hurting Charlene's feelings.

Unfortunately, I didn't feel this comfortable openly speaking my mind when attending ECF Bible study, let alone, clearly derive these conclusions, and it would cause some major grief and conflict until I learned to eventually stand up for myself. While I appreciated all of the love and support I received from my church mentors, I felt like something wasn't quite right. Constantly surrounded by men at West Point, I ached to hear a woman's perspective on how to compose myself as a respectable officer and handle issues unique to women in the military. But there wasn't even one female officer leading these Bible studies. It got to the point where the only place I felt like I could relax and truly let my hair down was the Cadet Chapel, singing in the church choir.

CHAPTER SEVEN

I first discovered my ability to sing like an opera lady in seventh grade. I was at home and just started imitating an opera singer I heard on the radio. It wasn't polished, but I sounded like a legitimate singer. Then one day in gym class, while changing in the locker room, I suddenly belted out an "Ahhhhh" in my operatic voice. I don't know what prompted me to do it. It was just an instinct in the moment. But my classmates were amazed. For the rest of the semester, they would beg me to do it again, and the acoustics of our locker room only amplified my voice. They were wildly entertained, and I loved making them laugh.

Because my parents already had me in piano lessons, they added some voice lessons too. My teacher for both was Dr. Jane LaRowe, a sweet, ninety-year-old, eccentric widow who used to drive a big van with a male blow-up doll in the passenger seat so she wouldn't appear to live alone. Unfortunately, her proclivity for blow-up dolls didn't translate into fun music lessons. She made me learn boring church songs that I didn't recognize—nothing majestic like opera or modern that I could relate to. I grew to hate both piano and voice lessons. But my father adored Dr. LaRowe and didn't care if I was bored.

One day, during a recital at a big hospice center, I had to sing a church song in an uncomfortable range that started with the lyrics, "Shackled by a heavy burden ..." The song was called, "He Touched Me." Even as a Christian kid, I knew about sexual innuendoes and thought about them while singing songs with lyrics like Jesus's "staff and rod." So I felt especially awkward singing "He Touched Me." Plus there was a really cute guy from school at the recital. I had no idea he took piano lessons from Dr. LaRowe, and we were mildly flirting before our performances. After he finished his piano piece, he rolled his eyes, indicating that he, too, was embarrassed. I finished my piano piece without incident, but when I sang about Jesus touching me, I wanted to crawl into a hole. Afterward, I gave the cute boy a look of solidarity, returning his eye roll.

Daddy was livid. He said I shamed him and Jesus. That was supposed to be a beautiful song edifying the Lord, and I ruined it—all to look cool for a guy. He chastised me for this for the rest of the time that I lived with him, often referencing how I threw away my singing career to look cool. I never sang again until West Point.

Every new cadet auditioned for the choir—it was one of the mandatory stations during basic training. The choir director asked us to sing our best rendition of "My Country 'Tis of Thee," and I belted out a dramatic, operatic performance. My classmates erupted into applause and the choir director delightedly announced, "You're in!"

I only attended choir a few times plebe year, but I promised myself I would make more of an effort yuk year. I noticed how regular choir attendance dramatically improved my singing technique. I figured this was an excellent way to serve God, and I enjoyed fostering a new hobby. I also had a soft spot for the guys who weren't shy about showcasing their nice voices. One especially nice voice came from a cute guy named Connor, a senior who also happened to be the president of the Cadet Chapel Choir.

Standing at a slender six feet two, Connor had a tall but gentle presence. He spoke softly and, as the choir leader, often prayed for us out loud. Unlike the average sexually charged women my age, open prayer became a huge turn on for me, taking precedence over big muscles. Something about me must have struck Connor too, because he started paying more attention to me and even began walking me back to my room after choir practice. My roommate quickly noticed the extra attention, especially when Connor invited me to tailgate with him after the next football game. In a highly restricted environment, this was his way of asking me on a first date.

As a senior, Connor was permitted to depart from academy grounds twice a week. As a sophomore (yuk), I could only leave a few times per semester, mainly during long holiday weekends or for ECF church retreats. Sometimes these retreats, although extremely fun, could be quite intense because cadets were encouraged to share their testimony with the entire group, chronicling the events that led to them to accept Christ as their personal Lord and Savior, and demonstrating how being saved has revolutionized their life's purpose. As a result, people would open up about their most innermost struggles—either because they thought they stood a better chance of having their sins forgiven by God, or as a way of freeing themselves of past sins in the hopes of not being judged too harshly down the road. It was easy to become fast friends with someone because over the course of only a few days we would learn many private details about one another.

It was during one of these retreats that Connor and I discovered we had a lot in common besides singing in the choir. We were both majoring in chemistry and also felt that it was important to prioritize our relationship with God. It felt amazing to have a respectable, attractive guy pay attention to me and know that he was there for me. We innocently held hands and hugged each other.

Back at West Point, we began dating. This entailed doing homework together, grabbing a pizza and bringing it back to one of our rooms, going on an occasional two-mile run and walking to choir practice together. Sometimes we even had breakfast in the mess hall after Sunday church. It felt exciting and validating to have Connor's companionship, and I ignored the fact that we often wore the same exact outfits when together. Unlike regular college students who get to take a crack at being real adults when they date, Connor's and my relationship looked strikingly similar to other cadets who were dating and not having sex.

In December, just two months after we became an official couple, Connor announced that he believed God had selected me to be his future wife. Despite my reservations about some of the marriage discussions I'd heard in Bible study, I was enchanted with the idea of romance. If this was God's will for my life, I was going to be the best wife possible. West Point didn't allow cadets to marry, so any potential wedding date was still at least two and a half years away. But it was never too early to being preparing for marriage.

My friend Anna also recently discovered her future husband when she fell in love with Bart, a civilian guy she grew up with who was away at Georgetown University. Like Anna, Bart was uber Christian. Unlike Anna, he had been sexually active. In fact, when they first got together, he was waiting to find out if he had impregnated an ex-girlfriend. After a few nerve-racking weeks of waiting, the ex finally got her period. When I questioned Anna about his commitment to Christianity, and if she was OK with him not being a virgin, she dismissed my concerns, blinded by her infatuation with Bart. Or perhaps there was a double standard for men and women.

Anna introduced me to the plethora of literature published for young Christian women in our position. Instead of reading books to help us with chemistry, or enhance our understanding of military tactics, we began reading *The Five Love Languages*; *His Needs, Her Needs;* and *Passion and Purity*. I finally discovered a topic I enjoyed reading about for pleasure, and Anna and the other Christian girlfriends and wives were only delighted to suggest more books to help me in my quest to become the perfect Christian wife.

I pondered how much physical contact I could enjoy with Connor while still being a good Christian. I knew intercourse was out of the question, but I constantly received mixed messages that confused me. Supposedly lust was a sin, but physical affection enhanced a relationship. So how far could we go? In God's eyes, what was physically acceptable for a dating couple? As we became more of a legitimate couple, I became hornier and wanted to do things with Connor, so I needed to know exactly what I could get away with and still be regarded as holy.

Sex was a hot topic in our ECF Bible studies. Sometimes it was easy to forget about global issues like famine and genocide because our Christian training focused more on controlling our hormones than on fixing the world's problems. But the messages our leaders taught us were too vague for me to understand my boundaries. Being told to glorify God in all of my actions didn't cut it and kind of creeped me out. I didn't want to be thinking about God as I lusted after Connor's penis. I had a difficult time reconciling the fact that giving him a hand job prior to marriage was evil, but post-marriage hand jobs were pleasing to my Lord and Savior. I needed better answers.

Some of my mentors said they didn't even kiss their spouse until their wedding day. I couldn't imagine what these mentors would think if they knew I had dry-humped my way to orgasms back in high school. So following their example was out of the question.

I thought maybe I'd find some suitable advice among my Christian peers, at least with my friends who were willing to talk about sex. Many preferred to avoid the topic altogether, even though their marital unions were only a few months away. When my friend Laurie and I teased Ruth, a senior who was getting married right after her graduation, she turned five shades of purple and clammed up. We pressed Ruth to explain herself.

"Stop, I don't want to talk about it," Ruth said.

"Why? Aren't you excited? We're so jealous," Laurie explained.

"It's embarrassing," Ruth admitted.

"But it shouldn't be," I said. "What does Rex have to say about it?"

"Nothing."

"What do you mean, nothing?" Laurie and I said simultaneously.

"We haven't discussed it yet."

"But Ruth, you're getting married in a few months!"

"I know. We'll figure something out."

At that moment I knew Ruth and Rex were doomed for a life of horrible sex. Not me. Despite being a virgin, I had made it a goal to be a total whore for my future husband, and my Bible study lessons taught me that it would be glorifying to God. So I was always happy to engage in a sexual discussion.

Colonel Mom (Charlene) appreciated how comfortable I felt delving into these topics. When she hosted a women's marriage seminar, she asked me to be her assistant, even if it was just for comic relief.

Amelia Harper, another senior, attended this seminar because her wedding was also just a few months away. I thought of Amelia as West Point's little angel. We both sang soprano in our respective choirs (she was in the Glee club) and were both frequently called upon for church solos. Her voice was soft and angelic, much like the genteel Southern belle demeanor she embodied. When I sang, it was with the rigor and emotion of a Broadway performer, which I thought was very reflective of my brash, sometimes dirty, inner thoughts and bold personality. I was an inferior Christian to Amelia. And here I was, anticipating Charlene steering the workshop toward sex, just so I could see Amelia's reaction.

When Charlene announced that it was time to talk about sex, everyone, not just Amelia, closed their eyes in embarrassment and offered sly smiles. Even Suzanne, the fiancée of my classmate Bob and who worked at West Point as a nanny, was shy, despite having a child. But she and Bob claimed that they never had intercourse and the pregnancy resulted from sperm accidentally traveling inside of her from naked dry humping. *Some mutant super sperm!* Sex was supposedly unchartered territory for her too. None of the ladies showed any interest in discussing sex, so the seminar concluded early, and Charlene and I joked about needing copious amounts of alcohol to compensate for how uptight everyone was.

Charlene had better luck mentoring some other cadets who approached her with candid questions. Brady, a gorgeous, California blond surfer confided that he was struggling with lustful thoughts about his fiancée, Elizabeth. Elizabeth was at the top of their class and had a rocking gymnast body, with size D breasts that matched her superior intellect, and an adorable personality to top her perfection.

"Of course you're lusting after her!" Charlene explained.

"Is that OK? I feel so guilty," Brady asked.

"Of course it's OK. I would hope you're lusting after her. That's normal. I mean, look at her. She's amazing!"

At least my circle of close Christian friends were more like me and enjoyed facilitating juicy sex discussions, especially when we were supposed to be doing our physics homework. Studying the "right hand rule" and "bodies in motion" changed the conversation from solving problem number four, to asking Eddie if he masturbated.

Poor Eddie. He was one of the few male cadets who had more women friends than guy friends, and at some point, he fell madly in love with each of us. He had a libido that matched his outrageous IQ, and he also had a reputation for having the biggest schlong on the West Point fencing team *and* a nickname for it. Our physics study group begged for him to reveal his nickname, but Eddie's lips were sealed. So were his palms. Not only was he saving himself for marriage; he also refused to allow himself to masturbate.

No one at Bible study ever even mentioned the word masturbation. Everyone completely avoided the topic. It never came up in my high school relationship with Tim or in my cadet relationship with Connor. Masturbation was a concept not even on the forefront of my mind, and

I didn't understand its importance and prevalence in a man's life until junior year at the breakfast table.

Every morning Shawn and Joe compared the porn they beat off to the night before. Monday morning conversations were the longest, as the weekend afforded them more time to review and react to more material. I knew that if I wanted to portray myself as an upstanding Christian woman, then I was supposed to scoff at the detailed descriptions of their magazines and DVDs. But I was intrigued, not only at how often these men needed to pleasure themselves, but also at how much better it made them feel. Maybe this was the solution to help Eddie calm down. So I made a suggestion.

"Eddie, you're super horny all the time, right?" I asked.

"Um, yeah."

"And you constantly obsess about your latest crush. And when you're turned down, it totally crushes you, right?"

"Maybe. What are you getting at?"

"Have you ever thought that masturbating would help? You know. Calm you down. Make you worry less about things. Help your hands stop shaking."

"No, I can't do that Laura."

"Why not?"

"Because it isn't right."

"Why isn't it right? Show me in the Bible where it says you can't masturbate."

"I can't. But I just don't feel right about doing it."

"Fine, but even my dad says it's a healthy thing that men should do regularly."

"That's gross, Laura!"

I felt sorry for how repressed Eddie was. His life seemed more difficult because of the physical restrictions he placed on himself. My non-Christian friends had it so much easier. They could proudly display their lust and seemed perfectly content doing so. I hated Christian guilt. Sometimes I wished I didn't have to be so damned holy. I started feeling like it was easier to relate to my bad friends versus my good friends. I much preferred joking about cocks than debating with chauvinistic men that the Bible's book of Ephesians didn't intend to subjugate women.

As I became more entrenched in the devout Christian community, I witnessed several young couples rapidly blossom into mature adults in serious relationships that were committed to serving God and spreading the gospel in their communities. These couples constantly stood up at church events and preached the importance of garnering our leadership skills to spread the gospel to the unsaved, and then they would pressure younger cadets like me to increase our involvement in the church.

They would also urge us to seek out "equally yoked" partners, a reference to the Bible verse that explains how important it is for oxen to share their workloads in order to not cause undue burden on one particular ox. (I imagine these oxen have huge schlongs.) Dating a weaker Christian, we were told, would hurt our spirituality, and inferior Christians unfortunately often had more influence than the better ones. Therefore, it was imperative to find a strong, equally matched Christian mate.

What exactly constituted a stronger Christian versus a weaker Christian wasn't exactly clear to me at the time, but it seemed like they used the same competitive West Point standards to measure one's Christian spirituality. If someone spent a great deal of time with church activities, volunteered to lead some church organizations, read the Bible every day (or at least claimed to) and never succumbed to lustful temptations, then that person was considered one of the Christian elites.

That was all well and good, except that I knew many cadets, including some who went to Bible study, that were very sexually active. I don't know how they mustered the energy to overcome the rules, homework, lack of sleep and a less-than-ideal dating environment to foster cadet love, but a lot of them did. Maybe overcoming these challenges and succeeding in the face of adversity were the inherent leadership qualities that attracted them to West Point in the first place. *If a school attracts brilliant, ambitious Type-As who can run marathons and ace physics tests all before breakfast, then maybe it should expect that the horny ones will figure out a way to get laid come hell or high water (or bombs and gunfire in a potential combat setting).*

Soon I would be privy to just how creative America's best and brightest could be. Sure there were library stacks, just like any other college or university, but these sex rangers did what any ranger would be inclined to do—head outdoors into the wild frontier.

West Point actually officially designates one outdoor area for cadet romance, nicknamed Flirtation Walk. There's a 1934 film about it, depicting the olden days when Flirtation Walk was a place for male cadets (since female cadets weren't allowed until 1976) to bring their dates for a walk after a formal ball. Many cadets proposed marriage here, which is probably what West Point's executive leadership had in mind when they incorporated Flirtation Walk into the rules and regulations—not my roommate Michelle and her boyfriend Ryan rolling around in the bushes, fucking like rabbits.

For others, Flirtation Walk was too cliché. These outdoor enthusiasts congregated in hipper places like the junior-year cadet parking lot and behind West Point's most famous monument—called Battle Monument—which is essentially a giant shaft with balls at its base. Others simply couldn't weather the elements and chose to do it indoors. A popular time was after TAPS, when cadets could sneak into their lover's room and hope the roommate was a sound sleeper. Poor Anna had to endure moaning coming from behind the dresser just two feet away because her roommate assumed she was sleeping. Anna complained to me continually but never had the gumption to say anything to her roommate.

Hearing about all of these sexcapades certainly provided me with an education not published in any West Point recruitment literature. I had no idea how important sex was to a lot of people and didn't understand why they couldn't follow the rules and restrain themselves. *What was the big deal with remaining celibate for four years?* That was my big plan.

Up to this point, Connor and I had enjoyed kissing and holding hands, but that was the extent of our physical contact. I hadn't dared to dry hump him like I did my high school boyfriend Tim.

CHAPTER EIGHT

Right before my high school senior year homecoming, I needed a date to the dance, and my friend Stacy suggested I go with Tim, a preppy, All-American-looking guy with light brown hair who looked like a young Kirk Cameron. To my surprise, Tim turned out to be a really nice guy and proper gentleman. Even my parents liked him—or at least that he had a 12:30 curfew and seemed responsible and respectful of authority.

Tim was also a virgin and never indicated that he wanted to change that. But soon we both got urges. The first time we held hands in a movie theater, I noticed an extra amount of wetness when I wiped myself in the bathroom. I noticed even more wetness after Tim and I kissed at the end of our dates. No one had ever spoken about this mysterious wetness, so I wasn't sure what to make of it. I sure as hell wasn't going to ask my parents.

After one of these dates with Tim, I laid in bed doing some computations in my head. The definition of sex that I learned in church was penile penetration. Therefore, anything other than penile penetration wasn't sex. I slept better that night.

At the end of another date, Tim pulled his mother's Buick into my driveway, turned off the engine and started kissing me. I was surprised by how much I liked to kiss, and by how much it made me want more. After a few minutes, I unbuckled our seatbelts, hopped onto Tim's lap, aligned the crotch of my jeans with the bulging crotch of his jeans and grinded away until I had the most blissful, intense, convulsing sensation that I had ever experienced. I asked Tim if he felt it, and he seemed to not understand what I was talking about. I didn't know this was an orgasm, or what an orgasm was, but I knew it must have been something serious, because I was too ashamed to look my father in the eye for at least an hour after it happened. But because Jesus didn't classify these actions as sex, I could partake in them and still keep my sparkle.

I worried my sparkle wouldn't shine as brightly if I stared at Tim's penis for too long. But maybe just a glimpse would be OK.

"I'm really curious what it looks like."

"Do you want to see it?" Tim offered.

"I do…but…I'm afraid." I hesitated.

"Why? It won't bite you…unless you want it to," Tim snickered.

"I'm just afraid that it's a sin and my father will be able to tell."

"What? Your father isn't a prophet."

"Well, he claims to be."

"You know that's bullshit, right?"

"Stop, don't badmouth him. I mean… I know, but I still feel bad. Maybe if I just stare at it for a second, it'd be OK."

"Are you sure?"

"Yeah. Just a quick peek," I assured Tim.

"Ok, here you go."

I allowed myself to look at Tim's penis for 0.37 seconds.

"OK put it back!" I ordered. "Wait," I hesitated. "Let me see it again."

"Are you sure? Are you damaged goods now?" Tim teased.

I silently prayed God would understand my curiosities and needs, and I begged for forgiveness.

"Yes! Let me see it again!"

"Here you go."

This time I allowed my gaze to linger a little longer, for approximately four seconds.

"Fascinating. It's so, firm," I marveled.

"That's because you keep teasing me."

"OK, I'm done. You can put it away."

Even though my father became sicker and more absent after my dates, I always felt guilty, like he and God were still watching over me. But I went with my instincts anyway because fooling around felt really good. But then the sexual interrogations began at home church.

In-between my Bible lesson and family prayer time, Daddy started asking about my extracurricular activities.

"Does Tim ever try to feel your breasts?"

My heart stopped. I couldn't lie. Not in front of God.

"Yes, Daddy," I admitted, lowering my eyes in shame.

"That's utterly disappointing, Laura."

I needed to quickly steer this conversation in a different direction.

"But I told him not to!" I bragged, like an obnoxious little girl proud of something silly like learning how to tie her shoes. "I told him it's not right, and he honored my wishes."

"That's very good, Laura," my father played right into my hand. "Just make sure he never does it again."

"Yes, Daddy," I promised him (and God).

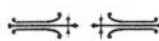

I made a point of telling myself that some of the things I'd done with Tim were far too inappropriate for the godly relationship I had with Connor. Sometimes in the presence of my West Point friends, especially the ones who refused to even kiss their significant other until their wedding day, I would feel a hint of guilt. I naturally assumed most of my Christian friends were virgins like myself, seeing how marriage was such a hot topic and premarital sex deemed to be a heinous sin.

One of my women's Bible study leaders, Lisa, delighted in training ladies like Anna and me to become good wives, I think because it allowed her to foster her own hopes and dreams of one day becoming someone's wife. Lisa, 24, was a single nanny who worked full time caring for the five children of two married West Point professors. I'm not sure how Lisa became a Bible study leader, because she wasn't officially affiliated with West Point. She may have volunteered, figuring that she was an example of living as a single Christian woman.

Finally, I thought, someone who may be able to provide me with a fresh perspective about what it means to live and behave properly as an adult. I was excited to join the group because Lisa was really fun-loving and had a great sense of humor. Always laughing, she loved to plan social outings and was generous with her affection, especially when we were having a bad day, which was almost always the case at West Point. Lisa easily kept my mind off of my pathetic college experience, and I hoped to learn a lot from her while enjoying a new friendship.

We indeed became fast friends, but our common interests stopped at wanting to be good Christian ladies. Lisa ached for nothing more than to be a wife and mother, and our Bible studies obsessively concentrated on these two topics. Every week we read Bible verses and wrote prayers about patiently waiting for a Christian man to come sweep us off our feet. Lisa's pain in waiting for that special moment was all too obvious when she would pray for patience and understanding, because God had chosen to not bless her with a good husband yet.

Instead of being angry with God, she believed that God had a perfect design planned for her life, which included an amazing husband. But it wasn't time for God to allow her to have that husband yet, so her faith required her to be patient and trust that God had her best interest in mind, and that when that husband appeared, no matter how long the wait, everything would be perfect and blessed. Looking back, it was like teaching a religious form of the Cinderella story, only worse. Lisa, along with many other church leaders, was teaching us to sit back and watch our lives unfold outside of our control, instead of taking action and making free choices. If the argument was presented to them in this manner, I'm sure they would deny having such a lack of control over their lives. But interspersed with Bible verses about having childlike faith, their lessons seemed to indicate that God manipulated our major life events like chess pieces on a chessboard.

Lisa's main advice to us cadets was to remain pure. She never specified the limits we should place on our physical relationships. She simply told us to act in a way that maintained our purity, and explained that purity was something each of us had to figure out in our hearts.

In the middle of one of these discussions, she suddenly broke down into tears. We all huddled around her with concern. Lisa then revealed that four years prior, she had dated a cadet she met at church and, despite their best efforts, hormones got the better of them, and they ended up having sex. I'm not sure how many times Lisa had sex before the relationship ended, but even four years later, she was completely devastated by what she described as her worst sin and complete moment of weakness. Lisa feared that no upstanding Christian man would ever want to marry her because she was damaged goods. "This is why you should set physical limits that will help you avoid sexual temptations," she urged us while drying her eyes.

Another reason I appreciated dating Connor so much was that, as a fellow Christian, he would understand this need to remain pure. One night, cuddled in the back of a bus returning from a choir trip, I nonchalantly mentioned something to Connor about our mutual virginity status when Connor suddenly cleared his throat.

"I'm actually not a virgin," he said hesitantly.

"What?" I gasped. Tears started to form in my eyes, as he recounted his first sexual experience.

A friend of his late father had set him up with a young student at a local college. What was supposed to be a casual date turned into him spending the night in her dorm room. He claimed that he wasn't even really into her and criticized her for having emotional issues. Then he said that he woke up the next morning to her sucking on his penis, and he couldn't resist the urge to have sex.

If a guy told me this story now, I'd respond with a loud "Bullshit!" But back then I didn't have a lot of experience with male desire. Connor should have just come out and said that he was set up with a gorgeous and brilliant pre-medical student with a great figure skater's body, and that he was ready to try sex. But my bullshit meter wasn't yet fully developed. My naivety convinced me that he was the victim, and I actually felt sorry for him.

I forgave Connor, just like Jesus would. But little by little, our fragile union began to crack. His charm wore off, and I started to see a side of him that not only made me uncomfortable, but sometimes infuriated me.

I first started noticing this less than desirable behavior during spring break in March. We decided to drive down to Florida to stay with my family. By now, I knew it was necessary to reveal to my parents that we were a serious and committed couple. Surprisingly and uncharacteristically, my parents took the news well and treated Connor with warm acceptance. In fact, during a Wal-Mart outing, when my father had Connor to himself, he told him that there are many ways for couples to experience physical pleasure, other than sex. My father encouraged him to explore back rubbing and other massage techniques. Connor seemed totally freaked out when he relayed this to me, and I was speechless.

The visit with my parents was a success. I was ecstatic that they were on their best behavior. Just as I was relishing how well things seemed to be going while driving back to West Point, Connor felt the need to criticize my driving skills. I knew I was a good driver and that Connor was just being sexist. His nitpicking exploded when I stopped to refuel just short of the DC Beltway.

"I'm going to drive the rest of the way," Connor said.

"Why? I'm fine. I don't need to rest. I can keep driving."

"No, I don't want you driving on the Beltway. It's dangerous, and you're not a good enough driver to handle it."

"Excuse me? I can't believe you just said that!"

"Laura, it's my car, and we do what I say," he insisted.

"No, I'm not moving."

We went back and forth viciously for a few minutes, until I realized that we would be late returning to school if we didn't stop arguing, and tardiness resulted in serious consequences. I finally relented (like usual) and switched seats. But I continued to berate Connor for being such a heartless jerk until he responded.

"Quit it Laura!" he yelled and slapped my leg.

"What the hell did you just do?" I screamed at him.

"Nothing. I didn't do anything."

"Yes you did! You just hit me! You just freakin' hit me, you asshole!"

"I didn't hit you."

"Yes, you did. So now you want to lie about it."

"Calm down. I didn't hit you. I was just pushing you out of the way because you were interfering with my driving."

I was astounded.

We rode in silence the rest of the way to New York. Eventually Connor got back into my good graces by being a little mushy and reminding me of our divinely ordained marriage.

Once we were back at school, life continued as normal. Organic chemistry was kicking my ass ; all I could do was try to keep up. I relished any time that I could hang out with Connor, who had recently started giving me gentle back rubs in my barracks room (only when my roommate was out) to lessen my stress, or maybe he had taken to heart what my father had suggested. We took our chances breaking the rules by closing my door, since cadets of the opposite sex weren't allowed to be in a room together with the door closed. Only the secretly gay cadets could happily enjoy private forays without breaking that official rule.

"Let me rub your belly with baby oil," Connor said one night.

"OK." I turned onto my back and lifted my shirt to expose my belly. I knew Lisa probably wouldn't approve, but Connor wasn't just some guy I was dating. He was my future husband. Plus, his massages felt really good. I closed my eyes as he proceeded to rub my belly with oil.

"Laura, can I tell you something?"

"Uhmm hmmm," I murmured and waited for him to say something about how much he loved me.

"I want six kids," he said. "And I can't wait for you to be pregnant."

"What?" I sat up and looked at him as if he had said an alien life form was protruding from his penis. I knew that according to everyone at church, bearing children was my primary purpose for existence, along with being a "helpmate" to my husband (like Eve was to Adam)—but six kids? And him fantasizing about me being pregnant!

"My mom had six kids," Connor explained.

"Yeah, but she didn't raise all of them at once," I countered. "She had three with your dad and then left and had three more with your stepdad. So it's not like she had to worry about six at any given time."

"But still, I want a big family. I love having that many brothers and sisters. Six is reasonable."

"Forget it. Two is enough. I'm not going to only be a mother my whole life. With six kids I'll have time for nothing else."

"But…"

"It's not up for negotiation. It's my body."

"How about we compromise?" Connor offered. "You want two and I want six. How about we settle on four?"

"You're crazy. I'm not discussing this anymore." I turned on my side and figured we could argue about this at a more appropriate time, like several years later. I certainly wasn't going to admit to him that ever since I was a little girl, I knew that I didn't want children.

But the biggest shock came one afternoon prior to departing for a church retreat. Connor and I were standing next to each other in formation as the cadet in charge was taking accountability of everyone. In normal Army formations, we were supposed to stand at attention and look straight ahead while remaining quiet. Church formations obviously didn't uphold these Army standards. It was perfectly acceptable to talk quietly as the head count was being conducted. For some reason, on this afternoon, when I was speaking softly to a friend standing beside me, Connor started chastising me in a firm manner.

"Laura, stop talking."

"Why? What's up?" I turned to look at him.

"You're being rude."

"No I'm not."

"I don't want to have to tell you again," he repeated, his voice raised. "This is a military formation, and you're disregarding the rules."

"Actually, this is a church formation. Stop yelling at me. You can't talk to me like that."

"I outrank you and you need to stop talking."

"Don't you dare try to pull cadet rank on me. I'm your girlfriend, not your soldier, and there's no need to act like this!"

Fuming, I stormed onto the bus. I didn't even want to sit next to him. I tried to sit with someone else, but Connor grabbed me and forced me down next to him. I proceeded to argue with him about how inappropriate it was to disrespect me in such a manner, but he stuck to his guns, claiming how important it was to maintain decorum in the formation.

I couldn't understand why God would partner me with someone so contrary to my independent spirit. Maybe we weren't meant to get married after all. Was a Christian union supposed to bring me so much angst? I knew I wasn't anything like my submissive mentors, but they were the only ones I felt I could turn to for help. Each and every one of them encouraged me to stick it out and make it work. When I reached my boiling point, Connor suggested we try couple's counseling.

Connor and I met with Chaplain Mark Baker, an active duty Army lieutenant colonel who had graduated from West Point in the early 1980s and served as the cadet First Captain—the highest ranking military cadet. Chaplain Baker looked like the spitting image of Chief Justice John Roberts—handsome, perfect and conservative. We spoke with Chaplain Baker about our constant arguing and how pressured I felt to stay in the relationship because this was God's will for our lives. Chaplain Baker absorbed what we had to say and briefly summed up our problems with two words: separation anxiety.

"Separation anxiety? What does that mean?" I asked.

"It's very simple," he responded. "You and Connor are about to experience a long-term separation when he graduates. This is so common, especially for military couples. Your emotions are heightened. You are more sensitive. Small issues get made into larger ones because of your fragile state. Arguing occurs more frequently. I counsel couples all of the time for this very condition. Just be aware of your emotions and try to relax and enjoy each other during your last few months together."

"See Laura, we're going to be just fine." Connor put his hand on mine.

CHAPTER NINE

Even though I wasn't convinced Chaplain Baker solved all of Connor's and my issues, I still enjoyed receiving counseling and wondered if he could help me deal with my parents. They were making this whole West Point experience seem a million times harder than necessary.

My organic chemistry struggles made me wonder if I was pursuing the wrong major, and maybe I shouldn't become a doctor. When I tried discussing it with my father, he screamed at me for wanting to give up too easily. His lack of understanding and support didn't seem right anymore, now that I had examples of other parents to serve as a comparison.

Most of the other parents made an effort to visit their children as often as possible. I understood that finances were rough, and my parents actually had to go on food stamps shortly after I started at West Point, but it still seemed as if visiting me wasn't a priority. The lack of funding also prevented me from going home except once or twice a year, and I usually relied on the generosity of friends and their families to have a place of respite during holiday weekends.

Instead of making the most of our phone conversations, since this was our only quality time, my father still harassed me about studying and boys. Then he would pick a fight and not speak to me for several days, and sometimes even weeks. My mother bugged me about upsetting him, instead of trying to smooth things over.

The worst of my father's control tactics happened back during my plebe year, when my high school friend Joey invited me to visit him and some of his buddies at the Coast Guard Academy. He threatened, "If you go away this weekend to visit Joey, we'll never give you financial support again." He didn't think it was appropriate for a woman to visit a man, even though Joey and I were strictly platonic. (He didn't see the irony of me living mostly among men.) My father's threat didn't hold any weight, as my parents only occasionally sent me a ten- or twenty-dollar bill, plus they had stolen my life savings (that "loan" would never be repaid). So I ignored my father and visited Joey. He went ballistic when he found out. He called Joey's mother, berated her for being a terrible mother and then called Joey's sister a whore. It wasn't the first time my father called a high school friend's parents and called their daughter a whore.

Back in high school, I suspected my parents were different, especially when I watched my friends interact with their parents in a carefree, harmonious fashion. When I complained to my parents, asking them to be more like the other parents, my father claimed they all acted different in the privacy of their own homes, and that they were just being nice publicly. I didn't have much proof, as my parents restricted my time with friends. At West Point, however, I spent many holiday weekends in the homes of my friends' families. It was the first time I was exposed to parents actually loving, supporting and doting on their kids. My initial thought was that it was obnoxious because I didn't realize it was normal.

I once asked Anna, "Don't your parents ever yell at you? You seem like you're more like friends."

Anna was like, "What? No, they don't yell at me!"

After that discussion, I was ready to seek guidance from Chaplain Baker. I didn't have high expectations, but he said something really profound.

"Laura, you have to live your life for Jesus, not your parents, and sometimes that can be in conflict."

He explained that the way my parents were treating me wasn't "God-like"—it was onerous—and, therefore, I didn't have to listen to them. Jesus would have encouraged kindness and being a good person. It was more important that I listened to God and put Jesus first, before my parents.

I suddenly realized that I would never be good enough for my parents. It disgusted me that while chastising me, they simultaneously had a large framed photo of me on their wall, in my full parade uniform, and they bragged to anyone and everyone about me going to West Point.

Their hypocrisy and using my accomplishments for self-glorification infuriated me, but my anger also made it easier to stop caring so much about pleasing them.

While my Christian community helped me to see that I could distance myself from my abusive family, they still implored me to cling to Connor. It reminded me of when my father used to talk about his "umbrella" during home church. He said that as a girl, I was under his umbrella, and then when it was time to get married, I would fall under my husband's umbrella. I supposed this was the time when God wanted me to change umbrellas.

My twenty-year-old brain was weary and overwhelmed. If I was going to make it through the end of yuk year, then I needed to buckle up for tough finals in physics, statistics and organic chemistry. While studying for our organic chemistry final, Anna asked, "Laura, why don't you push me down the stairs, and I'll grab you; that way, you fall too, and then we won't have to take our test."

"That's an awesome plan. I'd much rather go to the hospital with broken bones than take this damn test."

While we never executed our injurious fantasies, Anna did make the final more fun by handing me a candy bracelet to wear.

"Put this on before you get to class. I've got the matching necklace. I'll be thinking of you when chomping down on this candy."

I showed up to class in my drab black and gray uniform, bedazzled with a rainbow of candy strung on my right wrist. Whenever I needed a minor mental break in the middle of this intense exam, I chomped away at my bracelet. I not only looked ridiculous, but everyone could hear me breaking the hard candy with my teeth. But instead of feeling embarrassed, I delighted in my little conformist rebellion.

CHAPTER TEN

I needed to start pondering my future Army career and realized that it wasn't going to be medicine. West Point only had about eighteen coveted slots to medical school, and there were more than eighteen cadets who kicked my ass in organic chemistry. Even though I continued to make the dean's list and excelled physically, I knew I could never make the cut. But no other option appealed to me, especially since being a woman greatly limited what field I could enter.

During my time at West Point (1997 to 2001), a woman could enter the following career fields, or branches of the Army:

- Adjutant General's Corps (Human Resources Management)
- Finance Corps (Financial Management)

- Medical Service Corps (Hospital Administration, which seemed like a good alternative to being a doctor. However, this branch had very few slots, which would ultimately go to cadets who achieved higher GPAs—i.e. those who'd majored in easier subjects than I did—since branch selection went in order of class rank)
- Ordnance Corps (bombs)
- Transportation Corps (trucks)
- Quartermaster Corps (logistics, supplies)
- Aviation (flying helicopters, which required perfect vision without corrective lenses or surgery, i.e., not me)
- Air Defense Artillery (Patriot missiles, etc.)
- Engineer Corps (construction or topographical, since women were barred from combat engineering leadership roles)
- Military Intelligence (collecting and disseminating battlefield information)
- Signal Corps (communications and technology)
- Field Artillery (on an extremely limited basis)

Technically I could one day become a general through these career paths, but that was highly unlikely since women were barred from entering the combat arms branches (Infantry, Armor, Special Forces), which were more valued and respected in the Army. I was also alarmed to discover that entering the military through ROTC or Officer Candidate School (OCS) offered more career options, like nursing, psychology, anesthesiology, nutrition, public affairs, photography, journalism, social work and so many other fields that have a lot more relevance in the civilian world.

I studied chemistry because I wanted to be a military doctor. But when I realized this wasn't likely to happen, I thought about changing my major. I was fascinated with the brief exposure I had to psychology. Taking classes in that field sounded delightful compared to spending more time slaving away in various chemistry labs. I found human nature far more fascinating than studying the way chemicals react.

I also needed to select my summer assignment—what role I would play in training the younger cadets with basic training or at Camp Buckner. I knew this would be a challenge because my approach to discipline was not according to West Point norms. I hated yelling and saw it as pointless. Anytime an upperclassman had yelled at me, whatever they were saying went in one ear and out the other. As a yuk (sophomore), I was assigned to mentor two plebes and vowed to never yell at them and to treat them with the utmost respect. West Point is stressful enough. The last thing someone needs is for yet another person trying to prove something and taking it out on them. I believed my role was to be a nurturing safe haven for my plebes.

My philosophy would not gel with being a cadre member for basic training, nor did I feel like training new yuks in infantry tactics at Camp Bucker. Just when I was feeling desperate, I learned about the Beast Counselor role and submitted my application. Luckily I was accepted. So between sophomore and junior years, I spent the summer counseling and encouraging new cadets as they tried to survive their own basic training—something I was actually thrilled about. I couldn't believe that I was one of those new cadets just two years prior. It felt like a lifetime ago.

Connor graduated when I finished yuk year, and then I attended and graduated from Air Assault School—another West Point graduation requirement. (Air Assault School teaches helicopter familiarization, sling loading operations and rappelling. Getting to rappel out of a Black Hawk helicopter at seventy-five feet in the air was one of my most exhilarating experiences to date.) Then it was time to prepare for my Beast Counseling role, where the other cadet counselors and I trained with the psychology department—much nicer instructors than the chemistry department. I dug this touchy-feely stuff.

Right before it was time to receive our new cadets for their basic training, Anna (who was preparing to be a squad leader) and I had a heart-to-heart about our future at West Point. As we pondered taking more awful chemistry classes, Anna announced she was going to change majors.

"To what?" I asked.

"Arts, Philosophy and Literature. I can't wait to start taking more classes in that field! What about you? You can't possibly be looking forward to even more advanced chemistry classes."

"I don't know. I'm really torn," I told her. "I feel like we sacrificed so much in organic chemistry, and I'd hate to see that go to waste, so maybe I should continue with the major. But I really don't want to. I love this psychology stuff."

"It's never too late to change," Anna encouraged me.

I, on the other hand, despite the pit in my stomach, pushed aside my conscience and decided to stick with chemistry. For some reason, I assumed that people would be more impressed with the fact that I majored in chemistry rather than psychology, and that it would lead to more lucrative jobs down the road. But I secretly envied Anna and how effortlessly she abandoned her chemistry pursuit in search of a major that was more in line with her interests.

I would think of this decision often as I continued to struggle and deeply hate almost every single one of my chemistry classes. My only source of humor came from the two life-size skeletons on display in the back of the microbiology lab that my friend John and I maneuvered into sexual positions. Lab met every other week, and each session provided an opportunity for us to place them in new sexually compromising positions. We always wondered how long it would take for someone to notice. But every week we returned to lab, and there were the skeletons, still groping each other's genitals.

I was a natural at Beast Counseling. It felt amazing to find my groove. Some of the hard-core cadets teased that I was the West Point "milk and cookies lady," but I proudly fulfilled this unique leadership role.

As a counselor, the most common problem new cadets brought to me was, "I think I made a bad decision or mistake and am thinking about quitting." I listened with empathy, not judgment and gave them the best advice possible. Sometimes it was appropriate to encourage them to take one day at a time and see if they could make it through the next day. Other times it was appropriate for me to simply be the first line of defense and then send them on to a more qualified care provider.

One cadet said he wanted to quit because a friend of his had died just before he came to West Point, and he was dealing with a lot of grief. I referred him to Reverend Ron Fritts, a kind, civilian Presbyterian minister assigned to the West Point chaplaincy. After meeting they agreed it would be best for this cadet to leave and resume his civilian life. Right after making that decision, the cadet seemed incredibly relieved and confident in his decision.

Another day, as the new cadets stood in line to get their new rifles, I noticed a girl clutching her stomach when her squad leader made them all do pushups and flutter kicks. I discreetly pulled her out of line to ask what was wrong. She said she had had an abortion nine days before coming to West Point and was experiencing a lot of pain.

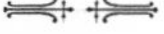

My mind immediately flashed to my twelve-year-old self, standing on the side of US Highway 19 in New Port Richey, forming a "life chain" with my father, mother and other pro-life advocates. We held "Abortion Kills" signs and chanted prayers aloud. Some drivers who passed us honked their horns in accord. Others lowered their windows and flipped us the bird. It was exhilarating, standing on this dangerous highway, evoking different emotions from the general public.

In his quest to deter me from not having sex (which could lead to not only eternal damnation, but also unwanted pregnancy), my father also made me watch several abortion documentaries. The narrators in these films spoke over scenes of loud, vibrating tools cutting up unborn babies and featured pictures of mutilated fetuses. One dead fetus in particular was still visibly intact and bright red, freshly killed from being drowned in a saline solution.

I was horrified and disgusted, but determined to not let my father see how grossed out I was. I watched with stoic silence, never flinching or looking away. When one particular image flashed on the screen, a dead fetus's face contorted into a scream, I silently swore that I would never allow myself to be in the position of needing an abortion.

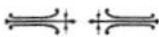

I pulled this young female cadet away so she could cry in private. "If you want to talk about it, you can," I told her. She spoke a little, telling me how her condom broke and how the father was also a new cadet, and I listened with compassion. (Although a few years later she said she thought it was funny and endearing how I initially turned gray, not expecting an abortion to be her excuse.) Pregnancy would have obviously interfered with training, but she also couldn't be a cadet and a parent. West Point explicitly prohibits cadets from being parents. She would have had to give the child away for adoption, or sign custody over to someone else. So she terminated her pregnancy and now was in both physical and emotional pain. After our talk she told me she would also like to speak to a chaplain. I only knew of male chaplains (we had an amazing woman chaplain who I unfortunately didn't meet until years later), so I asked the cadet if she would feel comfortable speaking to one. When she said yes, I arranged for her to meet Chaplain Fritts, and afterward, she felt relieved and confident that she could finish Beast. I also helped her obtain a profile, i.e. limited physical duty for the rest of basic training, which is common protocol when a cadet is sick or injured.

Other new cadets were simply intimidated and just needed a comforting ear and some basic advice. One super-skinny girl, who I had suspected was suffering from an eating disorder, told me she was so stressed out that she wasn't getting her period. I had her meet with a doctor who placed her on a birth control pill to help regulate her hormones. One guy came to me and proceeded to talk to me about philosophy for three hours straight. I think he was lonely and missed his brainy friends. Mostly, cadets just needed someone to lend a sympathetic ear. Their only contact with the outside world was a weekly ten-minute phone call and letters, of which they had barely any time to write. I remembered this lonely feeling all too well and wanted to do my part to mitigate the pain.

I loved being a counselor. It was one of the most rewarding experiences of my life, and not having the courage to switch to a psychology major would haunt me for many years.

CHAPTER ELEVEN

Junior, or "cow" year started right after my Beast Counselor assignment. The origin of this nickname most likely comes from the phrase "until the cows come home," since cadets used to not be allowed to leave West Point on holiday until the summer after yuk year. The women loved being called cows, especially those of us who had to buy bigger uniform pants and couldn't squeeze into our plebe "trou" (West Point's equivalent of skinny jeans). We also loved being called trou, a derogatory term used to describe a woman cadet, referencing how her hips and curves make the uniform trousers look funny.

The most monumental aspect of starting cow year is the service commitment incurred as soon as you step foot into your first class of the semester. People can actually attend West Point for free—up to two years—and leave with no strings attached (except your bruised psyche). But as soon as you start cow year, you incur an actual Army service obligation. So if you're kicked out of West Point for academic or behavioral issues between the start of cow year and graduation, you have to pay back your education by serving as an enlisted soldier in the Army.

I reluctantly dove right into a full chemistry course load: Quantitative Analysis, Biology, Thermodynamics and Modern Physics, along with Advanced Composition, International Relations and PE. Even though my brain and body were completely taxed, I dedicated even more of myself to the Cadet Chapel choir and became its president.

As president, I was responsible for rallying the troops, getting them to come to choir practice and keeping tabs on their morale. While I loved being president and singing with the choir, I hated the choir music. It was like funeral music—sad and somber. Several times I asked the choir master if we could change things up, but he always said no. He was only the third choir master / organist in the longstanding history of the Cadet Chapel, and he resigned a few months after I became president. We had interim choir directors, but not a lot of people came to our performances that year. I was convinced it was because of the dreary music.

Connor traveled from Missouri, where he was at officer training, to join me at the first ECF retreat of my junior year in Rainsburg, which is located at the foothills of the Allegheny Mountains in southern Pennsylvania. One night, a few of us gathered in the communal kitchen to discuss the church choir. Since I was Connor's successor to the choir's leadership, I wanted to bounce some ideas off him.

"Church is becoming a real drag for people," I said. "It's tough enough to have to wake up early on your only day off, and the services just aren't exciting enough to attract sleepy cadets. I think if we changed the tone of the music, it'll be more enjoyable."

"But you'd be messing with a lot of tradition," Connor said. "I don't think that's right."

"If that tradition is boring and doesn't encourage people to come to church, then what good is it?" I countered. "You remember how you struggled with getting enough people to come sing in the choir last year. I don't want that happening on my watch. I want to make church and choir as fun as possible for everyone."

"Well, I have to say that I completely disagree with everything you're trying to do. Plus, you know how I feel about women being leaders in the church. It's just not appropriate. So I don't think you belong in that role in the first place. A guy should really be leading the choir."

Not wanting to ruin a beautiful weekend, I made a joke about Connor just being jealous that I was a more proactive leader and worried I was going to improve on his reign. Secretly though, his chauvinistic attitude really did make me more determined to completely outdo him as choir leader.

Later that weekend Connor revealed that after training in Missouri, he was heading to Korea for his first official Army assignment. I was crushed, particularly since he hadn't consulted me before asking for that location. But there was nothing I could do about it. We agreed that when it was time for my Cadet Troop Leader Training the following summer, I would request to do it in Korea so we could be together. Connor left for Korea the night after my 500th night formal in January, the same night he performed oral sex on me for the first time (not a bad parting gift). Unfortunately, he wasn't very good at keeping in touch, which frustrated me to no end, especially when I experienced my third concussion in as many years.

My second concussion had occurred during a winter church retreat of my sophomore year—a ski trip to Pennsylvania. Having grown up in Florida, I wasn't exactly an expert skier, or even a good one. The hill was small but icy. When I saw a kid blocking my path on the slope, I skied away to avoid hitting him and ended up falling and hitting my head on a block of ice. The impact knocked me unconscious for about forty-five seconds. When I woke up, there were people standing over me. I was dizzy, and everything was blurry. The church retreat doctor had me lay down for the rest of the trip, left me with ice and frequently checked my vital signs. When I returned to West Point, a military doctor confirmed the concussion. It took about five days of feeling weird before I resumed normal activities, and I never thought anything of it except that I wouldn't ski again because I totally sucked at it.

As fate would have it, though, West Point assigned skiing as my PE class for my junior year. I wanted ice skating, but it conflicted with some of my chemistry labs. In the beginning of the ski course, we navigated easy bunny trails and gradually advanced to the intermediate blue hills. That was bad enough, but then we were suddenly told to traverse the big slope, which was super icy, narrow, steep and tree-lined. I was terrified but had no choice. I felt lucky to be alive after making it down the first time.

After that, the instructor said, "Now we're going to do moguls." I raised my hand and asked, "What are moguls?" He explained that they're a series of bumps in the snow. On my first attempt, the tip of my ski got stuck in a mogul. Before I knew what happened, my boot separated from my ski, I went flying into the air and landed on my face. I was rattled but didn't lose consciousness and skied to the bottom of the hill. I hoped and assumed I was OK, but my instructor seemed panicked and insisted I get checked out.

On the examining table, I suddenly had an excruciating headache and felt super dizzy. The doctor examining me wouldn't let me fall asleep; I think he feared I might lose consciousness if I did. Over the next two weeks, I visited the emergency room nine times. The pain was so intense, it often brought me to tears. I felt mentally handicapped—I was so out of it. Everything was blurry. I was like a vegetable in class.

My tactical officer (the officer assigned to my company), Major Muster, started treating me like shit after that, because he thought I was trying to get one over on the system, milking my "injury" in order to get out of class and other duties. Not that he had any ground to suggest this; up until this point, I was a good student and stayed out of trouble. He wasn't the only one punishing me for my incapacitation. During one of my visits to the emergency room, a civilian nurse named Janine accused me of faking my illness and reported me to my tactical officer, resulting in demerits and mandatory weekend study hall, even though Cathy from ECF tried to intervene on my behalf. *Perhaps this is one of the reasons why Keller Army Hospital is dubbed Killer Army Hospital,* I thought.

My primary care doctor at West Point suggested I spend spring break at Walter Reed Medical Center's head injury clinic. I had to get approval from my tactical officer, and while it should have been assumed, he played hardass. I later discovered that he wanted me to leave West Point altogether as a punishment for being sick, even though Walter Reed confirmed my injury with a post concussive syndrome diagnosis. Today it would be called a traumatic brain injury" (TBI).

I should have taken a medical leave of absence, but the thought never occurred to me. Fortunately, my doctor finally prescribed migraine medication that saved me. A few of my instructors were compassionate about my condition and didn't expect me to make up all of my missed work, but my Medical Radiation Physics (an elective, mind you) instructor gave me a D, obviously my first ever. After five months, I finally started to feel better and was able to wean myself off the migraine medication. But I received a 2.3 GPA that semester—my only semester not on the dean's list. My parents were aware of my injury but never came up to check on me. I expected my father to berate me as usual when my report card arrived. Instead, he told me, "I'm really proud of you. You went through hell, and you stuck it out." *I should get Ds more often!*

Cognitively, I was never the same. I always prided myself on my ability to study and concentrate for hours on end, but after that third head injury, focusing for long periods of time became next to impossible. I still feel those effects to this day.

CHAPTER TWELVE

After an incredibly tough cow year, I couldn't wait for my month of Cadet Troop Leader Training in Korea. Connor suggested we take a two-week vacation in Hawaii to kick off the summer. So first I would fly to Korea on the Army's dime and then we would travel to Hawaii together. I looked into hotels on Waikiki Beach and casually mentioned my travel plan progress after ECF Bible study one night.

"You can't stay in a hotel!" Cathy yelled.

"Why not?" I asked, perplexed.

"It's so bad!"

"How?"

"You'll be tempted to have sex!"

"No I won't. If I wanted to have sex, I could easily have had it by now. A hotel won't change that," I reasoned.

"But still, you'll look like you're having sex."

"What's that supposed to mean?"

"Devon, come over here and explain this to Laura," Cathy demanded.

They both lectured me about the impropriety of even sharing a hotel room with someone I'm not married to. When I said I didn't care what other people think, that I know what's right in my heart, and it's no one else's business, they said I wasn't projecting the image of a good Christian. They made me feel like a complete harlot.

Abbie Denali, another ECF wife, walked by and eavesdropped on our conversation.

"My brother-in-law is stationed in Hawaii and has a big house there on Schofield Barracks. You'll stay with him."

"Then it's settled!" Cathy said excitedly.

Ironically, the brother-in-law was gone for most of our trip and thankfully was kind and accommodating. I slept in the guest room, and Connor slept in our host's son's room, complete with race car driver decor. Even though we had plenty of privacy, Connor wasn't affectionate and refused to sleep in the guest bed with me. I couldn't figure out why he was so physically cold. I complained incessantly when he refused to cuddle, but he wouldn't budge.

We were now less than a year away from our supposed wedding date (the day after my West Point graduation), and he had yet to formally propose. In my mind, it only made sense that he would propose in Hawaii, the perfect romantic backdrop for a memorable engagement. But as our vacation progressed, I suspected it wasn't going to happen.

"You haven't bought me a ring yet, have you?" I inquired one evening near the end of our vacation.

Hesitating, Connor responded, "Um, no."

"I thought so."

"It's not that I haven't thought about it. I just don't know what to get you."

"But I've told you what I think would look nice, and we've gone looking for rings before. Didn't it occur to you to have one ready for Hawaii?"

"I guess not. I'm so sorry. Please forgive me."

"But what am I supposed to do now? Go back to New York, tell everyone that I'm getting married next year, and then when they ask where my ring is, have nothing to show them?"

"We'll get a ring this summer, I promise."

"Fine, but I'll just have you know that the surprise and romance of the moment is ruined. Thanks a lot."

We passed by many jewelry stores on our way to dinner, and Connor agreed to slow down and peruse them with me. I even tried on a few so he would commit my preferences and ring size to memory.

"I really like this one," I told Connor, marveling at how this particular ring looked on my not-so-dainty finger. "And it fits perfectly," I continued.

"It's really nice," Connor said, also admiring the ring. "Do you want to get it?"

"Not at a store like this. This is a tourist trap. You should only buy diamonds wholesale so you don't get ripped off." I replied, hoping that he appreciated my frugality.

"Well, let's see how much it costs," he motioned to the saleslady.

"Oh that's on clearance," she said. "Four-hundred and fifty dollars."

"That's it?" I had suspected this was one of those stores that purposely marks up the merchandise to ridiculous prices and then pretends you're getting a good deal by promoting major clearances.

"Yes, that's the final price," she answered.

I turned to Connor, "That's so cheap. They're not the biggest diamonds, and they're probably crappy quality, but the ring is pretty."

"If you want it, I'll buy it for you." Connor smiled.

I pondered some more and then agreed. "Yeah, let's do it."

Connor told the lady to wrap everything up and that he was ready to buy the ring. Then she said, "Cash only."

Connor turned to me with a disappointed look. "I only have three-hundred and seventy-five, and I already made the max withdrawal amount from the ATM today."

I thought quickly, "How about I go to an ATM and withdrawal the rest?"

"I feel bad asking you to do that."

"Don't worry about it. It's not your fault. I don't mind."

"You don't? Well that's nice. I appreciate it."

"I'll be right back," I said and ran over to an ATM to withdraw the remaining balance for my own engagement ring.

A part of me was definitely annoyed, and I immediately flashed back to a shopping trip with my mom where we walked past a diamond display in the mall. She was lamenting the fact that she had to pawn her engagement ring years ago and that my father would never be able to replace it. I wanted to roll my eyes at how much she depended on him for her happiness and well-being, but before I could begin a tirade of how she needed to do more things for herself, she offered, "You'll be able to buy your own diamonds, Laura." Maybe she got me more than I realized.

"I'll make it up to you, I promise," Connor said, as I handed the remaining balance to the sales lady.

I linked my arm with his. "Just make sure you're prepared to surprise me with it during a romantic moment. I won't wear it until you officially propose," I said as I handed the wrapped ring to him.

"Sounds like a plan," Connor promised.

When our vacation came to an end, Connor still hadn't proposed. I started calculating potential engagement possibilities as we ventured to Korea.

My training unit was located down in Seoul, an hour and a half bus ride from Connor's unit, which was located not too far from the demilitarized zone (DMZ) bordering North Korea. (A group of us from West Point had a fun guided bus tour of the DMZ, where we got to walk around a building that sits on the border and is used for peace talks. My favorite photo is where I have one foot standing in South Korea and the other in North Korea. A North Korean guard stood close by, ensuring we didn't do anything to threaten their country.) Our schedules would probably only allow us to be together on weekends, so perhaps we would get engaged during that time. I did have one entire week remaining with him before I needed to report for training, but I didn't want him proposing to me on his shitty military installation. I racked my brain for romantic spots in Korea.

Despite Connor's negligence, which didn't help with complicated logistics in Korea, I enjoyed working in a real Army unit and enmeshed myself in its daily life. My sponsor was a young woman lieutenant, a recent West Point graduate, who I remembered worked my new cadet basic training and supervised my first urinalysis. (She didn't remember me.) She was kind, laid-back and spent a good portion of my time there on an Australian vacation—so she entrusted her job to me. Wanting to make her proud (and not ruin things for her), I turned to her right hand woman for guidance—a senior noncommissioned officer (NCO), a.k.a. senior enlisted soldier, named Chandra. Chandra and I immediately bonded and made a great team. Chandra was in the Adjutant General's Corps, which solidified my decision to enter this career field.

Midway through my time in Korea, Connor and I planned an overnight stay at a nice hotel in Seoul. Because he hadn't proposed the previous two weekends, I assumed he was waiting for this special outing to officially become engaged. We spent the weekend touring the Korean War memorial, navigating the downtown streets and shopping at Lotte World, one of the largest shopping centers in the world. I was trying to absorb the culture and enjoy a fun adventure, but Connor was in a constant foul mood, criticizing the Korean food, culture and people for being rude. Instead of dining on ethnic cuisine, he insisted on eating at American chain restaurants like Bennigan's. When I wanted to go on some of the rides at Lotte World, he complained of a stomach ache. Finally, the weekend concluded, and I still had no ring.

"I'm sorry, but honestly, I just keep forgetting to bring it with me," he explained.

"It's my fucking engagement ring. How the hell can you forget something like that?"

"I don't know."

"Well, you obviously have some mental handicap that precludes you from remembering to propose."

"Laura, I don't want to fight with you now. Can we please talk about this later?"

We then spent a tense weekend trying to work through the same issues that constantly plagued our relationship. I was ready to give up, but Connor cried, explaining how his life was full of abandonment and disappointments, that he couldn't lose me after losing his mother to abandonment and his father to alcohol. He claimed that I was the most important thing that had ever happened to him, and he couldn't fathom life without me. I tried to empathize and promised to keep trying, as long as he did the same.

As my return trip to New York was now only a few days away, my coworkers made special gestures to recognize the time we spent together. I enjoyed nice luncheons, farewell gifts and well wishes. One guy in particular, a young West Point graduate named Alex who had an amazing ability to run two miles in under eleven minutes (while hung over!) arranged a bar-hopping adventure in the notorious party district of Itaewon. He was shocked that Connor hadn't introduced me to this fun area yet and invited him to come along. Since it was a Monday night, Connor immediately declined.

"Of course you're not coming," I sighed. "You're such a drag. Who cares if you don't get much sleep? I'm leaving in a few days. Don't you want to see me again?"

"I do, but I'm really busy. Please don't start another fight."

"No, I have to. We could have spent a lot more time together this summer, but you never would. I don't get it. I'm your future wife, and you don't even want to see me. What the fuck is wrong you?" I screamed.

"Please calm down. Go have fun. I'm going to make this up to you, I promise."

Despite bearing a heavy heart over yet another argument, I ended up going out with my new friends for what would end up my best night in Korea. Alex invited another young lieutenant who didn't drink much, so she and I nursed our girly cocktails while we cheered Alex as he downed hearty amounts of beer and hard liquor. He was the perfect host, extremely well acquainted with every bar in Itaewon. We ventured up the notorious Hooker Hill, and I was fascinated, witnessing prostitution first-hand. It was almost midnight, but many bar owners had their children running around in the streets. Being in this wild environment excited me. We stopped at one particular bar that always plays "God Bless the USA" at midnight, and we sang along rowdily, without a care in the world. *I wish Connor would just let loose and have fun like this*, I thought.

After our midnight song, for an early morning drink, Alex bought a kettle of soju, which is essentially the bottom part of a two-liter bottle of soda filled with soju and a sugary drink mix. I'd heard stories about people getting completely wasted on this concoction, so I gingerly took one tiny sip, and felt hotness pervading my entire insides.

"Want more?" Alex asked enthusiastically.

"I think I'm good. That was plenty," I replied. The other girl also only allowed herself a small sip, so I thought Alex would dump the remaining booze, but he guzzled it instead.

"Wow, that's impressive!" I yelled as we ventured back to the military living quarters. Alex got me back to my room safely and assured me that he would easily find a cab to his apartment. We said goodnight, and then I went to bed feeling buzzed yet refreshed.

I spent the next day saying my farewells to everyone and reliving the previous evening's events with Alex and the other lieutenant. Throughout the day, my thoughts wandered to Connor, and I suspected that he might surprise me with a visit to officially propose. Sure enough, when I went back to my room after work, he was waiting outside for me.

"Surprise," he said, handing me a bouquet of flowers and shyly kissing me.

"I thought you might be showing up," I said. "How long have you been waiting here?"

"It doesn't matter. All that matters is I'm here."

"How long are you here for? Can you spend the night?"

"Unfortunately I can't. You know I would if I could. But I really need to get back tonight."

"OK."

"Let's get something to eat. There's that nice café down the street. Want to go there and eat outside?"

"Sure."

We quietly walked, holding hands, but still experiencing a bit of hesitancy from our last major fight. After ordering dinner, we sat outside and idly chatted. Suddenly Connor stood up, his chair scraping loudly against the concrete, and knelt on one knee, pulling the ring out of his pocket.

"Laura Marie Westley," he said, looking up at me. "Will you marry me?"

I took a deep breath and looked Connor straight in the eyes. "It's about damn time!"

He smiled and placed the ring on my finger. We kissed and held each other for a few brief moments. The other patrons clapped. We were finally officially engaged.

"I need to catch the bus back soon," Connor broke the moment.

"OK," I said and we walked toward the bus station. We held on to each other until it was time for Connor to ascend the bus, knowing that this was the last time we would see each other until Christmas. I didn't cry as he departed. I just stood there waving and feeling completely empty. *Such is life with Connor.* I couldn't wait to get back to New York and reunite with my friends.

CHAPTER THIRTEEN

Despite suffering from a severe case of jet lag for an entire week, the start of my senior, a.k.a. "firstie," year buzzed with excitement. Everyone congratulated me on getting engaged, but I didn't dare reveal the circumstances. Life returned to a normal routine, with significantly more privileges as a senior. Now I could leave campus every evening, keep more civilian clothes in my room, adorn my floor with a rug and have my very own refrigerator! The only thing that prevented me from feeling on top of the world was the infrequency of Connor's communications. After not hearing from him for an entire week, I finally decided to discuss my frustrations with Anna.

Anna and I sat on the bleachers facing the parade field early in the afternoon on the Friday before Labor Day, planning our long weekend, basking in the sun. I decided now would be a good time to let her know what was really going on.

"Can I talk to you about Connor for a minute?"

"Of course, what is it?"

"I haven't heard from him all week, and I know he's available to talk. He hasn't taken a trip anywhere. He's just not calling me."

"Really?"

"The thing is, he does this a lot. I just never said anything, because I didn't want to badmouth him. But he ignores me a lot. I feel like I'm not important to him. And there's more."

"Like what?" Anna asked. I proceeded to tell her about the entire background of our engagement story. She sat there in disbelief.

"Are you willing to put up with that for the rest of your life?" she asked.

I contemplated fighting with Connor for years to come and realized I was being unfair to myself. "No, I deserve better," I said. "What would I do without you?" I hugged Anna tightly.

Then I ran to my room and called Korea. I was surprised when Connor actually answered.

"Hello?"

"Hi," I said curtly.

"How are you? How has your week been?" Connor asked.

I paused to take a deep breath. "Don't you think it's a little ridiculous to be asking your fiancée how her week has been?" I asked him. "Don't you think most engaged couples talk a little more than once a week? Where have you been all week? What were you doing?"

"I've been here, just busy. And then I went on a golf outing with some of the guys."

"So you could have called me, right?"

"I guess. I just didn't think of it. But I was eventually going to get around to it."

"Well, listen here, fuck face, I'm sick and tired of your excuses. You're a pathetic excuse of a man, and I'm taking my ring off right now. We're through."

"Laura, please try to calm down."

"Do you hear me? I'm breaking up with you. Don't you even care? Aren't you going to try and stop me? Here, right now, it's coming off," I yelled as I pulled my ring off and threw it on my desk. "There, it's fucking off."

"What am I supposed to do about it? You're going to do what you want."

"You're damn right I am. I never want to speak to you again. FUCK YOU!" I slammed the phone down on the receiver.

That was the end of Connor and me. Technically, we were engaged for fifteen days.

Unlike others who may cry for days after a breakup, I bounced right back after calling it off with Connor. I honestly felt more relieved than anything else, and I suspect he might have too. By then, I was used to not having him around and too busy to miss him. Every moment of every day was occupied with classes, mandatory training or duties, including another year as president of the Cadet Chapel choir.

Now that I was a senior, I was determined to push for more modern music. I presented my argument to the parish council, on which I sat with Chaplain Baker, Steve McKinney (Colonel Dad), Abbie Denali and other appointed church leaders. I felt Chaplain Baker subtly scoffed at me when I said the current church choir's repertoire seemed too old-fashioned and irrelevant. I could tell he hated being challenged, especially by a woman. I was the opposite of his quiet, submissive wife. In fact, one Sunday afternoon he had some choir cadets over for lunch after church. His wife didn't join us at the table, and instead, served us in silence. Instead of feeling sorry for her, her quiet subservience almost felt antagonistic to my bold persona.

Thankfully Colonel Dad had my back. He helped me convince the powers that be that they needed to get with the program if they ever wanted to fill the church with new cadets again. Not only did they acquiesce, they also allowed us to get the first set of drums in the cadet chapel—a huge deal. Some of the older alums were probably turning in their graves at the thought of drums being used in church music, but I didn't care.

Perhaps the biggest opportunity of serving on the parish council was being part of the search committee for the new choir director and organist. We hired Craig Williams—a brilliant, dynamic, kind, progressive Juilliard School graduate who still serves in the same position today.

Serving as the president of the West Point Cadet Chapel Choir allowed me to glimpse into the beauty of being part of a musical community. Unfortunately, other academic and military duties severely restricted my choir time. But I made the most of that limited time by transforming the musical program at the Cadet Chapel. Besides loving and nurturing my fellow choir cadets and inspiring them to sing better, I witnessed the dramatic improvement of my singing talent and performance confidence, shattered old traditions and incorporated more modern music into the chapel program. I felt proud knowing that my input could impact cadets for years to come, and that I had served my cadets, church leaders and fellow parishioners with all of my heart.

Every year the Cadet Chapel produces the Handel's *Messiah* oratorio. Professional singers are hired as the soloists, and the Cadet Chapel Choir sings the chorus part. Local musicians round out the orchestra, and the choir leader / organist conducts the entire ensemble. My sophomore year, one of our senior choir cadets, Josephine Appleton, sang the soprano solo. *I want to do that my senior year,* I thought.

I learn music by ear; if I can hear something, I can replicate it. When I went home for Christmas a few weeks after Josephine's performance, I saw that my father had CDs of Handel's *Messiah,* performed by the Atlanta Symphony Orchestra. He let me borrow them indefinitely, and I started practicing the soprano solo.

The superintendent (three-star general), a.k.a. Supe, in charge of West Point attended church at the cadet chapel about once a month. During my junior year he became accustomed to seeing me at the front of church, leading songs. That year the Handel's *Messiah* performance only featured civilian professional soloists—no cadets. Shortly after, he approached me.

"I want to see you up there next year, Laura."

I could have died and gone to heaven. Our beloved, revered Supe not only knew me by name, but also essentially commanded that I have the solo. *I will use this to make sure I get the solo next year,* I told myself.

"Yes, Sir!" I promised.

Besides having the Supe on my side, it was a no-brainer for me to have the solo my senior year. If work effort and dedication to the choir alone were reason enough, I was a shoo-in. Plus, I was vocally ready and had been singing along to my father's CDs for the past year and a half. I still needed refinement and consistent practice, though, so I practiced in my barracks room, despite everyone being able to hear me. I apologized profusely to one of my friends next door, but he insisted that he was insanely impressed with my singing and encouraged me to keep going.

I never prayed so hard as I did right before my solo. While I knew I belonged there, I was a little intimidated. I felt that the other soloists were out of my league and I was an amateur imposter, sitting among *professional* singers. I mean, just the day prior I was at the Army-Navy football game in Baltimore, saving my voice and withholding cheers (although with how much our football team sucked, there was nothing to cheer about), spending the entire fourth quarter in the bathroom, warming up under a hand heater. Now I had to switch gears from cadet life to opera singer. (Feeling like an imposter would become an all-too-familiar feeling throughout life, as I constantly push myself to try and quickly excel at so many new endeavors.)

I soaked in the grandeur of the cadet chapel, the 1,500 audience members, the one-hundred-plus ensemble, my gorgeous royal blue gown. (I refused to even ask permission to wear something other than my uniform.) This was my moment to shine, but I knew I was supposed to be glorifying God, not myself. So I prayed that my beautiful voice would bring everyone closer to Him, but I still wanted to kick ass. Thankfully I did well, and while I was relieved when it was over, it only made me want to do it again. Unfortunately, though, singing in the Cadet Chapel Choir was the last time I would sing grand solos for nearly fourteen years (drunken karaoke doesn't count).

As graduation approached, many of my classmates made plans to get married immediately after, including Anna and Bart (who would go on to have six children, to date). I later learned that six months after our breakup, Connor met a pastor's daughter at the church he attended years prior while at prep school. They married shortly thereafter. After racking my brain for months, trying to figure out why Connor insisted on dating me while he wanted to change so much about me, I realized it was more about him needing a wife, any wife for that matter, than actually wanting to be with *me.*

I felt torn about leaving West Point. On the one hand, I couldn't wait to escape the hectic academic schedule and restrictions of cadet life. On the other hand, I also knew I would never enjoy the same intense camaraderie that the unique, enclosed environment at West Point fosters. In addition, I was (for lack of a better term) a big fish in a small pond and enjoyed my seniority. For the last several months leading to the culmination of my academy experience, I wanted to revel in these intangibles.

My classes and workload were still ridiculous, but the increased number of group projects kept me afloat. I was so sick of homework, studying and having a difficult time concentrating in subjects I no longer cared for. By then, I was also the only woman in the engineering concentration of chemistry. All of the others tracked life sciences. I had changed concentrations shortly before my third concussion and was immensely grateful since math was so much easier for me than rote memorization, like anatomy and physiology (which I dropped while changing to engineering). So as the token woman, I was privy to even more boy humor and often the subject of their practical jokes. For my last chemistry final, my friend John hid condoms in my notes, and they all fell to the floor when the exam started. He also hid vintage Playboy magazines all over my dorm room. Every time I opened something, like my medicine cabinet, out came a naked woman from 1980. He even hid one in my pillow case. These practical jokes made me feel a special bond with my West Point brothers.

Despite the lack of concentration and motivation, I found out I would graduate with the Superintendent's Award—given to cadets who receive a 3.0 or above in all three areas: academics, physical and military grades. I would get to wear a gold wreath on my uniform for graduation. I couldn't believe I had survived four grueling years at this institution and hoped it would all be worth it someday. Reflecting back on my cadet career had me thinking back to my high school graduation.

I graduated high school with a perfect 4.44 GPA. But since Lisa McKay earned a 4.46, she was the valedictorian. (Lisa had an extra advanced class, as she opted to take AP Music Theory, plus my having attended a different school freshman year didn't allow me to squeeze in as many AP classes.) Despite coming in number two, and having the opportunity to give the salutatorian speech to my fellow seniors, my father ripped me to shreds. It was impossible to celebrate any accomplishments with him.

The night before my high school graduation, he had me rush him to the emergency room for an unexplainable pain, my mother in tow. My mother was terrified of driving even just a few miles from home, so as soon as I received my driver's license, I was often my father's chauffeur. Instead of partying with my friends, celebrating our last night as high schoolers, I had to stand there and watch him scream at the doctors when they tried to examine him. It turned out he had an ear infection.

I brought my father home from the hospital later that evening. The following day, on the morning of my graduation, he threatened he wouldn't be able to attend the ceremony because he didn't know if he would have to go back into the hospital. However, if I drove to the pharmacy and picked up a prescription for him, then he might be able to risk it.

Instead of focusing on my salutatorian address to a few thousand people and having one last opportunity to bid my classmates farewell, I raced to the pharmacy for my father's medicine. Then I ran into the audience right before the ceremony commenced and handed him his prescription. Far from grateful, my father started yelling at me for getting the wrong medicine from the pharmacist. I could have sworn I requested the correct one of his numerous pain pills; I remember having repeated the medicine's name over and over in my mind beforehand.

So with just a few minutes before I needed to march into the gymnasium with the rest of my class, both of my parents chastised me for being careless and threatened to get up and leave. I welled up with tears of frustration at my inability to coax them to honor my graduation. Then in typical martyr fashion, my father said he would suffer the pain to endure my ceremony before going back to the pharmacy for the right drug.

I walked to the back of the gym feeling crushed, but also determined to give the best speech possible. I knew my speech would be epic even as I wrote it, and I was excited to entertain everyone. I set it to the popular music throughout the big phases of our lives, starting with the theme music from *Star Wars,* to indicate that we were about to embark on a journey of our lives. Then it switched to "Stayin' Alive," since that's was a popular 70s song, and most of us had been born in 1979.

Then I started listing both major world events and significant accomplishments of our school's star athletes, like Jennifer Brady smashing the Florida State Championship record in the high jump—all set to carefully selected music for that time period. I thanked people like my teachers; golf coach; boyfriend, Tim; and my buddy, Joey, for being great friends. When I finished, everyone jumped to their feet and erupted into applause. Despite not being the valedictorian or class president (who also gave a speech),

I knew I won in entertaining everyone and making the traditionally boring ceremony enjoyable and memorable.

Afterward, the principal congratulated me and handed me an enormous framed certificate (on which River Ridge High School was misspelled "River River") for being the class salutatorian. Then she asked my parents to stand up and congratulated them on raising such a fine daughter. I had to fight a wave of nausea as everyone applauded them for being wonderful parents. If they had only known the torture and abuse I endured for years, only to have them continue it minutes before my speech.

That night my father went back into the hospital, and I stayed out until 4 a.m. going to different graduation parties. I came home to an empty house with no graduation presents, not even a card.

CHAPTER FOURTEEN

I knew well in advance that my father wouldn't be attending my graduation from West Point. For the past five years he had basically secluded himself in the confines of our home, barely venturing out to the grocery store, let alone to visit me in New York. He blamed everything on an unexplainable sickness. I didn't realize until years later just how much of a drug addict he was. I thought he was simply too lazy to put forth any effort to celebrate my accomplishments. For a while he pretended like he was going to try and make it, but I knew he never had any intention of attending. My mother came up as the family representative and joined me for the graduation festivities, which began two nights before graduation.

The baccalaureate service was a religious service for members of the graduating class, held at the various chapels all over campus. The Catholic, Jewish and Muslim cadets all had their own respective chapels in which to worship and celebrate. Not surprisingly, the Protestant cadets worshipped at the biggest and grandest chapel. My fellow cadets and I wore white formal uniforms, called India Whites—a white overcoat and slacks for men, white overcoat and skirts for women, both adorned with a red sash at the waist. For this service I sang a solo: "On My Knees," by Jaci Velasquez. It was pop—a stark deviation from my typical opera, so I had to practice and focus hard on doing it justice, as opera comes so much more naturally to me. I also had to push away images of blowjobs appearing in my mind whenever I sang "I get on my knees," in order to reflect how sacred the song is in worshiping the Lord.

It was sad knowing this was the last time I would sing at West Point, but also an amazing feeling to hear my voice reverberate through the chapel. Perhaps because it was my last opportunity to sing in that spectacular building with the world-famous pipe organ and symphony-worthy acoustics, I sang with more confidence and passion than I had ever exhibited before. My mother, sitting in the second row, right behind the Academy superintendent, started crying. I appreciated her sentiments, but at the same time, I sometimes felt her emotions were a little phony, because we had such a strained relationship. Nevertheless, I was thankful for her presence.

The following night (the night before graduation) was the gradation banquet. Again we wore India Whites, and civilians wore formal attire. The week prior to graduation, I had asked my friend Joon Kim, who was in the church band and played electric guitar for "On My Knees," to accompany my mother and me to my graduation formal. He accepted.

Joon and I had an interesting friendship built on a mutual interest in performing music at church together, crazy amounts of ambition and a sarcastic sense of humor. We could make each other laugh hysterically, and over time people started to notice our chemistry. But Joon could also be quite critical of me, when I least expected it. One time he told me I should sit and eat in a more lady like fashion and act like our fellow cadet Amelia Harper, and it pissed me off. He also tried shoving the Proverbs 31 description of women down my throat. I defended myself well enough and also sensed it was because he liked me, but didn't feel that he was supposed to be attracted to a woman like me. In a lot of respects, Joon's simultaneous adoration for and disdain of my personality reminded me of my father.

I felt closest to Joon when we performed together. We seemed to share a palatable sexual tension that made our musical performances intense. But instead of explaining these complicated details and feelings to my mother, I simply said I wanted to include Joon at my graduation dinner, because he's a special friend.

After the banquet, my mother departed for Colonel Mom's house, and Joon asked that I wait in his car while he went to his room to retrieve something. When he returned, he handed me two homemade CDs. The first one was a compilation of some of our favorite praise and worship songs we had performed, along with some of the corny ones we used to mock. Amid laughter and tears, I was touched by such thoughtfulness and then was nearly shocked when Joon played the other CD for me, a collection of cheesy romance songs I adored at the time. (I always badgered him to play Extreme's "More Than Words" on his acoustic guitar.) We sat there in silence, listening to the music, when Joon suddenly suggested that we continue listening in my room. While he moved his car to the appropriate parking lot, I bounded up to my room feeling both excited and slightly nervous.

Joon arrived shortly thereafter and immediately resumed playing the romance CD. He then grabbed me and started dancing with me. He held me tightly, and I closed my eyes as I pondered our closeness. Then I felt his face slightly shifting as his lips met mine in a passionate kiss. He was an incredible kisser, and this was the best first kiss I had ever experienced in my entire life!

After several moments, he stopped momentarily and then escorted me to my bed, where we proceeded to make out for what felt like both an eternity and too short of a time. This was the most romantic moment of my life. Had we both been willing to fornicate, we probably would have had amazing sex. Alas, we stopped ourselves from going all the way, or even removing a stitch of clothing—which happened to be matching gym uniforms. The thin fabric in our shorts made it easy to feel his boner pressing against my body. It seemed rather large to me, perhaps debunking the Asian stereotype about penis size.

The graduation ceremony took place in the football stadium. We wore our "full dress" uniform—our parade coat, reminiscent of what the flying monkeys wore in *The*

Wizard of Oz, combined with white pants and a red sash. We had to sit through a painfully long and boring commencement speech by Paul Wolfowitz, the deputy secretary of defense (under Donald Rumsfeld), before it was time to accept our diplomas on stage and then swear in as commissioned officers by raising our right hands and taking the oath of office. Then we threw our white hats into the air upon hearing those long-awaited words, "Class dismissed!" Everyone in my class simultaneously cheered and embraced our closest friends as we prepared to leave the Academy behind and embark on new careers as the Army's most junior officers.

As it poured rain, we were warned about an old Academy superstition: If it rains on your graduation day, you're going to war. It had also rained during our R-Day parade (first day of Beast), so hard, in fact, that we had to cut the parade short. According to Academy lore, you're also going to war if it rains on your R-Day parade. So we now had this double whammy threatening to send us to war. But war was the furthest thing from our minds.

To honor our new commitment, various organizations throughout the Academy hosted commissioning ceremonies where cadets select someone special to pin their second lieutenant bars, a.k.a. "butter bars," on their new Army green uniform. At graduation, it's tradition for the class that graduated fifty years prior to purchase and distribute butter bars to the new graduates. Just months before graduation, the class of 1951 published a white paper expressing their belief that women didn't belong at West Point or serving in the military. I wanted to laugh at the irony when the superintendent handed me my butter bars with a congratulatory note from the class of '51. *How could they still be allowed to sponsor us?* I thought and resisted the urge to throw the bars across the football field. Instead, I behaved and participated in the ECF ceremony Steve and Charlene sponsored, and I had both them and my mother pin my bars on the front lawn of the Cadet Chapel. After the bar pinning, we all enjoyed a lavish banquet.

My father's absence was painfully apparent throughout all of these events, as most graduates had several family members present. But it was while dining in the Cadet Chapel immediately after my commissioning ceremony that my mother, acting as if she didn't want to spoil my special day, dropped the real bomb—my father had gone into the hospital the night before. She fought tears. Everyone at our table immediately reached out to comfort her and lend words of support to me. I was livid. Why couldn't she have waited until the end of the day to tell me in private? *Because she can't stand not having sympathetic attention diverted her way, that's why.*

Dabbing her eyes with her napkin, she explained to my friends and colleagues that my father was very ill and in the hospital struggling for his life. I wanted to scream, "She's exaggerating! It's just another hospital visit that results in nothing productive!" As if sensing my doubt, she kept insisting that this time it was more serious and described the heart pain he (thought he) was experiencing as being "similar to palpitations." Anyone with half of a brain could tell that her incoherent explanation proved she was full of shit. But they all lapped up her half-truths and exaggerations, doting on her for the rest of the day.

I couldn't wait for her to go home and stop embarrassing me. I wanted to celebrate having graduated from one of the most prestigious institutions in the world without having to think about my pathetic family.

I lingered around West Point for a few more days, attending some weddings (singing "Ave Maria" in one of them) and bidding farewell to dear friends, especially Charlene, before driving down to Florida by myself.

Even though my bridal friends looked happy to finally capitalize on their love, I was relieved to not be one of them. Sure, it was scary embarking on a new life without the support of a husband, since my parents were no help, but not having to take a husband into account was worth being alone. Marriage, especially a Christian one, was a life I wasn't ready for, one that I felt was years away from happening.

When I came home, my father looked bloated, like he was pushing 300 pounds. The skin patch on his face—a flap from the back of his neck that was used to cover his hemangioma from childhood—was extra red and even more inflamed than usual. The first thing he said to me was, "Why aren't you going to medical school?"

"Because, I don't want to be a doctor."

"But you did from the time you were a little girl."

"Well, I changed my mind," I explained.

"It's because it was too hard, wasn't it?"

"Do we have to talk about this? Can't we just celebrate what I accomplished? Isn't graduating from West Point good enough?"

"No, Laura, it's not," he declared.

"I don't believe this!" I raised my voice.

"You only have a bachelor's degree. What are you going to do with your life now?" he demanded to know.

"I'm in the fucking Army is what I'm doing with my life now."

"But not as a doctor." He was relentless. Instead of letting it go, I continued to defend myself.

"No, I don't want to be a doctor."

"And what about getting your graduate degree?" He seemed to completely misunderstand the requirement of my Army service.

"Daddy, I have a five-year Army obligation, just like the rest of my West Point classmates. You've known from day one that if I go to West Point, I have to be in the actual Army for at least five years." I thought that would do the trick and get him off of my back. I was wrong.

"But some of your classmates are going to medical school."

"Only a few. The ones who want to actually be doctors."

"And they got better grades than you did, right? That's why they get to go to medical school."

"I'm not having this conversation anymore. I'm leaving."

"Well, you're a loser if you only have a bachelor's degree," he yelled as I walked away.

I went to my room and closed the door. I couldn't believe it. Here I was a graduate of West Point with a bachelor's of science in chemistry, a minor in nuclear engineering (and a PhD in keeping my sparkle!)—not to mention a commissioned second lieutenant in the United

States Army—and my father was calling me a loser! I had high expectations for this visit, hoping that my parents would feel inspired to treat me better and acknowledge how hard I worked and how good a person I was. But despite now being an alum of the most revered leadership institution in the world, they still didn't seem to get it. They probably never would.

I imagined the rest of my classmates celebrating with their loving families. Why did mine have to be so different? I couldn't help but wonder where God was in all of this.

Over the next few days, I tried to avoid my father as much as possible, opting to spend my time working out, eating and catching up on sleep. In three weeks I easily lost six pounds, which I attributed to the absence of mess hall food. My mom and I also shopped for my new apartment awaiting me in South Carolina. In July, just one month after graduation, it was time for me to report to Fort Jackson for the Adjutant General's (AG) Corps Officer's Basic Course (OBC). It was time to start paying back Uncle Sam for my "free" education.

CHAPTER FIFTEEN

Fort Jackson, South Carolina, just outside of Columbia, is home to Army Basic Training for new enlistees and advanced training for the AG (Human Resources Management), Finance and Chaplain's Corps. Sometimes AG officers are assigned to run post offices overseas, so the Army also required me to attend postal school, or what I fondly referred to as going postal. Post office training consisted of learning to punch buttons on a cash register and fill out the various customs and certified forms. This was definitely not rocket science, commensurate with a West Point education. Thankfully I had a fellow West Pointer to commiserate with, Carla Garret. I felt awful that we were in a class full of mostly nineteen-year-old kids who had just finished basic training, and Fort Jackson made a big deal about Carla's and my superior performance.

After *two months* of going postal, I entered my AG OBC class to learn all about being a human resources manager in the Army. My class consisted of forty students, most of whom were commissioned through ROTC, the National Guard and the US Army Reserves. I enjoyed this variety, especially being in class with students who were much older than I was and more experienced in life.

In daily lectures and quizzes, we learned all the pertinent regulations for writing and processing annual evaluations, awards and administrative actions—all functions we would manage in our Army units. Again—not rocket science. We also learned how to conduct accountability reports in both an office environment and combat setting, where the combat setting just seemed to add tents and walkie-talkie-like radios. Finally, we learned about casualty reporting and processing, the protocol enacted when a soldier is killed. The event is reported to the chain of command and then the family is notified in both an efficient and sensitive manner. All of this training was the pre-cursor to our real Army jobs and is similar to what a significant portion of the people in the Army end up doing—Combat Service Support. Contrary to its image, a far greater percentage of the military consists not of the core fighting forces, but of the supporting units—the behind-the-scenes people who make the military's logistical operations run smoothly. *It would have been nice if West Point gave a little more attention to this fact.*

I became lonely after initially reporting to Fort Jackson in July of 2001. Joon and I didn't last as a couple. He eventually told me he felt guilty for what had transpired between us physically, and that he could only do that with his future wife, and I'm not her. I took the subtext to be—*because you're not Korean*. I also had no idea what to do with all my free time. It felt weird not to have every moment of every day, including the weekends, occupied with mandatory duties and hours upon hours of homework. It didn't feel right relaxing, and I had yet to figure out if I enjoyed any hobbies. Maybe if West Point had been a little more lenient with certain restrictions and encouraged cadets to discover their inner passions, even if they didn't necessarily contribute to any academic achievements, I would have discovered some enjoyable hobbies. (Growing up with my father certainly didn't help in that regard either.) Since I felt too intimidated to explore other areas in life (like dating or, hell, even cooking), I fell right back into my comfort zone, embracing the same activities I did at West Point: working out, attending Bible studies and occasionally singing at a huge Baptist church near Fort Jackson.

At least I finally started reading for pleasure and discovered that I enjoyed dressing up and dancing with my fellow classmates at the local club—Banana Joe's. But I was hardly discovering myself or finding my niche in the grand scheme of life, which I feared would never happen. Life felt weird. I was in an intense incubator for four years, not to mention the eighteen years prior to West Point, and now I was a little lost in this new Army world. I questioned if I deserved the responsibility inherent with being an officer. I was an intimidated twenty-two-year-old who barely knew jack shit about the real world. Why would anyone in the Army want to follow my lead? Just as I was trying to figure out the kind of leader I would try to be for my five-year Army obligation, everything suddenly changed.

It was a Tuesday.

I just finished taking a quiz and walked into the class lobby area where the receptionist announced, "A plane just flew into the World Trade Center!"

Before I could ask where she got her information, she turned on the television next to her desk, and we watched another plane fly into the other tower of the World Trade Center.

My classmate, Carla, called her mother in a panic. Her mother informed her that a third plane flew into the Pentagon. (Later we found out that the top general of the AG Corps was killed in the Pentagon crash.) *We're being attacked. Could this be the end?*

After everyone finished the quiz and congregated in the lobby, we were all instructed to go home. Then we learned a fourth plane crashed in a field in Pennsylvania.

I drove the twelve-minute ride home, listening to the news on the radio, when the newscasters suddenly announced that the World Trade Center towers were collapsing. The sounds of crashing debris, victims' screams and cries from the announcers reverberated from my car radio into my shocked brain, as if I was in a dream. The tragedy itself was awful enough, but being in the military, and just three months after my West Point graduation, made me feel as if I would be affected more than the average American. While we had yet to know the source of these attacks, at the very least, I did know that some serious shit was going to go down, and maybe somehow I would end up becoming involved.

I got home and went straight to my television. Then my phone rang.

"Hello?" I answered.

"Laura, have you seen the news?" my father asked on the other line.

"Yes."

"Do you think you'll be shipped off to war?"

"I don't know."

I had a call on the other line and asked my father to hold on. It was my instructor at Fort Jackson, telling me to remain home until tomorrow. I then switched back to my father.

"I'm back," I told him.

"Oh my God, Laura. Did you just get called up for war?"

"Um, no. That was just work telling me to stay home for the rest of the day."

"Oh, I thought you were shipping off to war."

"It doesn't work like that, Daddy. You can't just amass the Army like that. Plus, I'm in training. I'm untouchable for at least several more months."

"Oh, thank God!"

Unfortunately, his sentiments quickly changed in the coming months:

"Do you think you'll be shipped off to war?"

"I don't know yet."

"When do you think you'll find out?"

"I have no idea. And why do you sound so eager?"

"Well, this is a big deal."

"I know it's a big deal, but it's not something to be excited about. It's not a game."

"I know that. It's war. The ultimate test of human fortitude."

"You're not forgetting that I'm your daughter, right?"

"But think of the medals they'll pin on your chest."

"I don't care about stupid war medals. I don't want to die!"

"But think of the honor!"

"Think of the fucking coffin they'll be bringing my body home in!"

"You have life insurance, right?"

"I'm done with this conversation! If dying for my country is what you crave, I'll NEVER be the son you wanted me to be. I refuse to die."

As I stayed close to the TV for the rest of 9/11, I couldn't help but think about what my father had said—shipping off to *WAR*. What did I know about going to war? Absolutely nothing.

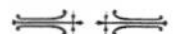

"Saddam Hussein Invades Kuwait" read the front page of the *New York Post* laying on the coffee table in my grandmother's Bronx apartment. I was eleven years old. *What is Kuwait?* I thought to myself. *And who the heck is Saddam Hussein?*

My family never spoke about the first Gulf War, but CNN was on so much in our home, I quickly came to recognize Wolf Blitzer. I also remember Bette Midler's song, "From a Distance," constantly playing in honor of our troops. The war seemed easy and over just like that—thanks to the heroics of General Norman Schwarzkopf.

Afterward, I barely paid attention to the news. I assumed that since we had "won" the Gulf War, we achieved permanent peace. My parents must have assumed the same thing because neither showed any concern about their daughter going into the military. Even when I was theoretically being trained for war, the thought of *actually going to war* never occurred me and probably nor to a lot of my classmates.

The closest I ever got to the military before going to West Point happened when I was a senior in high school. My school agreed to play at the Saddlebrook Golf Academy, not just one of the leading Florida golf schools, but actually a feeder school for the PGA and LPGA tours. Coincidentally, General Norman "Stormin' Normin" Schwarzkopf—the Desert Storm commander, American hero and 1956 West Point graduate—was enjoying his retirement at this lovely resort.

Even though we could've gotten in a shitload of trouble, my teammates and I drove around the golf resort until we found his house. (The Saddlebrook coach told us how we could find it.) I ran up to General Schwarzkopf's front door and had my teammates snap photos of me. Luckily, no one was home, but a part of me was disappointed. I fantasized about General Schwarzkopf coming outside and yelling at us, me stepping up to introduce myself and telling him that I had been accepted to West Point and was heading there in just a few short months. I imagined him being impressed with my chutzpah and offering to pose for a picture, and us becoming pen pals while I was at West Point. Clearly, if I was bold enough to trespass on his property, then I was bold enough to be West Point material.

⁂

When I returned to Fort Jackson on September 12, 2001, everything was different. We could no longer simply drive onto the post. Now it took three hours to pass through all of the brand new security measures that were erected overnight. Eventually everyone got the hang of these new procedures, and getting onto post only took a few extra minutes.

The following Sunday, I went to church services and quietly cried during the prayers, thinking *this is your time, this is going to happen, you're going to war.* I wasn't scared of going to war. It was just a known thing that was going to happen, that our country wouldn't let 9/11 go without responding in some major way. Even then, we knew that 9/11 changed the course of everything—for civilians, for the military, for the world.

And yet, it also felt surreal, like I was separated from what was transpiring. Whenever I'd thought of war, I always I felt disassociated from it. Even though I earned an A- in my last semester of military history, I found the subject of war to be boring and not relatable, although reading about World War II piqued my interest. At one point in my studies I became obsessed with the Holocaust and chose this topic for my international relations term paper. I was also obsessed with the nuclear bomb and wrote a paper about it for another class. At the time I was pro-nuclear bomb, because I was convinced it saved more lives than it killed—but now I'm disgusted I ever harbored those beliefs. (The same disgust, shame and brainwashed naïveté can be applied to my Florida absentee ballot vote for President Bush in the 2000 election. Unfortunately, I detached all of my chads, so my vote really counted.)

Regardless, I was emotionally distant. I didn't feel that fiery passion to speak out against the injustice of war because I didn't identify with it. Everything I did was about survival and checking the box.

What I didn't realize, however, was that all of the Desert Storm war stories we heard from our West Point instructors were nothing compared to what we were about to experience. A post-9/11 world would enter a new kind of warfare—fighting terrorism.

When I came home for Christmas that year, I rekindled my relationship with my high school boyfriend, Tim, who had never left the area, like most people I grew up with. Tim being back in my life felt comforting and grounding as the thought of war loomed over my head. Shortly after becoming a couple again, in February, toward the end of training, my assignment officer came to visit my class and said, "I gave your Germany slot to someone else who needed it. We need to figure out where you're going to be stationed." I didn't know what to say.

Then my father was diagnosed with colon cancer. His doctors had discovered a large tumor in his colon, one that had probably been growing for two and a half years. Between losing my Germany assignment and figuring I should be close to home, my assignment officer decided I would go to Savannah, Georgia.

In classic form, my father scheduled his tumor removal surgery on the day of my graduation from OBC. My absence didn't impact my graduation status, so it wasn't a huge deal, but I was disappointed that I would miss out on the festivities. I earned several awards, including one of the top academic students and the number one fitness woman in my class—something voted on by my classmates. It had no bearing on my future military career, but it made me feel popular and respected, and I felt sad to miss out on saying goodbye to my class. But I was glad to be at the hospital for my father's surgery, and it went well. He felt better immediately after having the tumor removed and recovered quickly. Afterward, they tested his lymph nodes, and because he had a mild to moderate chance of the cancer coming back, the doctor prescribed chemotherapy to err on the side of caution.

His doctor was very upbeat in the meeting. "You're really fortunate," she told my father. "Chemo isn't going to make you sick. It's going to make you feel better. You're going to be fine."

Of course, when we came home and my mom asked how it went, my dad said in a serious tone, "I have six months to live." The way he lied and manipulated my mother infuriated me. Immediately I chimed in, "That's a bunch of bullshit," which only made my father angrier at me. He convinced my mother that I was the one lying.

Since my mother couldn't drive him to chemo, and the neighbor who had been helping my parents with transportation also got sick, we agreed that I would request a compassionate reassignment from the Army so I could help them out. The military accepted my request and allowed me to stay home for two months. I simply had to report to an administrative unit at MacDill Air Force Base in Tampa, just to help out a bit, but my primary responsibility was to take my father to all of his appointments. In typical fashion, he spent much of the time criticizing my driving and nitpicking anything else in my life that was up for grabs.

After my father's first chemo session, I made plans to go to dinner with Tim.

"I'm dying, and you're going out to dinner?" my father asked.

"You're not dying, and Mommy is here with you," I responded.

But the more I wanted to hang out with Tim, the more my father got on my case. "Why do you want to hang out with Tim? Do you crave his penis?" he would ask me. I'd also frequently hear, "You're only here because you want to be with your boyfriend" and "You only got the reassignment because of that."

Disgusted with his gross accusations, I started to spend the night at Tim's place as often as I could, only returning to be my father's chauffeur.

I kept Tim's mom, Patty, apprised of everything with our lengthy, heart-to-heart conversations. Patty said that my father sounded just like her best friend's father. This woman always hoped that her father would change, but it never happened. Now that she was older and essentially stuck putting up with him, she regretted not cutting ties with him years earlier. It would have been too traumatizing to cut him off so late in both of their lives. But I was still young enough to decide what was best for me. I felt perhaps God was urging me to walk away. Knowing I had Patty's full support, especially since she was such a devout Christian and family woman, made this decision easy.

I devised and began to carry out my escape plan. Since I never planned to speak to my parents ever again, I wanted to take some of my childhood treasures from their home without them becoming suspicious. So over the next two weeks, whenever they were gone, I packed my car with small collections of mementos and my favorite Cabbage Patch Kids. Then I stored them in Patty's home and arranged for the Army moving company to make an extra stop there, since it was nearly time for me to report to my first duty station—Hunter Army Airfield in Savannah, Georgia.

On my last day in Florida, my father had a chemo appointment, and I drove him like usual. He was in an especially foul mood. Because he had weak lungs from years of being sedentary, he used a heavy oxygen tank that was difficult to maneuver, especially since he dragged it while I pushed him in a wheel chair. My father didn't like the way I pushed the wheelchair and started screaming at me in front of everyone at the hospital. I walked away, but then he pleaded with me in an even more dramatic fashion, forcing me to come back. Everyone around us was mortified. When we finally got home, his yelling only worsened.

"I don't have to take your shit anymore," I said, gathering the last of my things for my drive to Savannah.

"Yes, you do," he yelled at me.

"No I don't. I'm an adult now!"

"No you're not! You're just a fucking child!"

I walked away from him. That was the last thing he said to me.

My mother came home as I was ready to drive away. She could tell we had been fighting and asked what happened. Despite what had just occurred, she still sided with him.

"Can't you just be nice to him? Aren't you going to kiss him goodbye?" she asked.

"No, I'm done. I'm out of here," I slammed the trunk of my car and left. They had no idea I would never come back.

CHAPTER SIXTEEN

I drove to Savannah that evening in April 2002 feeling disgusted, angry and nervous about moving to a strange city and going to my first real unit. This would set the pace for my Army career. Underneath I felt a pang of excitement, but it was overshadowed with exhaustion and dread. I wanted to be back in the comfort of Tim's parents' home, but instead felt like, *Here we go, here's this onerous Army thing looming over me. Let's get this shit done.*

My five-hour drive gave me plenty of time to reflect on how my parents had treated me throughout my entire life. They used Proverbs 13:24, "Whoever spares the rod hates their children, but the one who loves their children is careful to discipline them," as justification for spanking me, but the extent of their physical punishment felt more violent than biblical. I was sick of them using the Bible to justify their actions, and I was on to their bullshit. They simply couldn't control their anger, and I was sick of it bringing out the worst in me.

While my father screamed and hit with a force far greater than my mother, her smacks and yelling still stung, sometimes even more profoundly. When I was four years old, I threw my underwear over my head and starting jumping on top of my bed. I thought I was hilarious and couldn't stop laughing. My mother demanded that I stop, but my hysteria made me unable to obey. I only stopped when she slapped me across the face. I froze in horror. It was the first time I ever felt one of my parents inflicting pain upon me.

Around the age of ten, I felt super nauseous and cried for my mother as I lingered around the toilet. She yelled, "Just throw up and stop crying about it." It wasn't until years later that I learned that mothers often stroke their children's hair and rub their backs when they felt sick.

When I became a teenager, I started fighting back. Any time my mother smacked me, I smacked her right back. Sometimes the rage she ignited in me made me feel capable of hospitalizing her, if I allowed myself to fully absorb my emotions. For the sake of my sanity and her safety, I had to suppress my true feelings.

I hated the person my parents made me become in their presence. Away from them, I was considered a wonderful person, kind hearted, generous, strong and funny. Many people thought I was optimistic. They would never be able to imagine I was a daughter who hit her mother. I felt utter shame picturing them observing me in my house, reacting to my mother's aggression, unable to contain my anger and be the better person.

In my father's presence, when I couldn't fight back, I turned on myself. Behind closed doors, I smacked my own face, punched my head and pulled my hair. I also threw things, needing an outlet for my pent-up energy. A few times I accidentally did this in front of my father, and he made fun of me for self-flagellation and said I reminded him of an ancient religious zealot.

Only one time my mother stepped in to defend me. During Christmas break of "firstie" (senior) year, my father went on a three-day bender of screaming, chastising our family and threatening to hurt me. On the third day, when I couldn't take anymore, still wearing my pajamas, I put my sneakers on and started packing, saying I was heading back to West Point. My father reacted by cornering me and threatening to unleash pain. When he raised a fist toward my head, I did the only thing I could think of to protect myself and put my foot on his crotch. "Go right ahead!" I warned, ready to castrate him if need be.

"Stop!" my mother shrieked, running in-between us.

Holy shit, I thought. *What's she doing?*

"Don't hit Laura in the head! After all that she went through with her head injury. Please, not her head!" my mother cried.

After catching his breath for a few seconds, my father walked away, and we didn't speak for the rest of my vacation.

I still hated my mother more than my father. Maybe something in me felt that fathers were allowed to be temperamental and flawed, but certainly not mothers. Mothers were supposed to protect the very product of their flesh. Many times I begged her to leave my father, but she refused. Many times she delighted in telling me that she couldn't wait until my father came home, so she could update him on the latest thing that I had done, knowing it would enrage him. I swore she felt some kind of victory whenever she would watch him beating me, satisfied that she instigated this round of punishment, instead of grabbing me and fleeing. Now armed with a steady paycheck, career and health insurance, I could flee on my own.

As I approached Savannah, I vowed to never be in this kind of abusive, violent dynamic ever again.

When I reported into my unit, there was a message waiting for me. "Your assignment officer called. You need to call him." *That's weird,* I thought.

I called my assignment officer not knowing why we possibly needed to talk.

"I don't know what's going on with your father," he said. "But you need to call him."

He went on to explain that my father called and said nasty things about me, claiming I lied to the Army about him being sick only so I could be close to my boyfriend. I was shocked. My father literally attempted to destroy my Army career before it ever even had a chance to start.

Mortified, I apologized to the assignment officer, who was thankfully understanding and kind. He even told me a story about his difficulties with his own father. He seemed to feel sorry for me, realizing that my father was insane. He even tried to guide me in how to respond, but I knew I would never follow through. I f I needed more evidence in my favor for cutting my parents off for good—this was it.

I hung up, walked over to a conference room since it was the only vacant room, and I started to cry. My father was dangerous, and I needed to protect myself from him. Just as I was contemplating how to essentially go into hiding from him, someone walked into the conference room. It was my new boss, Major Gregory Putte.

Major Putte wanted to know what was wrong. *Fuck. I can't tell my new boss about my personal problems,* I thought, but it was too late. He already saw me cry.

I tried to briefly summarize what happened. Thankfully Major Putte seemed to sympathize with me and responded kindly. But I was still mortified. It was difficult enough being a woman in the Army, the minority gender. Now I would be known as the woman with daddy issues.

Several months later, I had a dream. In the dream, I am scanning my childhood room to determine what possessions are most important to me. *In an emergency, what can I carry away in my suitcase? Will I take my most beloved Cabbage Patch Kid, my baby lion blanket and some photos from homecoming? What if there isn't enough time?* My heart is pounding. I suddenly hear footsteps pounding, and the sound amplifies with each step. They're coming closer. In a panic, I lock the bedroom door, grab my wallet and some official Army documents and stuff them in my bra. There's no time to pack. I must leave it all behind.

There is pounding on my door. "Open up!" my father screams. My forehead beads with sweat. "Open up now, Laura, or I will kick the door down." If he succeeds, which I have no doubt he could, I fear he will kill me.

As silently as possible, to pretend that I'm not behind the door, I climb onto my desk that contains piles of homework for classes that I finished years ago. I move a few stacks on top of each other so I can stand below the only small window in my room. The kicking commences. I hear wood splitting. He knows I'm in there; it's pointless to be silent. I need to bust out of this window ASAP.

I vigorously rotate my hand to crank open the three-paned jalousie window and use a pair of scissors to cut a hole in the screen. I hear more kicks and wood splitting. The door is so close to being destroyed. I rip open a hole and pull myself up to the sill and throw my upper body through it. Thankfully, we only have a one-story ranch home. I dangle for a split second and propel the rest of my body through, landing on the ground in a thud, just as the door to my room splits in half and my father enters. "I'll get you," he threatens.

My eyes adjust to the darkness. I have to flee and start sprinting in the woods behind our home. Any time advantage I think I have is a farce, because my father is chasing me, threatening to close in on me. I run faster. More distance grows between us, but just when I think I've lost him behind a big tree, something…more like someone… grabs me. A sharp pain in my side shocks me. My mother is stabbing me.

I don't scream for fear that my father will find me. Instead, I try to shove my mother to the ground. She doesn't budge. I should be able to overtake her petite stature, but the knife wounds only multiply. She is stabbing me to death. I can't help but emit a scream that I hope will wake any possible angel that could come to my rescue, but my sound is faint. I scream again.

Someone starts shoving me. "Laura!" They shove me several more times. "Laura, wake up!" My body shakes and I suddenly come to. It's dark. I hear a faint motor sound. My friend Ricardo is next to me, asking if I'm OK. I'm in a big tent surrounded by several people sleeping on cots.

"Laura, you must have had a bad dream," Ricardo says. I scan the area one more time as I recalibrate my mind. I finally realize that we are in Kuwait, on our deployment. I inhale deeply and exhale slowly, tears in my eyes. I thank Ricardo for waking me, ending the nightmare, and bringing me back to reality—where I know I have already escaped. But for the next number of years I always feel like I live in hiding.

CHAPTER SEVENTEEN

I began to settle into my new life at the Aviation Brigade, 3d Infantry Division at Hunter Army Airfield in Savannah. On my first day of work people said, "We're going to go somewhere, but we don't know exactly where yet. At any rate, we're on high alert, so if you leave the 250-mile radius surrounding this area, your departure needs approval from the chain of command." *Wow, that's really ambiguous,* was my first thought and then, *Shit, Tim lives more than 250 miles away.* So along with all of my fellow officers and soldiers, I started waiting to go to war. Only I gathered this wouldn't be Afghanistan. (We commenced Operation Enduring Freedom there in October 2001.) Apparently Saddam Hussein was stirring up some shit in Iraq, and we were pegged to respond if it got really bad.

In our first official 1:1 meeting (after the phone call debacle with my father), I formally met my boss. Major

Putte had graduated from West Point in 1986, but seemed different from my instructors who graduated around that time. His demeanor was kinder and gentler than your typical Army person, male or female. He was about six feet tall, thin and gawky, had thinning hair and rather pronounced acne scars on his face. Major Putte served in the Infantry prior to switching to the Human Resources Management career field—something the Army allows you to do after about a decade of service. I got the sense that he was his small Nebraska hometown star and went to West Point in order be that all-American kind of guy.

Before asking me to do any work, Major Putte wanted to make sure that I was comfortably settled into a new apartment. I was crashing at Anna's while she was away with her unit at the National Training Center, out in the California desert. Since Anna was stationed at Fort Stewart (our parent installation, because only the aviation assets were at Hunter Army Airfield), which was an hour away, I knew I would need to find my own place and told Putte that I had yet to secure my own apartment. He asked if I like the beach, and when I said yes, he strongly suggested that I consider searching near his neighborhood. I ended up finding a nice apartment on Wilmington Island, only a ten-minute drive from Tybee beach, and just about a mile away from him.

Putte showed concerned that I feel welcome at my new job. I don't know if it was my daddy issues incident, him being a good leader or just being a nice guy, Putte seemed to go out of his way to make sure I wasn't left alone. He took me to lunch every day and soon introduced me to his wife and eight-year-old daughter. Meeting families was the norm as we had many unit socials that included them. Before long, Putte started saying that I felt like another daughter to him. His acceptance was initially comforting, especially since I didn't know anyone else in Savannah, but playing this daughter role quickly became annoying and exhausting.

My new position was the Brigade Assistant S1—Major Putte's assistant—as he was the Brigade S1 / Adjutant. Our team also included Sergeant First Class Chase Richards (a nice, but lazy fellow with six children and two ex-wives, who I caught delegating work to me after Major Putte asked him to do it); Sergeant Calvin Hemming (another lazy guy who used his charm to weasel his way out of anything); and Specialist Cassie Fenda (a bright and cheerful woman who immediately befriended me and did more work than Sergeants Richards and Hemming combined). As a group, we were responsible for overseeing the administration of the Brigade, including accountability reports, awards, administrative actions and annual evaluation forms. Just as my Officer's Basic Course at Fort Jackson had shown me—rocket science it was not. But even the most menial tasks caused Putte to panic and, as his assistant, it was my job to both complete these tasks and keep him calm.

At first his sense of urgency made me feel like a valuable contributor to the war on terrorism. But I came to realize that each time I thought I finished a spreadsheet or Power Point presentation, he would have me change it because he didn't have anything better for me to do. He seemed obsessed with keeping me busy solely for appearances' sake. After a while, I just accepted that all of my work was going to require fifty reviews and revisions before he deemed it complete.

After a month on the job, my brain felt like it was beginning to rot away, and I was lonely outside of work. Luckily, Putte was totally cool with me exceeding the 250-mile radius to see Tim, so we fell into a routine of seeing each other every other weekend. But when I wasn't at work or with Tim, I needed something to do, so I enrolled at Webster University to begin working toward an MBA. Webster has satellite campuses on several military installations across the country, so I would commute up to Beaufort, South Carolina, for classes two nights a week. They didn't require any entrance exams. When I visited the admissions office on a Thursday, they asked, "Would you like to begin on Monday?" My tuition was covered by the Army, and if I finished within two years, then I wouldn't owe the Army any additional time. Not Harvard Business School, a common choice among West Point grads, but at least it was free and fed my hungry, aching brain.

Every time I left my desk, Putte expected me to walk into his office across the hall and inform him. Sergeants Richards and Hemming were free to come and go as they pleased, but Putte kept me on a tight leash, apparently just in case President Bush decided to initiate the Iraq invasion when I was picking up our unit's mail at the post office down the street.

One day I quickly went down the hall to use the ladies' room, and when I returned to my desk, my office mates told me that Putte was upset. I stepped into his office to find out why.

"I didn't know where you were," Putte said.

"I was in the bathroom," I replied, trying to temper my voice to remain respectful.

"Next time, let me know. I've already told you, I need to know where you are at all times."

"Yes, Sir," I said and returned to my desk, wondering why I was more essential than everyone else.

From then on, I informed him that I was leaving my desk every time I had to pee or take care of lady business. Instead of annoying him, he reacted with appreciation.

At some point, it dawned on me that I might be able to relate to Putte in a different way. I had picked up on some hints that he had a really twisted sense of humor, based on how he joked with the enlisted guys in our S1 shop. Initially, I was uncomfortable with how inappropriate it was for a superior officer to be so crude with his subordinates. It also made me feel torn on a personal level. Besides giving in to the flesh, my upbringing taught me that a good Christian woman isn't supposed to laugh at dirty jokes or take pleasure in worldly smut. Daddy was a total hypocrite, and I actually grew up with this kind of humor and secretly couldn't help but love dirty jokes, especially about sex—the raunchier, the better. Sometimes I pretended that I was offended, but that was only because my father taught me to do that (when he wasn't making me laugh at one of his own dirty jokes). So, while a part of me was offended, another part of me felt lucky to have a boss who could relate to his team almost like college buddies. After a while, I not only wanted in the club—I wanted to be his best college buddy, anything but the weird quasi-daughter role he assigned to me.

After trying out a few of my father's favorite dirty jokes on Putte, making him howl with laughter, he seemed to look at me in a new light.

"Laura, before I met you, I was afraid you'd be really stuck up, especially coming from West Point," Putte said.

"Oh no, Sir, I enjoy dirty jokes," I assured him.

"Good to know. We're a pretty tight-knit shop. Everyone here loved your predecessor, and they miss him. I'm hoping they'll grow to like you too."

In essence he threw down the gauntlet.

Throughout my West Point Bible studies, I learned how important it was to preach the gospel to my soldiers. Well, unless I wanted to be isolated and ostracized, I needed to join in on the dick jokes and leave Jesus at home. The goody-goody church girl crap just wasn't going to fly working for "Cousin Nasty," a *self-appointed* nickname Putte revealed to me after I told him my dirty jokes. Sometimes I felt guilty that no one would be able to tell I was a Christian. But being Putte's new best buddy and fast friends with all the guys in my shop helped me overcome that guilt.

I still attended church, but not quite as often, especially because I was traveling to see Tim on many weekends. Tim wasn't into church but still respected my beliefs and need to remain a virgin. Church also stopped seeming as relevant to me. I wasn't learning anything of substance that I hadn't already learned. Everyone else around me seemed to be fine without it. Perhaps it was indeed becoming irrelevant to my new life.

One evening my neighbor invited me to his Baptist church, where he played the piano. It was supposed to be a special evening with a guest pastor. Families all congregated with excitement, waiting to hear what extraordinary message emerged from this blessed man's lips. He climbed onstage in dramatic fashion, scanning his audience, pacing back and forth before releasing the loudest scream I've ever heard coming from a preacher's pulpit: "ORAL SEX IS STILL SEXXXXXXXXXXXXX!"

I guess I wasn't still a virgin in this man's eyes.

I didn't internalize any of his vitriol. I was indeed still a virgin, and the last thing I needed to hear, with so much turmoil going on in the world, was his obsessive disdain for mouth-to-genital contact.

Putte lived vicariously through Sergeant Hemming, who happened to be a gorgeous blond surfer. Every Monday morning, Sergeant Hemming shared his weekend sexcapades with our office, while Putte stood by listening, laughing and lapping it up. I took that as a cue that we should all ignore the fact that Sergeant Hemming was committing adultery on his hot, Ukrainian wife, and instead, cheer him on in his quest to defile all of the young, gorgeous women in Savannah—and in such detail! I justified listening to these scandalous stories—complete with every play and position—by deeming them valuable lessons on how to please my future husband.

The more I listened to Sergeant Hemming's stories and got to know my Army colleagues, the more I realized just how much of a minority I was as a virgin. Unlike my close friends at West Point, no one in the real Army seemed to be saving themselves for marriage. The fact that I had a boyfriend made everyone assume I was involved in a normal, sexual relationship.

The week after Tim and I spent a weekend at his parents' house (he was in-between apartment leases), my coworker and new friend, Hannah, asked me if we had dared to do the dirty deed in their home.

For a brief moment, I considered lying. I didn't want my virginity status to make people think that I was some kind of prudish weirdo. At the same time, admitting the truth would be an opportunity to finally take a stance for Jesus and maybe cleanse some of the guilt I felt about trying to fit in with Cousin Nasty. So I told Hannah that we didn't have sex because we don't have sex, because I'd never had sex.

For a moment, I thought Hannah was going to crash her sporty BMW that she had purchased while stationed in Germany. "Please don't tell anyone," I pleaded with her.

"I won't," she promised. And she didn't, for about two days.

Putte was one the first people to find out. We were alone in the brigade conference room when he told me he'd heard the rumor that I was a virgin.

"Is it true?" he asked.

I'd been taught to answer with a proud and resounding, "YES!" Instead, I bowed my head in shame and meekly admitted the truth. This certainly didn't help him regard me as a twenty-three-year-old adult. I went back to being his daughter instead of his best bud.

It didn't take long before the entire unit knew my virginity status.

"You know what your problem is, Ma'am?" Sergeant Hemming, the cheating sex maniac surfer, asked me.

"What?"

"You make way too big a deal of sex. You elevate it up here," he held up his arm, "like an opera song." Then he belted out his best rendition of a falsetto soprano. I laughed at the spectacle, but his words sunk in. It seemed like everyone was giving me a hard time for being a virgin.

Despite our eighteen-year age difference, Chief Warrant Officer 4 Ricardo Rojas and I became instant friends when we met at work. He was a Colombian immigrant who had been raised in New York and spoke with a strong accent. Muscular, average height and dark, he had entered the Army for the pride and appreciation of being able to live poverty-free in the United States. Ricardo was willing to bust his ass to make a good life for himself and his family. He was also a dedicated family man, having married his wife Camila when she was seventeen and he was twenty-two. But I soon realized that being married didn't stop him from having and expressing a very healthy libido away from his wife.

Ricardo and I shared many five-hour-long rides together on the weekends, because his wife and three children lived near Tim in Tampa. Ricardo's family settled there when the Army sent him to Korea for his previous assignment. (The Army has a dirty practice of shipping people off to Korea for a one-year unaccompanied tour after eighteen and a half years of service. Then if you actually want to come home after that year, you owe the Army a year of service for shipping you to your next duty station. So instead of retiring after twenty years, you end up retiring after twenty-and-a-half years. It's a brilliant way to squeeze an extra six months of service out of its powerless soldiers.) So Ricardo was eligible to retire in just under a year, and his family had begun establishing their roots in Tampa.

Through our many conversations, I ended up feeling closer to Ricardo than anyone else in the unit and was completely confident in his loyalty. Once we promised to be battle buddies if and when we ever went to war (a commitment to ensure that the other wouldn't die), Ricardo set out on his next mission—to completely corrupt me.

In Ricardo's mind, a twenty-four-year old virgin just couldn't exist, especially one with a serious boyfriend who *wasn't* a virgin. (Tim had lost his virginity back in college and by then had a total of three sexual partners under his belt.) Tim's ability to remain abstinent baffled Ricardo even more because he didn't believe that any red-blooded man in his twenties had the ability to keep it in his pants.

"Honoring my desire to remain chaste is noble!" I protested. But he still wasn't convinced. When I revealed that Tim and I recently delved into oral sex (remember "sex" to me meant penile penetration), trying to make our relationship sound more normal, Ricardo only obsessed about my sex life even more.

I think Ricardo sensed I felt conflicted about my religious convictions. He could smell desperate horniness emanating from my pores. This was also his last Army assignment before retirement, and he just did not give a fuck about rules or standards. He was a warrant officer, a rank between enlisted and officer, populated with technical experts that get away with murder because senior commanders heavily rely on their knowledge (one of the Army's best-kept secrets). So his attitude was uniquely rebellious; he had nothing to lose, and he definitely wanted to bring me to the dark side.

I didn't exactly protest his attempts. The dark side seemed like so much fun, especially when Ricardo created scenarios to test my devotion to being the pure and chaste woman I thought I was supposed to be. The more I laughed at these tests, the more he raised the stakes, and the more educated I became about all of life's naughty pleasures, of which I was purposefully depriving myself.

One day while driving down to Tampa, Ricardo altered our route so we could hit Café Risqué, the "butt-naked diner," on I-75, just south of Gainesville. It's essentially advertised as a strip joint with food catered to bored and hungry truck drivers. It sounded kind of gross to have naked women around food, but not gross enough to keep me from becoming completely giddy when we reached the entrance.

A big burly bouncer directed us into a side entrance and asked for our driver's licenses, saying he needed to hold on to them while we were inside of the building. He also told us to stay in the next room unless we wanted to pay a cover charge, and then we could venture off into the rest of the establishment. When I handed him my license, I wondered if he thought I was just another average young lady or a dirty whore.

Ricardo and I entered a room that turned out to be a sex-toy shop. I had never seen a sex toy before and marveled at the hundreds of varieties, shapes and sizes.

Despite the detour, we were still in a hurry, so we agreed that we wouldn't stay to watch the dancers. But we still had a decent view from the sex-toy shop. For the first time, I laid eyes on a naked stripper swaying next to a pole on a stage, right above an elderly gentleman nibbling away on a club sandwich. He seemed to be paying more attention to the sandwich than her performance.

I felt sorry for the stripper. The surroundings reminded me of a pimped-out Denny's. Ricardo let me stare at her for several minutes and then called my attention to the sex toys. I went through stacks of devices, reading the packaging, learning about all of the ways they can bring pleasure. I paused at something that looked like a strand of oversized pearls.

"I don't get it," I told Ricardo.

"Those are anal beads," he offered.

"What do they do?"

"You put them up your butt and then pull them out."

"Excuse me? Why? Why on Earth would anyone do that?"

"To feel pleasure," he explained.

"You feel pleasure in your butt?"

"Yeah, a lot of people do. And they're not just for women. Some men like them too, especially gay men."

"Wow, I had no idea," I said, and gingerly placed the package back on the shelf. Ricardo laughed.

I started wondering if the whole Army wasn't full of perverts and freaks.

CHAPTER EIGHTEEN

When Major Putte wasn't obsessing about Sergeant Hemming's sex life or my lack of a sex life, or color coordinating the latest Excel spreadsheet, he related to me less like his daughter, and more like his lady companion. When his wife was out of town, traveling for work, he often wouldn't dismiss me until well after everyone else went home. The first time he did this, it was under the guise of needing to finish a project, but eventually I realized that his wife's absence made him terribly lonely, and he didn't want to rush home to an empty house. (His daughter played several sports and didn't spend many evenings at home.) Sometimes we chatted for hours about our family lives and goals, and we naturally gossiped about our coworkers. It was during these conversations that we seemed to connect the most, not as boss and employee, or father and quasi-daughter, or even as raunchy best college buddies—but just as friends.

Perhaps this is why Putte panicked when he was ordered to go to Kuwait without me in the ADVON (i.e. advanced party). All of the other senior leaders were able to say goodbye to their staff members in a professional, friendly manner, but Putte practically cried at the prospect of not seeing me for three months. Not even 2,000 miles or an eight-hour time zone difference stopped him from calling me several times a day. But without him there, hovering over me and micro-managing my every move, it was much easier to do my job.

Theoretically, the war was about to begin. Since Putte was away in Kuwait with the entire executive staff, I was put in charge of all HR functions relating to the deployment for approximately 1,200 people. This involved ensuring everyone had up-to-date medical and administrative records (life insurance, emergency point of contact information, etc.). My unit's main lines of forces were the First Battalion, Third Aviation Regiment—the Apache Battalion; Second Battalion, Third Aviation Regiment—the Black Hawk Battalion; and our Headquarters Company, which included our Brigade staff. For administrative purposes, we also oversaw the Third Squadron, Seventh Cavalry Regiment, in which half of the forces had tanks and Bradleys (what I learned to drive at Fort Knox), and the other half of the cavalry had three troops (cavalry term for company) of Kiowa helicopters. Also attached to us was B/159—a Chinook helicopter company and D CO 1-58 AVN—an Air Traffic Control company. The 603rd maintenance battalion was also attached to us, as they would provide all maintenance and repair functions for our hundred-plus Humvees and trucks.

Going to war involved needing to send all of our helicopters, Humvees, weapons and gear to Kuwait, which would serve as our staging area. We packed and shipped everything on cargo ships that took three weeks to traverse the path from the port of Savannah to the port of Kuwait City. (When helicopters are shipped, their blades are removed, and they are essentially shrink wrapped in what looks like giant condoms.) The logistics involved months of planning, so even though there was no official order to deploy, it was a good thing we already had a plan in place.

Unfortunately, we were shortchanged some essential gear. The senior logistician in charge of our headquarters company had to decide who would get a new bulletproof vest and who would be stuck with the vintage, Vietnam-era flack vest that only mildly protected against grenade fragments. With these old pieces of shit, a gunshot wound would likely result in instant death. In his assessment of the company roster, he decided to use gender (i.e. those with a penis vs. those without a penis) as the criteria for getting a new vest.

"Well, the men, especially the enlisted guys, will most likely be in the front lines," he said when I demanded an explanation.

"I'm not buying it," I responded as flatly as possible. I didn't want to start a fight because we were friends, and it was helpful to have a logistician on your side.

"Ma'am, I'm sorry there's nothing I can do to get you the new vest. But I can promise you this. When we're out there, and shit hits the fan, I will personally look out for your safety and well-being."

"That's nice and all, but I'm still mad at you," I said, smiling, but also letting him know that I didn't appreciate getting screwed over. Then I dropped it, realizing the discussion would accomplish nothing.

Because we had been operating under a "what if" we're going to war pretense, we weren't able to prematurely acquire all of our necessary combat gear. This required legitimate deployment orders. After working in a hypothetical environment for nine months, I finally got my deployment orders just three days before shipping out. They simply said we were mobilizing to Kuwait, but it was obvious we would wait there to see what would happen in Iraq. I had already moved out of my apartment, packed all of my belongings into storage and made arrangements with my MBA instructors to do my coursework via email. But it was still a frenzy tying up loose ends at the last minute.

The day before we left, we had to go to the installation's central supply center to get the last of our gear. The civilian guy behind the counter issuing us the equipment was quite friendly. So I decided to turn up the charm and asked in my cutest voice,

"Hey, you wouldn't happen to have any of those new bullet proof vests back there, would you?"

"Do you need a new vest? You don't have one already?" he asked, mildly appalled that a cute little officer was in such a predicament.

"No, they didn't have enough, so I have to go to war tomorrow without one."

"That's horrible. Let me see what I can do," he smiled. He went into the back room and reemerged with a new vest, and it was just my size.

"Here you go, my dear," he said proudly.

"Thank you so much! Seriously, I can't thank you enough. You know you probably saved my life. After the war, I will come back and thank you personally if I'm still alive," I said melodramatically.

"Oh that's not necessary. I'm just doing my job and am glad I can help. I wish you the best, and please be safe out there. God bless."

Then someone told me it didn't matter that we had new vests because in order for them to stop a bullet, they needed to have the appropriate ceramic plates in them. Only the actual pilots in the Aviation Brigade got the ceramic plates. I simply shook my head.

Since we received our official deployment orders on a Tuesday, indicating that we were flying out on that Friday, I only had three days to pack my bags.

When you're packing for war, it's difficult to determine how many tampons you're going to need. To be on the safe side, I packed enough to supply all of the women in Iraq. Plus, I figured that tampons would be great for augmenting my first-aid kit—I could use them as plugs for bullet-hole wounds. I was also at a great tactical advantage, since I prefer the brand OB to Tampax. Not having a bulky plastic applicator to contend with would save me a lot of room.

Right before the deployment, I decided to go on the birth control pill. I figured it would help to have a regulated period, since I've never had a perfectly timed cycle.

I was also hoping the pill would mitigate my cramps. The last thing I needed was for my menstrual cycle to slow me down in combat. Another more serious thought kept sneaking into the back of my mind. *What if I become a POW and am raped?*

Granted, I assumed my captors would confiscate all of my possessions, but maybe I could hide my pill pack in my bra or underwear. I knew they would discover them if they raped me, but maybe having been on the pill up until that point would prevent a pregnancy. Regardless, as much as the thought of abortion terrified me, I would definitely get one if an enemy captor impregnated me.

When I told my boyfriend Tim that I was leaving on Friday, he freaked out—not because I was leaving, but because he didn't have enough advance notice to inform his boss. He was really nervous about being the perfect employee, probably because he had dated her sister and it ended badly. I thought he should have been using that as leverage to get away with murder, especially since the sister had cheated on him, and his boss had set them up, but instead, it made him terrified to ask for anything. Tim drove to Savannah Thursday night after work. As I finished packing, he bitched and moaned about how tired he was and then fell asleep on the couch. I remember thinking, *Are you kidding me? What kind of guy doesn't help his girlfriend pack for war?*

The next morning, January 24, 2003 (just three weeks after I turned twenty-four), Tim brought me to the gymnasium, where everyone had the chance to say goodbye to their families for about an hour before it was time to head out. Tim was getting really antsy about missing work and decided to head back to Tampa before the hour was up. "I should probably get back to work, blah blah blah." I wasn't going to pick a fight about it, but I was thinking, *What the fuck*. He was so obsessed with missing work, and I was about to go to war. I just couldn't believe it. But I couldn't dwell on it for long. Plus, his birthday was in two days, so even though his attitude annoyed me, I also kind of felt sorry for him.

We started to board the airplanes parked on our airfield—500 people per flight. They were normal commercial-type airplanes belonging to World Airways, a company contracted for military transport. Officers were told to sit in the front, while the enlisted members were told to sit toward the back of the plane. *Nothing like a little segregation reminiscent of Montgomery circa 1955 to build unit cohesion on the brink of war.* The captain in charge of the seating assignments took one look at my first lieutenant rank (I had been promoted to 1LT two months prior) and told me I could sit in the front row of the enlisted section. Then he looked at Ricardo's CW4 rank and told him to go to the front. Even though I technically outranked Ricardo, the Army values warrant officers over lieutenants, as it rightfully should. But Ricardo insisted that I needed to sit with him up front, and the captain agreed to his request. So we ended up in Row 1—first class, at that—but there wasn't any real service on the plane. At least I had more leg and reclining room.

We left around noon that Friday and had two layovers en route to Kuwait. The first was in Shannon, Ireland. We landed in the middle of the night, and to the misfortune of many thirsty soldiers, the pubs featuring loads of

Guinness were closed and caged up. Our second stop was in the country of Cyprus, just a quick fuel stop, where we were told we couldn't deplane.

Mid-afternoon the following day, we arrived at Ali Al Salem, an American Air Force base in Kuwait. We quickly loaded onto buses with curtains for security purposes. Shortly before our arrival, there had been a few attacks on American defense contractors, so a lot of people seemed extra paranoid. I was just annoyed that I couldn't tell where we were or what was going on. I was cold, starving and really needed to change my tampon, as my period came mid-flight. Unfortunately, we still had a two-hour bus ride awaiting us. Destination: Camp Udairi—a new, makeshift staging post for US troops in northern Kuwait. I tried so hard not to pee my pants. Thankfully my utter discomfort distracted me from contemplating the gravity of where I was and what I was about to do. In the Army, when things suck so badly, it's just easier to turn off your brain and go with the flow (pun intended).

PART 2

Temptation

CHAPTER NINETEEN

It was dark when the bus arrived at Camp Udairi. From what I could see after passing a long concrete barrier, there were several porta-potties, trailers and canvas tents. And a whole lot of fucking sand. We were clearly in the middle of the desert—no man's land.

The first thing I did was run to a porta-potty. Of course, with my luck I now had to contend with my period. After peeing and changing my tampon in the dark, I stumbled out into the vast desert, found my assigned tent and collapsed on an empty cot. It didn't even occur to me that our tents, which slept sixty-five people, were co-ed. I was too exhausted.

Fortunately, our chain of command agreed to allow the new arrivals to sleep for as long as necessary to help overcome jetlag. I slept for the next fifteen hours, waking only intermittently to wonder if I should change my tampon, but too tired, too cold and too far away from the porta-potties to deal with it.

I woke to someone kicking my cot.

My eyes slowly focused on the figure of my boss, Major Putte, standing over me, practically glowing with excitement.

"Get up Laura!" he bellowed.

Utter dread manifested throughout my entire body.

"Come on Laura, you've slept long enough. It's time to get up," he repeated.

"Why?" I moaned. "I'm still sleepy."

"Because I want to show you around. You'll wake up soon. Come on, wash your face and grab your stuff. I'm parked right outside the tent."

I lay there for a moment trying to psyche myself up. But I knew if I didn't move it, Putte would just come back in to pester me. He was my boss after all.

Reluctantly, I dragged myself from the cot and, after quickly changing my tampon in the porta-potty, slowly walked to the waiting SUV, where Putte eagerly awaited. My sleepy state obviously annoyed him and directly contradicted his enthusiasm.

"Cheer up, Laura! There are so many cool things I want to show you. It's good to finally have you here," he beamed.

He then proceeded to drive around in circles, or so it appeared, as I looked at our base camp in its entirety for the first time. "This is our dining facility," Putte said, pointing to a group of tents identical to the ones that we slept in and whose canvas color matched the bland expanse of desert sand that continued as far as the eye could see. I had no idea how I was ever going to learn my way around the camp because everything melded together.

"Now we'll head to our work area," Putte cheered while fumbling with the radio to find a station. Hip-hop music seeped from the intense static as he drove along the outer circumference of the inner camp area. It was interrupted by classical music with a distinct Arab sound. Putte explained that it was the Muslim announcement of call to prayer.

The tour was over almost as soon as it started, as there wasn't much to show of our dismal camp. But Putte wanted to keep me in the car with him. So he started explaining some of the basic camp rules, including a strict schedule allowing only a few showers per week because we had to ration water. And good luck finding warm water. Soon enough, like just about everything else in the Army, this lack of showering became a competition—not for cleanliness, but for who was conserving the most water. Both men and women bragged about limiting their showers to one per week and criticized anyone who they perceived to shower more than their fair share, even if it was within camp rules.

As Putte pulled up to my sleeping tent, concluding the tour, I contemplated visiting with some coworkers I hadn't seen in the past few months. "Want to go to dinner? Are you hungry?" Putte eagerly inquired.

I was famished, and I felt like I couldn't reject my boss's invitation. This set a precedent for every dinner and nearly every waking moment, for that matter; Just like in Savannah, Putte could barely let me out of his sight.

Our food was prepared by locals—not Kuwaitis, who are inherently wealthy, as the government gives its people money from oil subsidies—but third-country nationals who come to Kuwait to earn better wages than their country of origin. In trucks the size of semis, they prepared overcooked beef, potatoes, sautéed veggies—basically middle school cafeteria food—and served it in the huge dining tent. When the eggs were creamy, the guys would joke that the Hajis were jerking off into our eggs. (Haji was a derogatory, racist term to describe these third-country nationals.) Regardless, it really did a number on my stomach.

After that first dinner, I ran from the cafeteria tent for the neatly organized formation of blue and white porta-potties—and braced myself. Unfortunately, while the government was spending millions and millions of dollars on high-tech weapons systems, they cut corners on the basic necessities for the troops, evident with the food, uncomfortable cots and lack of sufficient warm water. But the most egregious insult was that the Army paid to have these porta-potties, eventually used by 12,000 soldiers, cleaned *only once a week.* With all of us eating a steady diet of powdered eggs and leathery Salisbury steaks, it did not make for pretty conditions.

Every time I used a porta-potty, I had to conquer my disgust and fear. First, I stood outside, staring at the blue and white structure with intense focus. Then I took three deep breaths, and on the fourth breath I inhaled everything my lungs could muster. Then I ran inside, slammed the door shut, ripped my pants down, did my business, pulled my pants back up and raced out of there before allowing myself to breathe again. If I couldn't finish my business in this one breath, then I took my hand and cupped it over my nose and mouth, only allowing myself the shallowest of breaths. It's amazing what I learned to accomplish with that one free hand, just so I wasn't found unconscious on top of the toilet.

One day a violent sandstorm raged through our base camp, knocking over several porta-potties. No one was caught inside, but I felt sorry for the poor workers who had to clean up the mess. Sandstorms were common, so to prevent it from happening again, the workers put sandbags on the floor of the porta-potties. Soon enough there was an accumulation of piss all over the sandbags.

Putte once asked all of us how much money it would take to eat our powdered eggs off the sandbags. I said a million dollars. Putte thought I was nuts and said he'd do it for a thousand. Captain Preston Niles said, "Shit, I'll do it for a hundred." But then he chickened out when we came up with the cash.

After my initial fifteen-hour nap, I realized it was Sunday, January 26—Super Bowl Sunday (the Tampa Bay Buccaneers vs. the Oakland Raiders). Our chain of command arranged to have a huge projection screen in the cafeteria tent so we could watch it live on Armed Forces Network, a military channel. (Sadly, AFN had no Super Bowl commercials.) Since our time zone was eight hours ahead of Eastern Time, it was in the middle of the night and bitter cold. There were a few space heaters in the tent, but nothing sufficient to improve the temperature. There was also non-alcoholic beer, but I stuck to water since I wasn't a beer drinker and didn't think there was a point without a buzz. Ricardo and I both cheered loudly for Tampa Bay. When they won, I remember feeling proud of my home team, but also wondered, *Why am I here and not there?* It made me sad to see everyone partying and having fun on the television screen while I felt like I was in hell, albeit a cold hell.

I called Tim the next day, to wish him a belated birthday and tell him about Camp Udairi and the weather. I complained about having to be with Putte again and then told him how much I missed him. It was good to hear his voice, and he did his best to cheer me up. Other people had to wait in line for hours to use the only two public phones at Camp Udairi, but there was a phone in our work tent, so I typically could make calls as I pleased, as long as I had privacy. So I called Tim once a week and also wrote very long and descriptive letters, thinking they would be like journal entries.

I also wrote to my friend Colleen, who lived in Rhinebeck, New York. We met through Connor as he had been tailgating with Colleen and her husband, Woody, since he was a child. (Connor was also from Rhinebeck.) Colleen was like a combo surrogate older sister / mom figure, and she had actually met my mom during a few of her visits to West Point. Even though Connor had stopped speaking to Colleen and Woody, they made it a point to be there for many of my major milestones, including the Handel's *Messiah* solo, graduation, and they even visited me in Savannah shortly before my deployment. Colleen was my most consistent friend and started sending me huge care packages full of treats to share with my unit.

Other friends sent me letters and packages, too, even parents of friends. Apparently being among the first forces on the brink of war was a big deal to them, and I appreciated the time they took to wish me well. Letters were our lifeline to the outside world because a communication infrastructure at Camp Udairi barely existed. Internet access was painfully slow, even for official Army emails. I heard that many of the top leaders, including the generals, resorted to Hotmail, as it was much faster than our secure email lines. To think that today people go to war with Facebook, Skype and plenty of other apps that allow free video conferencing is unreal, although that's how I remain in contact with my friends who are still in the military and deployed. Back then, going to war was completely isolating. And if we ran out of shampoo, it's not like we could order more on Amazon. Actually, we were inundated with care packages of shampoo and other toiletries, so much that we had to leave them behind and pass them along to the units that followed behind us.

On Monday, my first day at work, everyone in my department teased me about how excited Putte was to reunite with me. Apparently, he'd been talking about it for weeks. Instead of feeling flattered, I felt anxious realizing that my three months of independence were over, and now I would be subject to his controlling whims. I almost wished that he could head back to Savannah and let me take over his job in the desert, especially because in his absence, I had received accolades from numerous counterparts who told me I was more competent and enjoyable to work with. Now that I was back in his domain, I once again had to execute whatever ridiculous idea he thought up, in addition to letting him know my every move.

Other soldiers were dealing with their own headaches, like General Order #1, the Army's official list of prohibited activities for soldiers while deployed, including alcohol consumption and sex. At home, we could do what we wanted (within limits) on our down time. But while deployed, the Army owned us 24/7. Some of my fellow soldiers were extremely pissed off about the restrictions. But rules were rules, and there were serious consequences for violating General Order #1.

Colonel Weeds, the Aviation Brigade Commander (and Major Putte's boss), apparently didn't trust that our desire to live was strong enough to keep our hands off each other. Without any prompting from his higher-ups, he asked our unit JAG officer, Captain Arnold Carpenter, to augment General Order #1 and make it even more restrictive.

With his West Point education and Duke law degree going to waste, Arnold was eager to execute this task. Like me, his brain was rotting away as we passed each day in the Kuwaiti desert merely waiting, much like Groundhog Day, wondering when this war was going to start. Arnold, a brilliant overachiever who could have been making millions in Washington DC courtrooms, was instead sitting on a metal folding chair inside of a tent, writing the amendment for General Order #1. Because I was his only friend in the unit, he let me sit next to him while he poured his energy into the document as if he were drafting a new constitution for a liberated Iraq.

I set up next to him with my economics homework. Determined to not let the war derail earning my MBA, I tried my best to delve deeply into the fascinating subject of supply and demand graphs. But Arnold's frantic typing made it difficult to concentrate. I couldn't help but wonder, *What is he writing?* How could he possibly create new rules about sex and alcohol without specific guidance from Colonel Weeds? Was Arnold going to be relentless and suggest horrible punishments that could send us to jail? When he started chuckling, I couldn't contain my curiosity any longer. I begged for a sneak preview. Arnold eagerly obliged.

The new and improved General Order #1, Amendment 1 strictly prohibited masturbation. And just in case the officers and soldiers of the Aviation Brigade needed clarification as to what constituted masturbation, the amendment explained that men were "not allowed to fondle their penises in any way, shape or form." Unlike a lot of the Army treatment I was accustomed to, Amendment 1 was an equal opportunity amendment: female masturbation was also prohibited, including such activities as "inserting either fingers or objects, such as ChapStick, into the orifice."

I laughed harder than I had in months. I always knew Arnold had a perverted side to him, but I couldn't believe that he had the audacity to submit this to Colonel Weeds for approval. I also wondered if Arnold realized that women need something bigger than a tube of ChapStick to feel any ounce of pleasure. Not that I had ever masturbated before, but even virgins know that size matters!

I didn't say anything to Arnold because I didn't want him to change the document. It was perfect. And oh, how

I wanted to be a fly on the wall, observing Weeds's reaction to the examples. Would he appreciate Arnold's explicit descriptions of all possible sexual scenarios (which would make it easier to enforce)? Would he have the balls to publish something so prurient? Arnold and I could barely breathe until we had an answer.

Sadly, Weeds deemed the language too graphic and requested a rewrite. Arnold reluctantly watered down the new amendment to simply say "no masturbation." But I made sure to inform as many people as possible of its original wording and true intent.

Now armed with his weapons of masturbation, Colonel Weeds started a sexual inquisition. He began with what he assumed to be the low hanging fruit, our unit's married couples.

"Do you think Hannah and Kevin are doing it?" he'd ask random soldiers.

Hannah was our tenacious and loveable Battle Captain, a leadership position much like that of a hospital charge nurse. We bonded over our minority status as the only non-aviator female officers on brigade staff. I admired Hannah's brains and would have trusted her to lead me anywhere. But our male bosses overlooked her intelligence because she was four feet ten and had an X chromosome. She tried to compensate for it by working harder than anyone else in the unit, staying well past the time everyone else went home. When you could pull her away from her computer, Hannah was hilarious and a fun gossip. Four years my senior, she anticipated all of my dumb lieutenant mistakes and kind felt like an overbearing, yet endearing Jewish mother.

She was also the spitfire in her marriage to Kevin, a six foot three soft-spoken Kiowa pilot who commanded one of our cavalry troops. I was always curious about how their significant height difference worked out when they were between the sheets. According to Hannah, when two people are lying down in bed next to each other, their height difference is negligible, especially if they're naked. Good to know!

With a lot at stake, though, especially in Kevin's career, Hannah and Kevin didn't dare violate General Order #1. They wouldn't even kiss at the end of a long day, when Kevin would stop by our unit's sleeping tent to visit. Public displays of affection (PDA) are generally frowned upon in the military, but none of us would have complained if they wanted to embrace after an exhausting and stressful day. In fact, we kept egging them on to have their way with each other in some secluded spot out in the middle of the desert. We needed something exciting to pepper our boring days. Plus, it was early enough in the deployment that a few orgasms weren't going to jeopardize national security.

Their willpower astounded me. But on the occasion of their wedding anniversary, we all pretty much knew that General Order #1 was about to go to hell.

It was difficult to determine if they were the first violators because a startling number of single women suddenly became pregnant. Since the Army lacked the medical facilities and technology to pinpoint the conception date, and these women likely conceived the night before we left Savannah for Kuwait, they were shipped home with no punishments.

The morning after Hannah and Kevin's wedding anniversary, we prodded Hannah relentlessly until she admitted that, yes, they indeed violated General Order #1. She literally glowed as she admitted it. We privately applauded her accomplishment, not wanting anyone suspicious to catch wind of the conversation. But Colonel Weeds must have sensed her post-sex aura, because he gave her the silent treatment for the next several days.

As mentioned, we lived in large co-ed tents, sixty-five people practically crammed on top of one another. Only three inches separated my cot from Candace's on my left and Ricardo's on my right. Apparently Colonel Weeds didn't want it any other way. In fact, when some of the older women in my tent hung ponchos and towels to create barriers around their cots, so they could change their clothes with a semblance of privacy, Weeds ripped them down. "Aviation Brigade will only have desegregated tents!" he declared.

How dare these women attempt to destroy unit cohesion by denying their male counterparts the ability to watch them get dressed! To make sure this would never happen again, Amendment 2 was born: "No barriers will be erected in the tents."

It was just more nonsense to distract us from war preparations. I didn't want to change in front of sixty-four other soldiers, but I was too tired, apathetic and cold (winter in Kuwait is chilly) to bother carrying my clothes to the showers. So I became the master of the quick panty change inside of my sleeping bag. I also fell back on a vital skill I acquired in the seventh grade locker room, when I didn't want the other girls to see my mosquito bite breasts, and fed my bra through the sleeves of my shirt.

Because some of the men in my tent were old enough to be my father, I was especially careful to prevent a full frontal and often turned toward Candace and Hannah, just in case my shirt flew up. But after two months of this grueling ritual, I became careless and counted on everyone's apathy to not stare and use me as illegal masturbatory material. My plan worked with everyone, except Ricardo. Sleeping just three inches away from me was all of the inspiration he needed to execute his daily ritual.

Someone typically turned our sleeping tent's lights off at approximately 10:30 p.m. each night. While most of us nestled into our sleeping bags, hoping to drift off to sleep and temporarily forget our deployment misery, Ricardo chose to celebrate his predicament. And he wanted to make sure I didn't miss the party.

"Laura," I heard soft whispers requesting my attention. The first time this happened, I ignorantly turned to Ricardo and asked what he wanted.

"Look," he said, holding open his sleeping bag. When my eyes adjusted to the darkness, I could see him showing off his erection.

"Stop," I said, not wanting to encourage him or have one of our coworkers catch me staring at his boner.

"You did this to me, baby," Ricardo explained.

"Put that away and go to sleep," I demanded as softly as possible, hoping no one could hear me. Within seconds,

I heard a repetitive swoosh-swoosh-swooshing sound, Ricardo's hand moving back and forth against the nylon sleeping bag. I pretended to sleep for the next two and a half minutes, until he let out a sigh.

"All finished," Ricardo announced.

"Shhh," I whispered, horrified.

"Check this out," he demanded.

I refused to budge.

"If you don't look over here right now, I'm gonna get loud," Ricardo threatened.

"Fine, what is it?"

"Look," Ricardo exclaimed as he pulled a soiled sock out from his sleeping bag.

"Ewww gross! You're so bad!"

"Good night, my love," Ricardo replied, as he threw the sock on the floor between our cots.

"Good night," I said, relieved it was over.

This continued on an almost nightly basis until we left our camp to launch the Iraq invasion. Nothing could stop him, not the cramped sleeping tent, not the lack of privacy barriers and certainly not General Order #1, Amendment 1.

Eventually it seemed as if the topic of masturbation dominated every conversation in Kuwait. "I usually go rub one out in the porta-potties," I'd often hear from my male colleagues. I was shocked. I could barely stand to go to the bathroom in there. How in the world could someone sustain sexual arousal in a literal shithole?

Back at West Point, I spent most mornings at the mess hall breakfast table hearing stories about what porn the guys had jacked off to the night before (porn was banned, but they easily hid it in their foot lockers and then disposed of it when they sensed an inspection was pending). That was when I first learned the importance of this daily routine. But I completely forgot about it while preparing for war. I assumed other things took precedence. I was wrong.

Hopefully taking the time to rub one out would allow these warriors to better focus on the task at hand: not getting our asses blown up in combat. Maybe their routine would increase my chances of coming home in one piece.

Unfortunately for Colonel Weeds, all of this talk about General Order #1 and not giving in to our most fundamental desires ironically filled our combat environment with even more sexual electricity. By the time we were ready to ~~invade~~ liberate Iraq (we weren't allowed to use the word "invade"—we were ordered to use the word "liberate"), I couldn't stop thinking about sex. Imagine how the non-virgins felt.

CHAPTER TWENTY

"Hurry up and put your gas masks on!" our commander instructed us.

We were sitting in our brigade headquarters tent, listening to the nightly intelligence updates before dinner. Typically, these updates were mundane, and all of the disseminated information would become obsolete twelve hours later. My favorite update was when Colonel Weeds told us that when we launched the ~~invasion~~ liberation, we would encounter no resistance. He painted a picture of the Iraqi military and civilian populations welcoming us with open arms, just as in 1991's Desert Storm, when hundreds of Iraqis could be seen surrendering on the news. He didn't specify there would be balloons and confetti, but that image popped into my mind.

A lot of people were really eager to go to war. They'd been in the military for years, trained for it and wanted to fight for their country. I didn't necessarily want to get shot at, but I did like being part of the biggest news story in the world. This was clearly an important historical event—or at least it would be once it got started. But at the moment, most of us were completely bored out of our minds.

We weren't training or practicing shooting our weapons. Instead, we woke up, went to breakfast and sat in the work tent all day long, doing busy work. In my case, that meant spreadsheets for Putte, ones no one else would ever see. It was exactly like being in Savannah, except we were out in the middle of the desert, far from any form of civilization. I often thought, *Can't we just get on with it?*

On this night, however, intelligence reports detected movement in a neatly organized formation, starting in southern Iraq and heading south in the direction of our Camp Udairi.

"Gas masks, now!" our commander yelled again.

Well isn't this exciting? I scrambled to put my gas mask on.

I wasn't scared. If an element of the Iraqi army was indeed trying to pick a fight with us in Kuwait, we had three mechanized infantry brigades around us that could and would handle it. But I was confused by the gas masks. We were only supposed to put them on if there was a threat of nuclear, biological or chemical warfare. Intelligence only detected ground movement. *Was there something they weren't telling us?*

We stood in the headquarters tent with our gas masks on for about twenty minutes. Then we heard something scratchy over the radio—an intelligence update.

"Everyone, you can remove your gas masks," our commander instructed us. "The threat is no longer viable."

Great! Now we could go to dinner.

"What was it?" we all asked, eager to know what had caused the panic.

"Turns out it was a heard of camels."

Camels! If this was any indication of what was to come, then this was going to be a long-ass war.

Note: everyone in the United States joins the military voluntarily, but deployments are involuntary. There's also usually a time limit for deployments, but this deployment was indefinite. This was one of the few times deployed US soldiers had no idea when they were going to be able to go home.

We weren't even at war yet; we were just passing time in Kuwait. I hoped that war would be as boring as our time in Kuwait because if I ended up in a firefight, I'd likely die. I could barely shoot my 9mm pistol.

⟜⟝

The irony was that West Point, the ultimate training ground for future officers, gave us the opportunity to practice shooting an amazing arsenal of cool weapons. Besides qualifying on the M16 rifle, the weapon typically assigned to enlisted personnel, I played with the M249 squad automatic weapon (SAW), the M60 PIG machine gun, and an AT4, which is like a bazooka rocket launcher.

I also got to throw a live hand grenade, fire a M203 grenade launcher and even shoot a 50-caliber machine gun mounted on top of a M1 Abram tank at Fort Knox. But the one weapon we never touched at West Point, despite it being the weapon typically assigned to officers in the regular Army, was the 9mm pistol.

Thankfully, my father had taken me to a gun range my senior year of high school. "You're going to head off to West Point in a few months, and you've never touched a weapon before," he told me. "You can't act like a scared little girl the first time you pull the trigger."

I can't say I actually gained any skills that day, as my bullet holes sprayed all over the paper targets, but at least I gained the exposure. Even though it only lasted a few hours, the outing turned out to be one of the few special bonding adventures I'd had with my father when I was in high school.

The next time I touched a 9mm was as a lieutenant, on the gun range in Savannah. I was a frazzled mess that day. The night before I was the assigned as the staff duty officer, tasked with conducting random security checks all night, despite there being regular military police patrols. Even if I found a terrorist lurking around the unit area, all I had to defend myself was the clipboard I held because staff duty officers don't carry weapons.

The next day I stood on the shooting range under the hot Georgia sun, running on no sleep and not having touched a 9mm pistol in over five years.

"Hurry up, Laura! We're getting hungry," Major Putte shouted from the bleachers. I thought Putte would be more inclined to help me with my technique, seeing how he was a former infantryman, wore the expert marksman badge on his uniform and was responsible for mentoring me. Not to mention, we were supposedly going to war in the near future and would likely have to fight the bad guys together.

"Can you just pull it together and qualify already?" he yelled. "We don't want to miss the Hooters lunch special! You're going to make us late."

Beads of sweat rolled down my face as the rest of the ten superior officers in my unit—each one hungry, cranky and horny—started yelling at me from the sidelines. I was the only one keeping them from a lunch of spicy hot wings and bodacious breasts.

With everything I could muster, I finally qualified after seven attempts, and we made it to Hooters, just in the nick of time.

After lunch, I assumed Putte would sit me down to strategize on how we would work to improve my skills, which he must have noticed were sorely lacking. Instead, he chose to mock me in front of everyone.

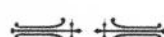

Later, when I found other units' ranges to practice at, he came up with every excuse to not let me go, including in Kuwait.

"Sir, the headquarters company is hosting a gun range this afternoon," I announced, several weeks after arriving in Kuwait.

"That's nice. And?" Putte looked up at me.

"And I'd really like to go," I responded.

"Why?" Putte asked. For a moment I thought he was kidding, but his stare indicated otherwise.

"Because we're starting a war any day now, and I haven't fired a gun in over six months."

"You don't need to go."

"Excuse me, Sir?"

"Stay here. You don't need to go."

"But I have to go. I'm not comfortable with my shooting skills."

"I need you here."

"What for?" I snapped, barely able to control my mounting rage.

"There's a report Weeds wants finished, and I need your help," Putte answered.

"But Sir, can't that wait a few hours?" I tried to reason. "This is really important. I can't go into Iraq without being proficient at my weapon."

"You'll be fine. You don't need to worry about that. It's not like we're going to need to use them."

"Sir, you can't assume that. That's not fair. And you of all people know how badly I suck at shooting. You remember the qualifying range. You can't possibly feel comfortable letting me go to war without some extra practice!"

"Ah," he brushed me off. "I'm not worried about you," he said.

"I promise I'll finish the report as soon as I return from the range. Please let me go, Sir," I begged, trying to hide my trembling.

"No, and don't ask me again. There will be another range before we head up north."

"You'll just find something else for me to do," I muttered under my breath, beyond livid.

Apparently, Putte's priority wasn't to make sure that I could properly defend myself against enemy forces—it was to keep our common area nice and tidy, especially when the general in charge of all deployed forces was scheduled for a VIP visit.

"Laura, I need for you to find three soldiers and sweep the hangar."

"Excuse me, Sir? Did you say you want me to sweep the hangar?"

"Well, not you specifically. You can make the soldiers do it, but you need to supervise."

"Sir, how can we possibly sweep away all of the sand when we're in the middle of the desert?" I went on, hoping he would abort the mission.

"I know it can't be perfect, but do your best. There's brooms in the corner over there."

With my head and shoulders slumped, I approached the first group of junior enlisted soldiers I saw in the hangar and humbly explained my predicament. When I told them that there was no way in hell that I was just going to stand by and watch them work, they generously agreed to assist. For the next thirty minutes, we swept the sand out of the hangar into the sand outside, which the wind just blew right back in. A few colleagues walking by actually asked us, "What the fuck are you doing?" When I thought the hangar was as clean as it could be, I thanked and dismissed the soldiers and put the brooms away.

Then Putte peered down at the ground in several spots.

"Laura, go get those soldiers back here and sweep for twenty more minutes."

"Sir, there's no way in hell I'm going to do that."

"Fine," he said, "but that just means you'll have to do it yourself."

"Fine," I replied, and dragged the broom around again, yielding the exact same result. When I was done, Putte told me to go find some pastries.

When I returned with enough pastries and beverages to make Martha Stewart proud (apparently pastries were included on the food service department's combat packing list), Putte told me to make a nice arrangement on the table. Then he completely redid everything, claiming that the Cokes should go before the Sprites, which should go before the punch.

The general finally made his appearance and led an intense meeting with officers far above my pay grade. I thought I was finally going to be released, but Putte ordered me to man the refreshment table, in case I needed to hand the general a snack. I waited for an hour and a half, observing some last-minute war-gaming, while the pastries and drinks remained untouched.

My friend Hannah also struggled to achieve her male boss's cosmetic standards on the brink of war. As battle captain, it was her job to consolidate complicated operational plans and constantly update them based on daily intelligence updates. But no matter how in-depth, comprehensive and downright smart her work was, Colonel Weeds constantly hounded her to make changes.

"Hannah, your charts need to be color coordinated. This area should be green, this one red and I like yellow for this part."

Unfortunately, Hannah didn't have the luxury of stopping at an Office Max to obtain a color printer. But Weeds, having an aversion for being without survival gear, ensured his combat packing list included the appropriate printer that would produce colored charts to his heart's content. Hannah slaved away on our battle plan, resubmitting it in an impressive binder that even included color-coordinated tabs. Unfortunately, she still missed the mark.

"Hannah, the holes you punched are out of alignment, and it makes the papers askew," Colonel Weeds miffed. "I want a neat stack. Reprint this and fix your holes."

It seemed ironic, that these male leaders were obsessing about such girlie things. I imagined that if I had a chain of command comprised of only women, they would be acting far more professional. I couldn't believe that the general public thought men were better equipped to be leaders because of their stable emotions. Putte and Weeds were anything but stable, and I felt like a pawn in their silly games—games that deterred us from actually preparing for war.

If I allowed myself to think about how ill-equipped we were, I would become paralyzed in fear. It didn't matter. I was stuck. Better to turn my brain off and hope for the best. The only thing that kept me going was imagining my bank account increasing exponentially, since I had no living expenses. My only consolation was thinking, *At least I'll have a shit ton of money when I come home.*

Occasionally a thought crept up about my parents. I tried to picture them watching the news, wondering what was going to happen to their daughter. What hurt the most is that I didn't think they cared. My death would make no difference in their lives, since I was already gone forever. But I couldn't dwell on the tragic way I had to divorce them. I had a new mission of survival to focus on—a literal war.

CHAPTER TWENTY-ONE

Standing at just five feet four, Colonel Weeds was much smaller than what I had imagined he would look like before he took command of our brigade. But he had some decent muscles to compliment his small stature, and he looked a lot younger than a lot of full-bird colonels. He came to us from the special operations community, specifically the 160th Special Operations Aviation Regiment (SOAR), whose most famous (and tragic) mission was depicted in the movie *Black Hawk Down*.

Because Weeds wore a 160th patch on his right shoulder (indicating combat participation in this unit), we thought he had fought in Somalia. But he didn't regale us with any war stories like commanders typically do, so we eventually surmised that he was never actually there.

What confused us even more was the movie director's chair that adorned Weeds's flashy office. Since the words

"Black Hawk Down" were stitched across it, we naturally thought Weeds might have flown in the movie. He even told us that the movie producers interviewed him and put the segment in the special features section of the DVD. When I checked it out, I was rather impressed and proud to work for a Hollywood badass. But after digging a little deeper, I learned that Weeds was simply the officer-in-charge of administration and logistics for the stunt pilots and their aircraft. In essence, he was the stunt pilots' bitch boy.

More than anything, Weeds dreamed about going to war. Being in charge of seventy-six helicopters, two lieutenant colonels, two majors, eight captains, two lieutenants, several senior enlisted personnel and our helicopter battalions wasn't enough. Weeds needed something more to make the Aviation Brigade his own and portray him as the supreme warrior.

Weeds adored the movie *Gladiator* and told us how much he admired and identified with Maximus, the character played by Russell Crowe. He loved Maximus so much that he was inspired to change our brigade's long-standing, historic motto "Wings of the Marne." This was a reference to the 1918 battles of the Marne in the First World War, when French, British and American troops held off German forces and launched a counter-offensive, which would eventually win the war. Weeds ordered us to instead chant "Strength and Honor," the phrase Russell Crowe chanted when he was about to fight in the arena. Many of us were appalled by this idiotic and disrespectful move to rewrite history. We rebelled by chanting our new motto incorrectly—instead of saying "Strength and Honor," we chose to say, "Strengthen On Her."

War couldn't come fast enough for Weeds. Every day we had Fox News—*Fair and Balanced*—playing 24/7 in our work tent, letting us know if war was coming because our chain of command really had no clue. Every day it seemed like the information from higher headquarters changed. But the *Fair and Balanced* news anchors seemed to reassure us that war was coming any day now.

When we were back in Savannah, the 3d Infantry Division had technically been under an alert, which meant that we could be called up to deploy within 24 hours. But we didn't own any combat gear, and it would take weeks to ship our aircraft and Humvees to any war zone, so none of us expected this alert to come to fruition any time soon—except Weeds.

Instead of waiting for the Pentagon to issue us deployment orders, Weeds took it upon himself to precipitate two premature deployments to Kuwait. This is why Major Putte left three months before I did. I have no idea who he knew in high places to have this ad hoc mobilization authorized, but he did it, unnecessarily ruining Christmas for many of his troops.

When the entire brigade finally made it to Kuwait, under official, legitimate deployment orders, Weeds was excited to rally his troops. Channeling another favorite movie inspiration, Lieutenant Colonel Hal Moore from the movie *We Were Soldiers* (Mel Gibson's character), Weeds formed the entire brigade in one of the aircraft hangars and gave us a motivational speech about venturing off into war. I may have been inspired, had he not announced that he was going to get shot down—twice.

I couldn't help but think back to my military history class at West Point, when we studied Napoleonic warfare. Reading about all of Napoleon's battles and the gross number of troops who died simply to fulfill his glory, I could only surmise one theory: He must have had a really small penis. I applied the same theory to my own chain of command. There could be no other explanation for their motivations and behavior.

Now in Kuwait, the mood was becoming increasingly antsy. We watched Fox News's *Fair and Balanced* coverage of Colin Powell giving his presentation to the UN, trying to prove that Saddam Hussein had weapons of mass destruction. I thought, *Can't we just make a decision?* If we weren't going to war, the fallout of deploying tens of thousands of troops unnecessarily would be a disaster. Since we were practically there, evidence of weapons of mass destruction didn't matter to many. They simply expressed, "Let's go get that fucker."

Then one day, somebdy just said it: "Pack up. Tonight we're going to move out."

It didn't take a lot for me to pack. I gathered my thirty bullets and three decrepit magazines with springs so old they threatened to cause a misfire, and I tucked them away in the various pouches affixed to my pseudo bullet-proof vest. Then I was ordered to pack my trailer full of Colonel Weeds's personal belongings, more specifically, home decor to adorn his tent. I would end up driving into

Iraq with his gourmet coffee pot and plethora of knick-knacks. I felt more like a furniture deliveryman than a defender of the free. But I figured if all hell broke loose, maybe I could win the hearts and minds of the Iraqis with cute presents.

We left our canvas tents behind, but brought the Humvees and mobile tents. In the late afternoon, we drove for two hours through miles and miles of flat sand to another spot in the middle of the desert near the border of Kuwait and Iraq. It looked so identical to where we'd just left that if you weren't paying attention, you'd have no idea we'd actually gone from one place to another.

Two nights before we crossed the border, we set up some small work tents and slept on cots outside our Humvees. We had separated from the cavalry on the way, so our brigade now had about 700 people. After two months of dealing with those disgusting porta-potties, I was so excited to move out of our base camp. But we had a new problem. For some reason, we weren't allowed to leave any trace of our presence behind. So burying our crap in the sand was out of the question.

Luckily, some clever handymen in our unit invented contraptions with plywood, a makeshift toilet seat and a large drum to collect our waste. At first I loved how these stalls had no ceilings, just a constant supply of fresh air. But then we were ordered to burn our shit.

My chain of command actually generated a shit-burning schedule on a Power Point slide. My shit shift was in the evening, just as the sun was setting. It almost made for a nice campfire setting, if the logs we were burning were made of wood, not shit. It didn't take long for Putte to start asking how much money it would take for us to eat hot dogs roasted over these shit fires.

On top of the shit-burning shifts, our new amenities consisted of absolutely no concealment. There wasn't even a tree to hide behind when it was time to do my business. Sometimes a female friend was available to partially cover me, which was OK for urinating, but I felt uncomfortable passing my bowels in front of her.

My modesty changed completely, however, when late in the evening I noticed vague flickers of light shining on my bare ass while in the middle of going number two. I looked around for the source of light. It was coming from my fellow coworkers back at our staging area, several hundred feet away. They were using our military issued flashlights.

Instead of screaming across the desert, I decided to show I had a sense of humor. After wiping my ass, I stood up and shouted in their direction. "You wanna see my ass?"

"Well, if that's what you want, then you got it," I turned around, dropped my pants, and bent over, mooning everyone. Cheers and applause emerged for my performance. I laughed out loud as I returned to the staging area, where the guys thanked me for my generosity. It was the least I could do to ease their tensions before going to war.

We still didn't know exactly when we were going to cross the border. The next day, I had an onset of really bad cramps. In an attempt to sync my menstrual cycle with President Bush's ~~invasion~~ liberation timetable, I skipped my birth control pack's placebo pills and moved on to the next pack. Supposedly this would allow me to miss my period. But it wasn't working, and I started experiencing an extremely heavy period. *Just my luck,* I thought. *But at least I have plenty of tampons.*

Talk around the work tent seemed to indicate that we would probably be going into Iraq the next morning. The Apache helicopter battalion geared up to launch their mission of blowing up some observation posts just over the border into Iraq. I assumed at this point that no Iraqi would be stupid enough to be waiting there, and the mission seemed like a waste, but who was I to offer my opinion?

During the mission, as other pilots bombed the observations posts (that indeed had been unmanned), the Apache Battalion Commander, Lieutenant Colonel Jeff Radcliffe, became overzealous and over-torqued his Apache (flew it too hard), forcing him to make an emergency landing. He had to wait there, technically on Iraqi soil, until a maintenance test pilot arrived (via another helicopter) to power up his helicopter. After an all clear, they returned to the Kuwait border.

Lieutenant Colonel Radcliffe would end up receiving an Air Medal with Valor for this mission, because he was "stuck behind enemy lines" and "risked enemy fire." When we eventually returned home to Savannah, Boeing (the manufacturer of the Apache) hosted a grand ceremony where Radcliffe was presented with his award. Even though I personally liked Radcliffe, from the moment I heard about the outcome of his mission, I knew it was all utter bullshit.

This incident set a precedent for the confusion and obfuscation that would paint my entire war narrative—forcing me to trust none of my leaders, from my boss all the way up to President Bush.

CHAPTER TWENTY-TWO

The sound of explosions woke me up in the middle of the night. The sky looked like a fireworks display celebrating the Fourth of July, only it was in the wee hours of March 21. I sat up thinking, *Alright, it's happening. We're really going to war.* Then the soldier next to me, a woman who was suffering from depression and really shouldn't have been there, suddenly threw on her gas mask. Following her lead, I put my gas mask on too. Then I realized we were the only ones wearing them.

"Don't ever do that again!" I yelled at her. "You just made me think there was a gas attack, and that's how bad information gets disseminated."

I felt bad for yelling at her, but she totally freaked me out. We later learned that the explosions were Tomahawk missiles being shot into Baghdad from nearby cruisers parked in the Persian Gulf. I couldn't think about it.

If I thought too deeply about what we were doing and where we were, I would become paralyzed with fear. I forced myself to concentrate on action, not thought. Besides, I had no control—everyone was making decisions for me. The only way to get through this without losing my shit was to remain detached. In that respect, maybe it was fortuitous that I was having the worst period of my entire life, because it momentarily distracted me.

Two months after our arrival in Kuwait, we finally launched the ~~invasion~~ liberation of Iraq. Back home, where it was still night time on March 20, President Bush announced to American citizens via the Oval Office that "coalition forces are in the early stages of military operations to disarm Iraq, to free its people and to defend the world from grave danger." In other words, it was time to get Saddam Hussein out.

We left our temporary camp for the Iraq border at noon on March 21, 2003. It was odd to have a leisure morning on my first official day of war, but who was I to question our departure timeline? (Alicia Campbell, a notoriously glamorous woman in the Black Hawk battalion, even had time to apply her usual thick layers of mascara.) I wasn't aware of this at the time, but our cavalry support ground forces crossed late on the evening of March 19, and Lieutenant Colonel Mike Fuller—our Brigade S3 / head of tactics—crossed early on the 20th with 3-69 Armor (of our infantry division) and a Marine Corps Explosive Ordnance Disposal (EOD) team.

~~Invading~~ Liberating Iraq commenced by getting in our Humvees, single file, and driving at two miles an hour with our headlights on. Thankfully Major Putte was assigned to go in a separate vehicle, so the ~~invasion~~ liberation provided me with a huge reprieve. (Even though Ricardo and I were technically battle buddies, he also had to move ahead in a separate vehicle, so I also had a reprieve from his masturbation.) I shared my vehicle with two nice enlisted soldiers who enjoyed joking around and the manic depressive one who had donned her gas mask unnecessarily. I pretended as if we were the Griswolds of *National Lampoon's Vacation* trying to find Wally World.

The border was just dirt and sand with wire, an orange construction cone, and a few uniformed men from the UN directing us into specific lanes: "You go into lane five. You go into lane three..." One of them instructed for my vehicle to enter Iraq via lane five.

Once we crossed from Kuwait into Iraq, we passed another UN soldier standing beside a UN cone with a cardboard sign taped to it that read "Welcome to Iraq." There were no Iraqis on the Iraq side, and no Kuwaitis on the Kuwait side. I sat in the front passenger side of the Humvee, like a tourist, snapping photos of a truck that had been on fire. Until I had the film developed, I didn't realize that the tarp next to it concealed dead bodies with some guts sprayed askew. Mostly, it was just a desolate no man's land. I lowered my camera and took it all in. *Were we really at war?* It was so anti-climactic, yet still surreal.

We drove for hours seeing nothing but sand and, later that evening, a Bedouin man in a white tunic traversing the desert with a camel. We had no idea where he came from, or where he was going, but he was completely unfazed by us driving through, almost as if we weren't there.

Over the course of next three weeks, we would drive a total of 500 miles up to Baghdad, all at two miles an hour, and always with our headlights on.

Initially we only stopped driving temporarily to refuel the Humvees and relieve ourselves. (I also used these stops to brush my teeth and wash my hair with water bottles and travel sized Salon Selectives shampoo and conditioner, which had a strong, refreshing scent.) Since we were living out of our Humvees, my toilet paper and tampon hoarding had come in handy, and my Humvee was fully stocked. But the one thing I wasn't prepared for—the one combat skill I was least trained in—was going to the bathroom in front of my coworkers. When you're maneuvering through enemy territory with bombs and missiles flying overhead, you can't just wander off to do your business in private. I imagined the obituary: "Young army lieutenant dies of gunshot wound to her bare ass."

My solution to the bathroom dilemma was to use the Humvee's back and front doors to form a "V" that covered me in the perfect spot. Then I kicked a small hole in the dirt with my boot, crouched down only a little—so the doors still covered me appropriately—and did my business right there, with a bunch of my fellow soldiers hanging out just a few feet away. I thought my plan worked and that I buried my poop and tampon sufficiently, until Sergeant Hemming asked me, "Ma'am, are you on the rag?" At first

I was mortified and would have given anything to go back to burning my shit. But I quickly got used to it.

To avoid these humiliating situations, some people purposely dehydrated themselves. Hannah told me she didn't take a shit for nine days. Not me. As we kept driving toward Baghdad, not only did my period keep on flowing (talk about shedding your blood all over the battlefield)—I had crazy bowel movements. The MREs made my poop green and enormously large. It felt like my anus was ripping apart whenever I had to go. My poor soldiers who had to witness this. Many of us came home with chronic stomach problems and digestive issues.

There must have been logic to when and where we stopped—maybe our commanders were waiting for battles to finish ahead of us—but no one told us anything. Most of us didn't have a radio or a map, and the Humvees kicked up so much sand we couldn't see a damn thing. When we heard bombs and shooting nearby, we just hoped it was friendly and not enemy fire. It was confusing and frustrating to wander so aimlessly, or to *feel like* we were wandering aimlessly, especially when we were basically one long, slow-moving target.

Fed up with the lack of information, I stormed over to Lieutenant Colonel O'Neil, our doofus executive officer, at one of our fuel stops.

"Sir, what are we doing? Where are we going?"

"Don't worry about it. Everything's under control," he answered stiffly.

"Can you at least tell us what's going on? People are going crazy."

He shrugged his shoulders. "It's classified. And if people are upset, tell them too bad."

I walked back to my Humvee. What a moron.

On March 31, we finally stopped and pitched our first camp, out in the middle of the desert. I took a much-needed shower, which felt nearly orgasmic. Unfortunately, things didn't feel great down below when I cleaned myself. I had detected a burning sensation several days earlier, and now I realized what it was. Baby wipes didn't suffice in cleaning myself for the past eleven days, and now I had a vaginal yeast infection. (I guess Newt Gingrich wasn't entirely wrong in 1995 when he declared that females in combat would get infections.)

"Wake up! Put on your gear and get in formation!"

Intelligence reports indicated Iraqi forces were about to penetrate the perimeter of our camp, and we needed to defend it.

We all fumbled for our helmets, pseudo bulletproof vests and weapons. Major Putte started giving out orders, pairing us up, and telling us to take position in different spots. "You and you go over here; you and you go over there… Laura, you stay with me." Up until that point, I had barely seen him on the convoy, but now he wanted me to be next him.

When everyone assumed their positions, we were formed in three overlapping circles. I had switched my pistol for a rifle, but it seemed like if we were going to get into a firefight, we would end up shooting at each other because of our circular formation. Knowing how awful my aim was, I was ideally positioned to annihilate my entire company.

I waited with Putte, picturing these theoretical Iraqi forces marching into our base camp of hundreds of soldiers armed with an arsenal of destructive weapons. I thought, *there's no way this is really happening. Who would be so stupid as to antagonize us like this?* Instead of being scared, I couldn't help but shake my head and laugh, wondering if this was something like when we were back in Kuwait and had to protect ourselves against a fleet of camels.

In the middle of waiting for the Iraqis to kill us, Putte asked if I wanted to scope things out through his night vision goggles. I said sure, but admitted that I didn't know how to actually use them. So he stood behind me, adjusting the knobs, telling me where to look, when suddenly I felt his body pressed up against mine. If he wasn't scared shitless, I definitely would have detected a boner. *Holy fuck, is Putte copping a feel?* I thought. Normally I would defend myself, but I stood completely frozen. *I should say something*, but I couldn't. We stood there for several unfathomable moments until Putte cleared his throat.

"Um Laura, I'm going to go over there now and am gonna wait this out with Sergeant H. But I won't leave you alone for long. I'll send someone over to keep you company."

He must have remembered that I sucked at shooting a gun (90 percent his fault) because Sergeant Hemming just happened to be one of the best marksmen in our unit. So in short order, my boss didn't let me practice shooting a gun, then he copped a feel when he thought our lives were being threatened, and now he was abandoning me right before a potential firefight. Some leader. Some West Point graduate!

Soon Ricardo came prancing over, laughing hysterically at our predicament.

"Your boss sent me over to protect you," he joked.

I busted out laughing and knew that we would be ok.

Not long after, a soldier came over and dismissed us, telling us to go back to bed with no explanation. When I poked around, asking for more information, the intelligence officer on duty said, "Oh, it was nothing. What we thought were enemy forces turned out to be the headlights on the Humvees of our sister brigade."

I went right back to sleep. I had this overwhelming feeling of being a waste, not contributing anything of significance. And it was getting harder and harder to take any of it seriously.

Wanting to see if I could have my yeast infection treated, the next morning I paid the brigade doctor a visit and, since it was April 1, decided to have a little fun.

"Doc, I'm late," I announced.

Doc froze. The consequences of getting pregnant at war were serious. In addition to sending me home, Colonel Weeds would probably kick me out of the Army for violating General Order #1.

"Holy shit, Laura, what did you do?" He was practically shaking. "I can't believe this."

"Is there any way I could get a ride over to the CASH (combat support hospital) to get a pregnancy test?" I asked. Doc sat down, shaking his head. When I saw that he was on the verge of tears (he really liked me and hated to see me get in trouble), I blurted out, "APRIL FOOLS!" He then gasped and threw his arms around me, laughing, "THANK YOU JESUS!"

Thankfully, he had the right medication: Diflucan. The yeast infection went away within two days, as did my period—finally! I like to think they both went into hiding, like Saddam.

My sense of humor was helping me to survive some ugly situations—but what happened next was no joke.

CHAPTER TWENTY-THREE

In the very early morning on April 2, Sergeant Richards woke me up asking for the special laptop on which we kept all of our soldiers' confidential personal information.

"Why do you need it?" I asked while handing it to him, thinking his request was odd. He wouldn't tell me, which was even more strange. I was too tired to think about it and went back to sleep.

When I fully awoke and walked around, I noticed an unusually somber mood. At first, Major Putte wouldn't tell me what happened, but I demanded, "This is my fucking job." So he told me. Six of our guys died in a Black Hawk helicopter crash. I felt like I'd just been punched in the gut.

It was the second time I was like, "Holy shit, we're dealing with death." A couple of days prior, during a nightly intelligence update, we heard that an Iraqi suicide bomber killed two soldiers in our division. The Black Hawk crash was the first casualty in our aviation brigade, and it hit me really hard. I quietly cried myself to sleep that night. I had met one of the late pilots in Kuwait—such a nice guy, a West Point graduate who after the war was slated to go to Harvard for his MBA, and then teach at West Point. We had agreed to become study buddies since I, too, was studying for my MBA, and when we met, I was in the middle of an economics assignment.

Later in the morning, we gathered to listen to an official announcement: "The crew was flying to relieve another crew, and at the time we lost radio contact with them, they perished." That's when the war became real for me. April 2 would haunt me for nearly a decade after, until the psychotherapy I sought finally healed me of this tragedy.

That afternoon, a crew flew out to the crash site to begin covering the remains.

The next day we left.

The transition was so quick and shocking. The worst tragedy had just happened and the war continued on. It also hurt because I thought these men had died for nothing. Years later a therapist posed a question that helped to mitigate some of my pain: "Did it ever occur to you that they might have loved what they did, and perhaps this was the most honorable thing they could imagine doing for their country?"

At the time, I didn't see it from their perspective. I only felt resentment that we moved on like nothing ever happened. The crew that retrieved the remains stayed behind to investigate the crash, but the rest of us pushed forward to Baghdad.

Colonel Weeds, acting in true wannabe Hollywood badass fashion, also went to the crash site and actually made the guys retrieving remains stand in front of the crashed helicopter and take a picture with him standing in the middle, posed like some great big hero. I found out about it about a month later when I was sent back to Kuwait as a purchasing agent to procure supplies depleted during our convoy. Weeds handed me the roll of film to develop and said that he wanted to mail copies to the late soldiers' families. We were all disgusted. I never followed through on his order.

Any time I heard we were in a "battle," I became suspicious. It seemed like we either exaggerated details for the sake of looking glorious, or we completely overreacted to non-threats. During convoy stops, Major Putte routinely rallied a bunch of bored soldiers to kick in doors of abandoned buildings, hoping to ignite some fight. I rolled my eyes watching as I peed and gassed up my Humvee.

Our unit planned to have firefights, but I couldn't tell if they actually happened, whether or not we instigated them or if they were fabricated. What I observed was that intelligence would indicate if there was a point of interest—this could be something like an Iraqi military installation or a warehouse that supposedly housed a weapons cache. Then our helicopters would fly over these areas. Even if nothing was there, we blew it up anyway, and then our chain of command reported, "We had a battle." I never knew what or who to trust.

I never knew how much danger I was in. Regardless of whether or not our battles were real, shit was constantly blowing up everywhere. Life became an orchestra of bombs and rockets detonating all around us. The sand we kicked up from our Humvee tires made it impossible to see where they were coming from or where they landed, and without a radio or any explanation from the chain of command, I was utterly clueless. *So much for studying years of warfare tactics at West Point,* I thought. *Talk about fog of war!* To cope, I laughed and joked to the other soldiers in my Humvee, "I hope that's American!" while driving on ahead to our unclear objective. It felt like a gauntlet of slaughter, but I couldn't allow myself to think about it. So I shut my brain down, hoped for the best and relied on my sense of humor to get me through each and every explosion.

I suspected any battle was completely of our own doing and unnecessary. I worried we put ourselves in far more danger that the Iraqi forces presented themselves, just so we could claim some kind of victory and revel in the glory. I expressed my frustrations in those lengthy letters to Tim.

From a battlefield tactics perspective, we had Apache helicopters that were supposed to do the fighting from a safe distance, afforded by the long distance range of their hellfire missiles. Black Hawk helicopters transported the high-ranking officers who were supposed to observe the fighting, such as Colonel Weeds. Apparently the fighting didn't occupy him enough, as he used to bring Pepperidge Farm sausages and cheeses onto the flights and torture Candace (serving as the air battle captain) by asking if she wanted to take a bite of his sausage. Then the Kiowa helicopters of the cavalry conducted reconnaissance missions and encountered plenty of resistance, but they were now following the orders of the assistant division commander for movement (ADC-M), so Weeds couldn't claim any of their victories, nor did he dictate any of their moves. Their movements were coordinated between the ADC-M, cavalry commander and their tank assets. Sometimes the Kiowa helicopters would get shot at by Iraqis using surface-to-air missiles or rocket propelled grenades, and their pilots exuded bravery for surviving these fights and progressing on ahead. Theoretically, their actions in destroying any threats made it safer for us to proceed on to Baghdad. But the rest of us were support elements and not supposed to be in battle. This left me not knowing how to answer someone whenever I was asked if I saw combat. I don't know what the fuck I witnessed, but I believe I only survived by sheer luck.

Two days after the Black Hawk crash, in the middle of the night, someone on night duty told us there was a scud missile nearby and ordered us to put on all our chemical gear. Ricardo was sleeping in his Humvee, but he came into my small group tent to wait with me. I gave him space on my cot, and we cuddled in the fetal position the whole time. No one said anything about Ricardo and me lying together on the cot. There was nothing sexual about it. We were just holding each other as we waited to see how things panned out. Eventually we heard the all clear, and took off our gear. We'd made it through another scare.

The next day we were back on the road to Baghdad.

Most of the roads we drove over were unpaved, so there was always a concern of driving over unexploded ordnance (un-detonated bombs or missiles) or getting stuck in the sand. Our Humvees were old. They frequently broke down or got stuck. Luckily we had the 603rd maintenance battalion to bail us out. On this particular morning, my Humvee wouldn't start. Somebody had to radio in to the 603rd on my behalf, and a mechanic fixed it in about thirty minutes. But then I had to hurry to catch up to my position in the convoy. The people occupying the vehicles directly in front of and behind me didn't wait and had left without me.

Tensions were high as we rolled along for the third week through more of the same monotonous landscape. To avoid getting stuck in tire tracks, we were told, "Spread out, don't drive in a single file for this stretch, but don't stray too far because of possible unexploded ordnance."

I was in the passenger seat of my Humvee with my driver, Tammy, the depressive junior enlisted soldier who should have never deployed. Suddenly, our brigade chaplain, Major Julio Colton (who sounded just like Mike Tyson), broke formation and drove up next to us in his own Humvee.

"Get in the lines!" he yelled.

"What?" I yelled back.

"You're all over the place. Get in the damn lines!" he waved his arms.

I looked over at Tammy like, *What the fuck?*

Chaplains weren't allowed to have weapons, so their assistants had to be on extra alert to defend them both with only one weapon. This meant that the assistant had to be on guard scanning the battlefield from the passenger seat while the chaplain did all the driving. Our chaplain had literally been driving non-stop for nearly three weeks through a sandy hell. No wonder he was losing his mind. Plus, he was a total weirdo and prima donna who despised playing Army.

It was like a classic road rage scenario, except we were two Humvees in Iraq, driving side by side, with the chaplain and me shouting each other.

At one point the chaplain actually pulled in front my Humvee and slammed on his brakes, purposely cutting us off. Tammy slammed on her brakes. Then the chaplain got out of his Humvee and stormed over. Meanwhile, everyone else drove away.

"Just drive around him!" I told Tammy. But she froze. The chaplain came up to my window, shouting and threatening to pull rank and report me for insubordination.

"I don't care what you fucking do," I yelled. "Get back in your vehicle!"

It dawned on me that I just cussed out the chaplain—me, the Christian girl. Even though I had started to lose my faith, I still wanted to try and be good and certainly not swear at God's representative. But the Chaplain was a loose cannon who could have easily injured us.

When we got to the next fuel stop, I went straight up to Putte and O'Neil and warned them about my altercation with the chaplain.

"We heard allllll about it," Putte smiled.

"Kudos to you for cursing him out," O'Neil added. Then they high-fived me.

April 10, 2003: Baghdad. After weeks in the empty desert, it was amazing to see lush green banks of the Euphrates River, the longest river in Western Asia, and the surrounding rural neighborhoods. I wondered how the Iraqi people ate, since so much of the country is barren desert, but seeing the river revealed some crops and irrigation lines. Gradually, we saw more houses and civilization, everything the color of khaki and caked with a thick layer of dust.

In Baghdad itself, droves of people were looting everywhere. Unlike the phrase, "everything but the kitchen sink," I actually did see a man carrying a kitchen sink down the road. There were no police officers, authority figures or Iraqi soldiers—just civilians who waved at us and gave us a thumbs-up as we passed. Even though sentiments would change a few months later, it was heartwarming to be welcomed in this manner.

Just the day prior, Iraqi protestors pulled down a massive statue of Saddam Hussein in Firdos Square, symbolically ending his twenty-four-year presidency. He had become president of Iraq on July 16, 1979—just six months and eleven days after I was born.

We went straight to the airport, which was deemed secure since our armor (tank) battalions had arrived there before us and seized it. The Baghdad International Airport became our new home away from home.

CHAPTER TWENTY-FOUR

I walked through the Baghdad International Airport (BIAP) and entered an office building, feeling like an explorer who discovered a new land. I wanted to soak everything in and permanently etch it in my mind. Up until this point, the desert landscape of our ~~invasion~~ liberation was nothing like I had ever seen, and I only saw a few people en route to Baghdad. So I had yet to witness the war's impact on actual Iraqi people. But now, standing in this office building, I grasped so much.

The office building looked like a typical American office, only it seemed dated, like I was watching a TV show about an office from the 1970s. There were cubicles with papers, books, stationery and office equipment. The desks had paperwork that looked like it was abandoned in a hurry. I tried to imagine the Iraqi workers in here, going about their day, griping about their jobs, gossiping about one another and wondering what the hell was happening to their country. I pondered how long they lingered until they were told to leave. I worried about them being scared and if they were now safe.

The main difference between this office and the ones back home is the walls were lined with big posters of Saddam Hussein. When I went through the books on the shelves, I noticed many of them were about the dictator. His face was everywhere. I thought of the movie *Office Space* and how Jennifer Aniston's character was required to wear fifteen pieces of flair to show her dedication to her job. Well, this job seemed like it required 915 pieces of Saddam flair. I swiped some books and posters, knowing they would make awesome souvenirs. I figured no one would notice they were gone; that is, if anyone was ever to return here. If so, the remaining 900 pieces of Saddam flair would be plenty for these unfortunate workers.

The executive offices were in an adjacent building. They had large windows and fancy furniture that had been punched and blown up, presumably by our soldiers who seized the airport. I noticed that someone had taken a shit in the corner. I imagined the soldiers releasing all of their anger and pent-up fear by unleashing hell upon these mahogany desks and overstuffed couches. I was both disgusted and fascinated.

Someone announced that we needed to find our own rooms to live in. This particular building was rather intact, minus the damaged furniture, so it seemed suitable. I claimed a small corner office on the fourth floor that hadn't been desecrated. It had sliding glass doors that opened onto a patio. Then I foraged through the rest of the floor to find some curtains, a coffee table, chairs, everything except a kitchen. My cot would serve as my bed. A few days later, when I toured one of Saddam Hussein's forty-five Baghdad palaces (the one across the street from the airport), I picked a few roses from his beautiful garden, put them in water and enjoyed fresh flowers in my new room.

Major Putte asked to be my roommate, but I had already promised Ricardo that I would room with him. I could tell Putte was gravely disappointed by the look in his eyes, but for the love of God, *why would I want to sleep in the same room as my boss?* One time, however, when he and his wife had me dog sit at their house, instead of putting me in one of their several guest rooms, they had me sleep in their bed. And the sheets weren't clean. I had to pretend as if I wasn't creeped out by this arrangement, for fear of offending them. Now I had to hold back the same disgust.

Once I finished decorating, I had quite a cute studio apartment and felt like it was a little sanctuary from the chaos and destruction. We still had to eat from our mobile kitchen and mess tents outside, and with no running water, we had to go in the dirt. But the accommodations sure as shit beat sleeping in a Humvee or tent. Soon we dubbed our building "Hotel California."

Life quickly fell into a routine. In my group, we still had plenty of paperwork to process, especially accountability reports. Major Putte also asked me to write sympathy letters on behalf of Colonel Weeds for the families of the six soldiers who died in the Black Hawk crash on April 2.

And he assigned me with writing the narratives for their posthumous awards.

To get a better sense of what exactly happened on the day of the crash, I spoke with Sam, a fun, spirited Black Hawk pilot who was one of the few women pilots in our brigade.

Sam was my West Point classmate, and we met studying for an economics final at the end of our freshman year. We never hung out after that, but we always said hello while passing each other in the hallways. Sam married a fellow West Pointer who graduated two years ahead of us. West Point seemed to be a natural default for Sam, as many ancestors on both sides of her family went there, including Edgar Allan Poe, who had been adopted by one of her great uncles. (Poe was expelled from West Point in 1831.) Sam was a stellar Black Hawk pilot with a reputation for incredible skills, especially after dark under night vision goggles. When Sam was asked to relay the events to me, so I could document them with the Bronze Stars with Valor and Purple Hearts I needed to include, she was stoic, barely comprehensible and clearly still in shock about the tragic event.

As Sam described it, the Black Hawk that crashed was flying to relieve her of the mission she was flying because she exceeded the eight-hour flying maximum for that day. In the crash, she lost her commander and her "stick buddy" co-pilot, who was also her best friend. (Her co-pilot randomly happened to fly with the commander instead of her that day.) Sam also lost two of her crew chiefs and two fellow pilots. She would later name her first son after her stick buddy (first name) and commander (middle name).

After speaking with Sam, I heard the formal investigation concluded and revealed that the cause of the crash was spatial disorientation. This happens when a pilot's perception of the horizon becomes askew, which can easily happen in a desert setting, especially at night. When pilots use their own sense of direction, instead of relying on the helicopter's instruments, it can catastrophically result in the pilot flying straight into the ground. A similar accident and fatal crash happened in another unit when we were all still in Kuwait. The pilots and crew perished before even having gone to war.

To make the families feel better, Putte advised me to not write "pilot error" in the award narratives and, instead, write that there had been the potential for enemy fire. Like so many details about this war, it was fabricated. But at least in this case it felt like the right thing to do. They were dead. Why not let them be remembered with honor? But knowing the truth would haunt me for years to come.

I wanted to do my best job ever writing these letters. At twenty-four, this was the first time I needed to write with emotion. I tried to put myself in the shoes of the families and internalize what they would be feeling once they learned of their loss all –in the voice of a male colonel, the soldiers' commander. That afternoon, in the loud and bustling workspace of the Baghdad International Airport, I tuned everything out and wrote to each family, desperately hoping that the words brought some measure of comfort to them.

Dear Mr. and Mrs. X,

The officers and soldiers of the Aviation Brigade join me in expressing our deepest sorrow over the death of your son, Chief Warrant Officer <>. He was part of a crew that was on an air movement mission to ensure command and control of the Brigade could be maintained. Contact with his aircraft was lost along the route of flight, and at this time, we are unable to determine the cause of the accident. As a parent myself, I know you have suffered a tremendous loss and though there is little we can do to ease your pain, we would like to extend our thoughts and prayers to you and your family. During this time of sorrow, we hope it may be of some comfort in noting that <> is a true American hero who was proudly serving his country in support of Operation Iraqi Freedom.

During this operation, I had the opportunity to fly with <> on numerous occasions. He was an incredible pilot and instructor who made a tremendous impact on our brigade this past year. I came to rely on <> for important missions, because I knew he was the best man for the job. His loss is felt deeply by everyone who had the privilege to know him.

As you know, on April 9, 2003, the soldiers and families of the Brigade Rear Detachment held a Memorial Ceremony at Hunter Army Airfield in Georgia. An additional memorial ceremony for the soldiers of the brigade was held on April 12, 2003 at a field site in Iraq. The soldiers of the Aviation Brigade, as well as many others from the division attended the ceremony. <>'s First Sergeant sang a special song, and two members of his company wrote and performed a song in his honor. It was *a touching experience, highlighting the wonderful memories your son left with his comrades.*

May God keep you safe and be with you through this most difficult time.

Charles M. Weeds
Colonel, U. S. Army
Commanding

The memorial service took place in one of the airplane hangars at the Baghdad airport. We all lined up in formation, facing the six rifles, boots and dog tags that were set up at the front to represent each perished man. We recited a few prayers, and Lieutenant Colonel James Cooper, the Black Hawk Battalion Commander, gave a short speech. Then Colonel Weeds read each man's award citations for "exceptionally meritorious conduct… in support of Operation Iraqi Freedom." It was a beautiful and poignant formal ceremony. I really wanted to cry but was groomed, just like everyone else, to hold it all in. So I dutifully stood there, stoic, yet traumatized.

Against this somber backdrop, Ricardo wanted me to join in on his nightly ritual of fun, especially since we now had privacy. Every night, after work and dinner, we congregated in our Hotel California studio apartment and bitched about our day, making fun of our crazy circumstances. I also imitated the jerks we worked with, which made us laugh hysterically, especially when I acted out how I thought they might behave in bed with their respective significant others. (In my mind, Lieutenant Colonel

O'Neil wore his gym socks and dog tags to fornicate while mumbling incomprehensible grunts.)

To relax before bed, Ricardo also loved reading magazines about sex, and then he shared the stories with me. I was an eager listener, but I also wondered if he ever bothered to read about anything other than sex. Even though sex seemed to be on everyone else's mind, I wondered if Ricardo bordered on an unhealthy obsession.

Surprisingly, Ricardo said he missed his wife. I was taken aback, because his actions with me didn't fit his statement. So I asked more about their relationship. He explained their long history together and the kind of teamwork it took for them to make something of themselves. He also told me that they had an understanding with respect to sex. I gathered this meant she wouldn't leave him if he cheated on her or that maybe she also cheated on him. Perhaps this was necessary in order to survive twenty years of marriage to Ricardo, since he was always hyper horny and the Army often took him far from home.

Ricardo disclosed that he spoke to his wife about wanting to teach me more about sex. He told her how sheltered I was, and that he needed to help change that.

"She thought it was a good idea," Ricardo explained.

"Shut the fuck up!" I responded in shock, perplexed but also grateful that she cared about my "education" and didn't see me as a threat.

After my shitty and terribly sad day writing the sympathy letters, I wanted nothing more than to retreat to my room, crawl into my sleeping bag and laugh with Ricardo. These evening retreats were becoming paramount to me getting through each day, even though I had to deal with not only Ricardo's need to masturbate, but also his new obsession with getting me to join him. Now that we had a private room and a possible blessing from his wife, the only thing holding me back was my own volition. But that was starting to change, especially after witnessing such tragic losses from the war.

On this particular night, when Ricardo asked if I cared to join him, I thought, *Fuck it, I need to feel good and alive,* so I told him, "Yes."

"Oh dear, I'm so excited!" he yelped.

"I know, I know, but let's not make too big of a deal about it." The last thing I needed was him psyching me out with too much enthusiasm.

"OK honey, I promise it will be very nice."

"Thank you."

"You know, when a woman pleasures herself, it's the most beautiful thing in the world."

In that moment, I wanted to feel beautiful. Not just desired by others, but beautiful for myself. I deserved to feel beautiful and be beautiful. War was ugly. Denying my femininity in all of these crazy military environments made me feel less of a woman. Well, not tonight.

Ricardo turned off the overhead light and used our flashlights to try and create a soft glow. If we had been anywhere else, I imagine he would have lit some candles.

"Thanks for the mood lighting," I laughed.

Ricardo suggested that I play some soft music, so I put my Norah Jones CD into my Sony Discman and put one earphone in, leaving one ear open to hear Ricardo's guidance. After lying there for a minute, soaking in the romantic music, he asked if I was ready to begin.

"Yes," I said, feeling nervous, excited, only mildly guilty, but more importantly—beginning to feel alive.

"Pull your shorts down," Ricardo instructed.

I followed instructions, feeling open to new sensations and possibilities.

Instead of whipping his penis out, Ricardo focused solely on me, telling me to slightly spread my legs and caress my folds with my finger. He remained contained while I opened myself up. I could tell that he was doing everything within his power to restrain himself. Then when he explained where to touch, he moved his hand toward me, asking if he could show me directly.

"No," I said. "I don't want you to touch me."

"Why not? It's OK. This is beautiful, not dirty."

"Still, it feels wrong if you touch me there. I want to do it myself."

"This is all about you," he promised.

I fell into a trance-like state, feeling aroused and full of pleasure. After touching myself for a while, exploring how my body reacted to different levels of pressure, Ricardo couldn't take it anymore.

"Do you think you will come?" he asked.

"I'm not sure. I'm really enjoying this, but I don't know if I'll actually have an orgasm."

"That's OK, dear. It's not necessary."

I felt relieved that he wasn't expecting me to finish.

"But I must say, you are so incredibly beautiful and sexy, and I'm so turned on. Would it be OK if I take care of myself now?"

"Of course. Go right ahead," I responded, appreciating the fact that he actually asked this time.

As I continued feeling wonderful pulses of arousal in my most intimate parts, Ricardo removed his pants and grabbed his fully erect penis. He moaned as he stroked his shaft and watched me stroking myself. I moaned too, entering a connected bliss that felt new and exciting. We were experiencing a very special moment together, and nothing about it felt wrong. I pressed on myself more firmly and vigorously as he stroked himself harder and faster.

Our moans grew louder as our spirits felt entwined in some kind of bond that I knew could only be created in this unique war environment. Ricardo practically screamed when he finished, with sweat pouring all over him. My pulse was racing toward the finish line too, only I never quite reached it. But that was OK. I felt alive anyway.

I fell asleep to Norah Jones, feeling like a legitimate woman who was empowered to take charge of her own pleasure.

I woke up in the wee hours of the morning with my stomach feeling like it had turned inside. Something was drastically wrong. I ripped the earphones off my head (so much for sexy Norah Jones music coaxing me to sleep) and ran to the balcony grabbing the first thing I saw—my laundry bucket. I managed to close the balcony door behind me (Ricardo was still sleeping) before heaving violently into the bucket, wondering *what the hell could be making me sick?*

As soon as I finished I had to shit my pants—so urgently I knew I would never make it down the four flights of stairs to the slit trenches outside. So I ripped my shorts down and released my guts into a grocery bag that happened to be laying on the floor just inside of the balcony. I cleaned up with several baby wipes and set the bag aside to discard later. I wanted more sleep. But as soon as I lay back down, the cycle repeated itself. More vomiting. More shitting in grocery bags. I ended up filling four bags. To dispose of the vomit, I poured water into the bucket and flung it over the balcony, hoping no one was passing by underneath. Never had I reached such a low point in my entire life. Death would have felt more pleasant.

Apparently hundreds of others in my unit were also plagued with the same illness—dysentery.

Due to the lack of running water, any time we needed to use the bathroom, we had to run outside to use the big slit trench dug in the ground. There were only three makeshift stalls serving hundreds of people, so many times I found myself crouching down close to this trench, once again with no concealment. To maintain some semblance of dignity, I pulled the end of my shirt down as far as it would reach, hoping it would cover my crotch and ass. At this point, I would have given anything to go back to crapping next to my Humvee! Unfortunately, our vehicles were now locked away.

As the weather warmed up, the slit trenches became infested with flies, and apparently, our dining tents weren't far enough away from the trenches. So the flies roamed between our shit and our food, making hundreds of us violently ill. (I will never be able to eat gluten or lactose again for the rest of my life, and doctors think that my digestive problems started here. Thank you, Army.)

I felt better about my predicament the day Donald Rumsfeld came to visit with a pretty, young woman aid accompanying him. She wore a nice dress, panty hose and high heels. When she asked us to point her in the direction of the restrooms, we all busted out laughing. Someone escorted her to the slit trench, and we had the best time watching her figure out how the hell she was going to pull this off. Four of the civilians she traveled with stood around to shield her, their backs turned to give her privacy, so it's not like we were complete voyeuristic perverts. We just delighted in civilians sharing our misery. Secretly we applauded her efforts—she was such a trooper—but I guarantee she never volunteered to return to Iraq.

A lot of the men didn't leave their rooms to pee; they just pissed in empty water bottles. I was jealous of their anatomy until I realized that I could cut a bottle in half, empty my bladder into it, and then pour the contents into another bottle. I too could pee in the convenience of my own room. Like any neat and tidy woman, I threw these bottles away. But a lot of the guys let them accumulate—to the point where our unit command sergeant major had to issue a formal memorandum prohibiting the collection of urine bottles in a room.

Between the disgusting bathroom conditions and Major Putte still breathing down my neck at work, I was ecstatic to learn that my ass was going back to Kuwait.

CHAPTER TWENTY-FIVE

Prior to the ~~invasion~~ liberation, my unit had assigned me as the brigade purchasing agent, the person in charge of buying depleted supplies mid-combat. I was happy to accept the position. If my country needed me to shop, then dammit, I would shop, and I would make my country proud. From then on, I dubbed myself the Combat Shopper.

When I first arrived in Kuwait from Savannah, I visited an Army finance office at one of the permanent American bases south of Kuwait City, where an acquisition corps officer briefed me on the rules of combat shopping. I had to submit receipts to account for all of my spending; I couldn't spend more than $2,500 at one vendor; and if I lost the cash, the Army would recoup the loss by directly deducting money from my paycheck (ouch). Then he told me that when I was finished spending the first ten grand,

I could go to any Army finance office and withdraw ten grand more, over and over again. My eyes widened at the thought of shopping with an unlimited supply of cold hard cash.

After the formalities, the officer turned me over to a finance clerk, "What denominations would you prefer?"

I had no fucking clue. Up until this point, I think the most cash I had ever carried was $300. I had *no idea* what a wad of $10,000 even looked like! But I figured that in the midst of this ~~invasion~~ liberation, it would be difficult for business owners to make change from big bills. Plus, I had no idea what the exchange rate was from US dollars to Iraqi dinar, so I thought it was prudent to request mainly twenty-dollar bills, sprinkled with a few hundreds, fifties, tens and fives. The clerk counted out the bills for close to ten minutes; then she handed me a *five-inch-thick wad of cash.*

When I returned to our base camp that evening, Major Putte told me that Colonel Weeds wanted me to store the cash in our brigade safe. I wasn't aware of the safe and was skeptical.

"No way, Sir," I replied. "This cash isn't leaving my side. If something happens to that safe, the Army comes after me for the money, not Colonel Weeds."

What I really wanted to say was that I didn't trust Weeds as far as I could pee standing up. He would never defend me or cover the loss of the money if it happened to disappear due to his negligence.

But where *was* the best place to store the cash? I didn't have a purse or backpack and didn't wear my pseudo bulletproof vest 24/7, so stashing it in there didn't feel secure enough. Another option was to stow it in my bra like I'd seen women do in the dance clubs near Fort Jackson. But there was no way a five-inch wad of cash was going to fit into my 34B bra—though it would have been hilarious to walk around the war looking like I had a nice, new fake set of 38DDs. After some deliberation, I decided to put the cash in my cargo pants pocket. From then on, every night when I went to sleep wearing my gun and my money, I felt like a true gangster.

After settling into Baghdad, our unit was running low on many basic supplies. Since all of the local markets in Baghdad were still closed, Colonel Weeds decided to send me back to Kuwait to go shopping, and, wow, did he have a long shopping list for me.

I don't know what excited me more—disrupting the monotony of life in Baghdad or getting the fuck away from Putte. Either way, I was about to taste the freedom of showering, pissing and eating without first asking for permission.

Master Sergeant Pete Harley was assigned to accompany me on my shopping journey to Kuwait. Many of the soldiers and officers were terrified of Pete. He was like a younger, blonder version of the Gunnery Sergeant Hartman character in *Full Metal Jacket*: gruff, old school, broad framed, loud raspy voice, extremely patriotic and loved the *Fair and Balanced* Sean Hannity from Fox News. Pete embodied the typical old-fashioned senior enlisted stereotype.

When I found out that Pete and I were going to be working together, I made it a point to get to know him better. I figured I could get to his soft spot by seeking his advice, which actually wasn't such a bad idea—I was a dumbass, naïve Lieutenant who could stand to learn a thing or two about the Army from a soldier with twenty years of experience under his belt. I asked him technical questions, advice about Army stuff and how to deal with the morons, especially Major Putte.

"Your boss *is* a moron," Pete said. "And he's probably in love with you."

So it wasn't just me. It felt good to be validated like this.

Pete didn't like a lot of people we worked with, but he took a liking to me because I was humble (despite technically out-ranking him as lieutenant). In fact, he appreciated the gesture so much, he started opening up to me—a little too much.

He told me about the love of his life, Lizzie, an Air Force sergeant he'd met while on a six-month deployment to Italy. They had had an intense connection, amazing sex and fell deeply in love. But after the deployment, they returned home to their own lives and respective spouses.

They never resumed the physical love affair, but they continued to communicate via long and passionate love letters. One day Pete showed me some of his love letters.

It seemed like an odd gesture, but also somewhat endearing and kind of flattering that he wanted to share them with me. So I agreed to read them.

Imagine my surprise when each love letter described not how much Pete missed Lizzie and was thinking about her constantly, but his desire to pull her hair, shove her hard down onto the bed and choke her airway.

I was simultaneously terrified and intrigued. It wasn't difficult for me to picture Pete doing violent things, but I didn't understand what this had to do with the love of his life.

I wanted to get to the core of his psyche and understand what compelled him to be turned on by such physical aggression. When I asked more questions, he happily showed me more letters. I couldn't help but wonder, *Is that what people are like?* I'd never read anything like that before, nor was I introduced to the concept of sexual fantasies. I never imagined that someone could fuck someone else with just their imagination, or that one would project such carnal lust on paper and mail it to someone else.

The night before we left for our Kuwait shopping trip, Pete asked me to read a *twenty-page letter* he had just finished for Lizzie. I sat down to read a detailed description of her getting gang-banged by ten different men, and all of the different ways they had their way with her, tossing her around "like a rag doll." Meanwhile, in the letter's fantasy, Pete sat in the corner, stroking his nine-inch cock, enjoying seeing the love of his life get raped by ten men. It took me nearly an hour to read the whole letter. It was far more violent and vivid than the other letters he had shown me. Despite the content, he was actually a very good writer.

"What do you think?" Pete asked, eager for my reaction.

"It's definitely different," I said as gently as possible, not wanting to hurt his feelings. He trusted me and was being vulnerable by letting me read it. I suspected he was very lonely.

I very gingerly asked him questions about Lizzie to gauge if this would be OK with her. He was like, "Oh, Lizzie would fucking love it. She's a goddamned champ! She fucks like a champ, and she swallows cum like a champ."

After describing her this way, I said, "Oh, then this letter is perfect."

"Awesome." He took the letter back with a big smile on his face. I could tell that he felt validated.

"Well, thank you for sharing this with me," I said, backing out of his room. "It's getting late, so I'm going to sleep now. See you in the morning. I'm so glad we're getting the fuck out of here tomorrow."

"Fuck yeah," he nodded, folding his letter in an envelope. "Night, Laura."

I smiled. When enlisted soldiers felt comfortable calling me by my first name, it showed that they regarded me more as a friend than a superior officer, and I really liked that.

I went back to my room and didn't tell Ricardo anything about Pete and his fantasies. I felt that would be violating his trust. Instead, I focused on enjoying a fun night of laughter and then said goodbye to Ricardo. I wasn't sure how long my shopping trip would last or when I would see him again.

CHAPTER TWENTY-SIX

Pete and I flew in one of our unit's Black Hawks from Baghdad to Kuwait's Camp Doha. Camp Doha is an established military installation, complete with bathrooms, flushing toilets and showers. Colonel Weeds's shopping list included cleaning supplies, USB thumb drives, external hard drives, CD-ROMS, and a lot of random shit that wasn't yet available in Baghdad. Thankfully, Pete and I were given access to an SUV and a cell phone, but no maps or GPS devices (Google Maps hadn't been created yet), so we had to figure out Kuwait City on our own.

Pete read more into my friendship than I'd intended. When we walked to the breakfast tent on our first morning in Kuwait, he asked matter-of-factly, "Laura, would you like to have sex with me?"

A few months prior I would have been taken aback—I *should* have been taken aback—but I wasn't. At this point I had grown so accustomed to Ricardo's advances, Putte's passive-aggression and trying to survive all of the come-ons, let alone the war itself, that I didn't even flinch.

"That's very nice of you to ask, but no thank you," I said sweetly.

"OK, but just so you know, I brought condoms with me," Pete continued.

"You brought condoms with you?"

"Yeah, in case you wanted to fuck."

I thought now would be a good time to tell Pete the skinny.

"Oh, well, just so you know, I'm still a virgin. So, I'm not looking to have sex *at all*."

Pete laughed, "Yeah, me too."

"No, I really am," I insisted.

It took Pete a few days before he believed me. "No shit?" was all he could muster. It was as if I told him I was an alien from another planet. For a moment, I wondered if I made the right decision being honest with him.

Pete started confiding in me a lot. While deployed to Saudi Arabia during Desert Storm, his wife spent all of his hard-earned money. When he returned home and discovered his empty bank account, he became violent, and during one of their altercations, he held a gun to her head. My gut sensed that Pete had severe anger issues, like a lot of people in the military. (Unfortunately, the military is an environment that not only allows superiors to yell and scream at their subordinates, but it also glorifies violence upon the enemy. As a result, character flaws such as anger issues often are embraced and rewarded instead of denounced.) I told myself, *I need to be careful around this guy.*

When I revealed I was a virgin, I worried Pete was going to be persistent like Ricardo and continue to harass me until I gave him something like a token peek at my nipples (something Ricardo forced me to do before the ~~invasion~~ liberation). Thankfully, he backed off right away.

For our first shopping trip, we wore civilian clothes: Pete in jeans and a T-shirt, me in jeans and a long-sleeved shirt. (Prior to deploying, we were all instructed to pack one civilian outfit, just in case.) Pete insisted on driving—no surprise there. In the passenger seat of our SUV, I soaked everything in.

Kuwait City is a beautiful, large, cosmopolitan city (population 2.1 million). It's located at the tip of Kuwait and surrounded on three sides by the Persian Gulf (technically, Kuwait Bay). It has beautiful beaches, paved highways, a massive soccer stadium, stately buildings with columns and several ornate mosques.

Driving was a challenge because traffic was insane and nobody seemed to follow any traffic laws. People barely stopped at stoplights and didn't use turn signals. They aggressively cut us off without warning. Pete took this as an opportunity to drive with the same recklessness. I tried to say something, but he totally ignored me—until we got into a fender bender with a Kuwaiti citizen's car. The Kuwaiti driver was very kind and spoke English, but he had to call the police. In Kuwait, driver's licenses are temporarily confiscated after causing an accident, so the police had to take Pete's away. So we had to go back to Camp Doha and complete an incident report. Pete was livid, but all liability was covered by the Army, and he eventually got his license back.

After Pete's accident, I insisted on driving. I had traveled abroad before going to Kuwait, but always in organized trips. Now, with driving an SUV through the city, sunglasses on, pockets full of cash, and the wind rushing through my hair, I felt more alive than ever. This was my adventure to discover a new country (without bombing the shit out of it). As it turned out, I was awesome at traveling and exploring. Despite not having a map or any knowledge of Arabic, I grew to know Kuwait City rather well in short order.

Kuwait seemed a lot like me. If there was ever a place obsessed with virginity preservation, it was Kuwait. The country is known for being emancipated with respect to other Middle Eastern countries. Women are allowed to pursue an education, work, drive and vote. But couples aren't allowed to date before getting married, and women are discouraged from exposing their bodies in public. Outside of the home, many women wear a full-length, long-sleeved black abaya, which covers their clothing underneath. They also wear a hijab or black veil to cover their heads. Some even wear a burqa, which covers everything from head to toe, except for the eyes. To my surprise, the ladies walking around in black burqas totally turned Pete on.

I didn't get it. He told me many times that his ideal woman is a blonde, all-American "brick shit house" with "big fucking fake Double-D titties"—in other words, Pamela Anderson (if she wasn't Canadian). These Kuwaiti women, many of whom only exposed either their faces or eyes, were nothing like his porn-star fantasies. But every time we walked past a new group of women, especially in the shopping malls, Pete unabashedly moaned and announced to me that he had a raging hard on.

Sometimes he even stopped, stared and offered a flirtatious smile and "hello." Luckily the husbands or fathers of these women were nowhere in sight, especially because a lot of them smiled back at Pete.

"Pete, what the hell is going on?" I asked, trying to calm him down and ensure he didn't cause an international sexual harassment lawsuit. "Aren't you being way too forward with these women? We're in one of the world's most conservative countries."

"Laura, you don't get it. Can't you see that these women fucking love the attention I'm giving them?"

"What? They do? How can you tell when they're completely covered?"

"Easy. Look at their eyes," Pete explained. "See that one over there?" He pointed to a woman seated at the far corner of the mall's food court area, talking to a friend. Only you couldn't actually see her mouth moving, just the flap of cloth attached to her burqa, which allowed her to slip food underneath. "Do you see how much eye makeup she's wearing?"

I studied her eyes carefully and then realized I never saw anyone wear that much makeup, except for *Cosmo* cover models. She was going for the sultry, smoky look with dark blue-gray shadow caked on nearly up to her eyebrows, and tons of eyeliner on her lower lid. And there was no way her lashes were real—100 applications of mascara couldn't create that glam effect.

She must have noticed us staring at her, because she turned her head in our direction, paused, blinked slowly and then softly giggled as she moved her head back toward her friend.

"See that?" Pete practically yelled. "She just told me to fuck her with her eyes. Goddammit I'm in love. This place is heaven."

Because our shopping trips didn't take all day, Pete and I had ample downtime to people-watch and thoroughly discuss his favorite topics: women and sex. His obsession with Kuwaiti women made me start to examine myself. What did random men think about me when I passed them in the streets? Isolated on an Army deployment, it's easy to have the attention of men when there are so few women to look at. But in a general setting back home, could I capture a man's attention? Did men find me pretty? Was pretty good enough? Did I have what it took to be sexy? Was it important to be sexy?

Every time a beautiful woman passed us, Pete used it as an opportunity to teach me a lesson. Like Ricardo, he had made it his personal mission to build my confidence so that I wouldn't restrict myself from experiencing life's greatest pleasure.

"Laura, check out that chick in the skirt. Even though it goes down to her ankles, and even though she has her hair wrapped in a scarf, look at how hot she is. You can tell she values her appearance, and she *knows* she looks good. That makes her confident. Confidence is fucking sexy."

I studied the woman, and took Pete's words to heart. I then looked down at my baggy jeans, sneakers and plain gray shirt, realizing that I had a long way to go.

Pete looked me straight in the eye. "Laura, I want you to understand that beautiful women are very powerful. A lot of women don't realize just how much they can influence and even control a man with their sexuality."

My brain exploded. I felt like an infant who just learned how to walk. I'd never heard anything like this before. But could you blame me? My father did everything within his control to sabotage my appearance. The Bible taught me to flee from any sexual temptation. It's not like there were any sexy women hanging out at church, so I didn't know any hot, confident women. And it certainly wasn't in West Point's training curriculum to teach me how to pick clothes that flattered my frame and accessorize with cute shoes and sparkly jewelry. So I literally was an infant in this department. But instead of dismissing Pete's lesson, like the society of my past would have implored, I was intrigued. Goddammit, I wanted to be sexy too!

As soon as Pete's message settled into my mind and heart, I asked, "Pete, can I be sexy like that?"

Without hesitating, Pete answered, "Of course you can. You definitely have it in you. I see it. I know you feel like you need to do this whole virgin thing, but I don't feel like that's really you."

Holy fucking shit. I froze and tried to process what Pete said. What did he mean by that ? Was he projecting his own fantasies? Was he saying this to get me in bed with him? Was this a reflection of his desire to corrupt me and bring me into his world? Or was he on to something? Did he get me better than I understood myself? Was my whole virgin persona a farce? Was I keeping myself pure because that's what I truly desired for my life? Or was I doing it out of obligation to my father, Jesus, fellow Christians, West Point and my country?

Something deeply shifted within me. I contemplated that perhaps it was time to start making some big changes—changes to be the person I really am—the *real* Laura Westley.

I wasn't sure how to start down this new path in the middle of Kuwait, isolated from everyone in my life, but there was definitely one thing this foreign environment provided—plenty of shopping malls. At least I could start small and buy some sexy new clothes—with my own money of course.

That was the ironic thing about Kuwait—while so many women opted to wear burqas in public, the shopping options were unbelievable, and the malls themselves were almost like nightclubs. Probably because alcohol is banned, and therefore bars aren't any part of the entertainment culture, the shopping mall appeared to be the epicenter of Kuwaiti leisure activity. They were bigger and fancier than in the States. The women who didn't wear burqas got all decked out just to go shopping, and because everyone was rich from government oil subsidies, they could afford to wear high-end designers like Gucci and Prada.

Every time we went to the mall, I felt like I was visiting a fashion show in Paris or Milan. These fashionistas seemed to be strutting as they perused all the designer stores. But what really confused me was that the burka-clad women also feasted on couture, buying up outfits worth hundreds and even thousands of dollars. Where the hell did they wear this stuff?

Watching them buy such beautiful things made me feel a little inferior and sorry for myself, but then I quickly remembered my American freedom and got over it. Thankfully these same malls had some more normal stores like Zara and Guess to fit my budget, although I avoided buying American labels because Kuwait marked them up 30 percent.

One afternoon I convinced Pete to join me in a makeup and perfume store. An adorable, blond-haired, fair-skinned woman, Camille, from Lebanon, immediately greeted us. Camille was my age and told me that she was a Christian and spoke French. I started speaking to her in my broken French, and Pete became quickly turned on by two young women conversing in French.

"Oh that's so beautiful, ladies!"

We told Camille that we were Army soldiers in the middle of the war, so she did the best thing she could within her power to make me feel better—and offered me a makeover. I couldn't help but laugh at the notion of my colleagues dredging through another awful day in Baghdad, while I got pampered with fancy makeup. But not a pang of guilt plagued me.

Pete watched intently as Camille applied many products to my face. She saved my eyes for last, and before starting on them, let me take a look in a mirror to observe her progress. I liked my reflection. I still looked like myself, but with some striking, colorful enhancements. I had worn makeup every day back in high school, but only wore it for special occasions after joining the Army. Being in the Army made me so self-conscious about looking too feminine, so I only wore enough to smooth out my skin tone. But after seeing how pretty Camille made me, I vowed to embrace it, even in an ugly Army uniform.

Camille asked what colors I wanted her to use on my eyes. Before I could respond, Pete interjected and told her to give me "sexy, seductive eyes." I thought this was going to look ridiculous with my green T-shirt and jeans, but he carried on about how he loved how all of the Kuwaiti women wore such heavy eye makeup. So Camille and I agreed to let him have his fantasy. When I batted my heavily made up eyes at him, he got weak in the knees, which made me laugh.

Pete and I usually ate by the water, snacking on delicious olives and feta cheese. Our designated eating spot, just outside of the massive Sultan Center shopping area, was nearly obliterated by a SCUD missile the day before the ~~invasion~~ liberation. We were up at the border, enjoying a pre-war barbeque, and I was catching up on some accounting homework. Suddenly, we were ordered to don our chemical gear. Fifteen minutes later we received an "all clear" and never knew what came of the threat. Now I could see it first-hand. Luckily the SCUD landed in the water, only destroying a small wooden dock. Had it veered just one-hundred feet away, thousands of people would have perished.

Meal time is when we extensively discussed my boyfriend, Tim, and my virginity. Like Ricardo, Pete thought it was completely impossible for a normal, red-blooded American man to be in a serious, nonsexual relationship. I told Pete that it wasn't because of lack of desire. Tim wanted to have sex with me, but he was honoring my wishes. Pete was like, "Bullshit, something's wrong with that guy."

After a few of these shopping trips, a Kuwaiti Air Force colleague we befriended told us he wanted to introduce us to two guys "who could get us anything." He rode in our car as we drove to an office building where a pretty, modernly dressed receptionist (still wearing a headscarf, albeit a colorful one) led us to a large conference room with vertical blinds on the windows. Seated at the head of the long oval conference table were two rich businessmen by the name of Luai and Shek. Luai (who was Kuwaiti) wore a white robe with a red and white-checkered headscarf. Shek (who was Indian) wore a short-sleeved, button-down shirt with khakis and lots of gold jewelry. They both stood to enthusiastically shake our hands.

Over a steady stream of delicious Turkish coffee, which gave me diarrhea, Luai and Shek told us their plan for how we could obtain every item on our shopping list. (Once we had everything, we would load it onto one of our Black Hawk helicopters at Camp Udairi and send it to Baghdad, since our helicopters routinely traveled back and forth between the two countries.) I felt like an important international business woman who was going to succeed at her difficult mission with ease.

In short order we realized that Luai and Shek weren't helping us to make money for themselves; they were already stinking rich. All they wanted to do was tell stories and bitch about Saddam Hussein. They were still bitter about him invading Kuwait back in 1990. They spoke about the oil he had stolen from Kuwait through secret pipelines. And they were incredibly thankful to the Americans and what we did for them in Desert Storm. Helping us was their way of expressing deep gratitude for our presence.

Every time we went to see Luai and Shek, they ordered delicious take-out food, poured Turkish coffee and showered us with attention. The contrast between Baghdad and this scene in Kuwait blew my mind. It was always a delight to visit them, and when they bombarded us with questions about Baghdad, we were happy to oblige with our wild stories.

One evening, Luai arranged for us to have a fancy dinner out with his younger brother, Halid. Halid had earned his bachelor's degree in London, missed the good life there and was considering returning there for an MBA. He was extremely wealthy, well-traveled, attractive and a suave young man who could do anything he wanted. Pete and I asked him about daily life in Kuwait, especially relationships. Halid reiterated what we already knew: young people aren't allowed to date, and women are pressured to maintain their virginity.

"But a lot of them get around this by having anal sex," he added. I almost snorted water through my nose. Anal sex hadn't even occurred to me. Even in a place like Kuwait, it seemed as if sex was always on everyone's mind. That night, I went back to Camp Doha with a head full of new questions and feelings.

CHAPTER TWENTY-SEVEN

Usually I slept in a warehouse on a cot with about one-hundred other women who were either stationed at Camp Doha or transient like me. But back on Easter Sunday, after one of our shopping excursions, someone told me I could sleep in a small trailer with about six sets of bunk beds, as there were some empty spaces. The trailer and beds were far nicer and more comfortable than the warehouse cots. The other beds were occupied by Air Force guys, who were also transient. Accustomed to sleeping around men, I didn't think anything of it and almost felt like I had the entire place to myself.

Lying on a real bed felt magical, and immediately I fell asleep. Then I woke up in the middle of the night feeling so damn horny, in desperate need of a release. Up until now, I had only masturbated with Ricardo, which yielded no orgasm. But tonight, all I needed was my imagination. I was ready.

I pictured Luai—not in his traditional Kuwaiti garb—but the photo of him on his business card in a fancy, modern suit. I didn't find Luai sexually attractive, but for some reason, this photo was doing the trick for me. Something about his eyes was very compelling, almost encouraging me to have my way with myself. In an ordinary situation, my thoughts would have seemed utterly ridiculous, but here they were working. I was completely aroused and felt myself dripping with wetness.

Let's face it. All of this talk about sex every day finally brought me to a point where all it took was a damn business card to get me going. At this point, I could have done it to anything. It was especially hot in that it was illegal, and I was surrounded by a group of strange and attractive men. I hoped I didn't make any noise, but I was in a nylon sleeping bag, which made a "whooshing" sound every time I moved. As I pictured Luai next to me, my heart rate soared, my breathing got heavier, my body became covered in sweat. I used one hand to stimulate my sensitive area that became so engorged with arousal, while I used the other hand to penetrate myself with one, and then two fingers. The more I penetrated myself, the more I imagined Luai inside of me, opening my tight and sacred area to a whole new world of empowered delight. Just when I couldn't take it anymore, my body exploded into an intense orgasm, and I convulsed for several seconds. Eureka!

I was damn proud. *Wow I can do this!* I couldn't wait to tell Ricardo. Then I had to stifle my giggles—how hilariously ironic that I did this on Easter Sunday in a Muslim country. *You go, Jesus girl,* I thought. *This day is about me resurrecting myself, not the resurrection of Jesus Christ.*

In the midst of celebrating my victory, I thought I'd heard some stirring. I panicked thinking that someone could tell what I was up to, and then I thought I heard some reciprocal whooshing... I suspected the guy next to me started taking care of himself, probably using my actions for his own masturbatory material.

While penetrating myself, I could tell that my vagina was opening more, and I wondered if I had done anything to my hymen. For a split second, I pictured my father scoffing at me. He was always obsessed with preserving my hymen, much like Islamic and other religious extremists are obsessed with the notion that women maintain absolute purity for their husbands or risk dire consequences.

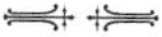

When I got my period, I begged my mother not to tell my father. I wasn't ready for him to know that I was no longer his little girl. I knew he wouldn't be able to handle it. Just three years prior, when I was eleven, I had a melt down that was difficult to explain to my parents.

"I don't want to grow up," I cried.

"Why are you worrying about this, Laura?" my mom asked.

"I can't grow up. Daddy will freak out."

"Why do you say that?"

"Because I know. I just do."

"That's ridiculous, Laura," my mom tried to assure me. But the tears kept pouring out of my eyes. When my father came home from work, my mom asked him to intervene.

"What's wrong, Laura?" my father asked, sitting me on top of his lap at the kitchen table.

"You're going to hate me when I grow up. I can't grow up!"

"I'll never hate you," he promised. But I didn't believe him.

"You'll start making fun of me. I just know it. When I start wearing a bra, you'll call me 'bra-bee-baa.'"

"No I won't."

While he never used this term, sure enough, he treated me differently after I started wearing a bra. My tiny breasts probably reminded him that I wasn't actually his son.

My mother broke her promise and told my father I had my period, just ten minutes after telling me she would keep it to herself. He shook my hand and congratulated me when I emerged from the bathroom, wearing a thick maxi pad my mother miraculously found in her bathroom, since she had had a hysterectomy several years earlier. I immediately fell to the floor, crushed.

I hated how messy my period was, especially when playing sports or exercising, so I asked my mother if we could buy tampons.

"Ask your father" was her default response for everything.

"You're kidding, right?" Only I knew she wasn't. Not even menstruation could get her to act like a mother.

I mustered the courage to ask my father about wearing tampons. I anticipated his response, which indeed was an immediate, "No." But I wasn't going to give up easily, so I graphically depicted the inconvenience and mess of playing sports and bleeding all over the place. I exaggerated for my benefit. I also quoted statistics saying that tampons don't tear hymens. It worked because he didn't immediately dismiss my efforts.

"I will consider it if your pediatrician says it's OK."

I knew victory was nearly mine because my doctor had good sense. Surely she would support my cause. My mother and I just needed to make an appointment with her and obtain her blessing. I thought this was an utterly ridiculous waste of time, but I was willing to do just about anything to wear tampons.

When my doctor patiently answered all of my mother's questions, I couldn't help but wonder if she thought my mother was a complete moron. Part of me suspected that she felt sorry for me. Sure enough, she assured my mother (and father by proxy) that my hymen wouldn't be impacted by a tampon.

The first time I tried to insert a tampon, it wouldn't go in. I asked my mother to help me, but she acted like she had never worn one before and tried to claim that the difficult insertion was due to me being a virgin. I knew that was nonsense and cried as I tried to jam it up in me. (At the time I didn't realize that Tampax tampons were too long for my anatomy, but fortunately I discovered the shorter OB ones just a few months later.) My father caught wind of the struggle and later that day blamed my poor golf practice on my need to wear tampons.

"I hope you're happy that Procter and Gamble ruined our Sunday golf outing," he scolded me.

⁂

Perhaps my father's harassment foreshadowed my need to never allow my period to interfere with anything—not even invading a country. Regardless, it was a good thing that my father was out of my life. If he couldn't handle me going through puberty, he would never have been able to handle me becoming a sexual woman. And after this special Easter Sunday, I was ripe.

A week and a half later, I shockingly ran into Ricardo. The Army was sending him home early in order to let him attend his son's high school graduation. I didn't know his request had been approved, since keeping in touch while I was in Kuwait was next to impossible. When I saw him walking around Camp Doha, I screamed and ran up to him. We embraced. We laughed. Naturally, we had a lot to catch up on before his departure.

The only privacy Ricardo and I could find was in the SUV I used for shopping, which was parked in a far corner by an empty warehouse. We kept the engine running for the air-conditioning as we caught up. I told him about the shopping trips, about Luai and Shek, about masturbating and getting a makeover, and how I was going to make some changes to my appearance in order to embrace my femininity more. He was really proud of me.

Ricardo told me how work sucked, morale was low in Baghdad, and I was lucky to be away. He also said he was going back home for good. In a few months, he would retire from the Army. This meant that we would never work together again. I let his words sink in and pondered proceeding in my Army career without him. I felt a pang of loss and grief at this prospect. When our arms touched, he reached up to touch my cheek. Suddenly, we leaned into each other and started kissing. It was the first time our lips ever made contact.

We passionately kissed and touched and embraced for three hours, with sweat pouring off us, and the windows steaming up. Ricardo gave me three orgasms just by touching me through my underwear. He came twice without even touching himself! Neither one of us ever removed a stitch of clothing. It was the perfect way to conclude and commemorate the war we shared together.

Afterward, we kept saying, "That was beautiful. That was amazing; I've never felt so alive in my entire life." We told each other that we loved each other. It wasn't as if we were in love and that he would abandon his family to be with me. It was a different kind of love—as friends, comrades and war buddies who would have died for each other—so deep and so powerful and so unique.

I also knew that Tim would never be able to make me feel anywhere near the way Ricardo made me feel. It made me think that perhaps I wasn't meant to be with Tim. *Not too long ago, I would have felt guilty about this, but this is what it's about. This is what life is about. Good for you for not feeling guilty about it because you shouldn't.*

I thought about how my old Christian community would consider Ricardo and Pete bad people and sinners, but at the same time, they made me feel more accepted and understood than anyone from my past. A lot of what I had been taught was about repression, suffering and martyrdom, and about holding my feelings in check. In the military, the Christian community was even more intense. Feeling good wasn't supposed to be a priority. They considered feeling good a drug Once you get a taste of it, you need more and more, to the point where that takes over your relationship with God and Jesus, which were the only relationships that mattered.

I was obviously taught that sex was only to be enjoyed within marriage, but then once you get married, sex could and should be wonderful. The message was: repression, repression, repression, then marriage, and then bliss. But a lot of Christians I knew who were married had sexual dysfunctions. One of my friends told me she sees images of Jesus Christ when she tries to enjoy sex with husband. Another couldn't allow herself to have an orgasm and was plagued by her religious past. Sexual enjoyment and fulfillment, I came to realize, isn't a light switch. You can't go from shutting it down to suddenly turning it on.

After the make-out session, Ricardo went home and we stopped working together. I loved him, but he wasn't the kind of guy I would want as a romantic partner, boyfriend or lover. I didn't have these fantasies about him leaving his wife and us being together. Even if he were single, I wouldn't have dated him. He wasn't educated enough for me. He was too much of a sex fiend. He was the kind of guy that would cheat. There was also a huge age difference between us. I was twenty-four; he was forty-two, married and had kids. I also really liked his family and would never want to do anything to hurt them.

I thought about his wife, but I didn't think she would care. He seemed to indicate as such when he told me she knew we had a special kind of friendship and that she supported him mentoring me in the ways of the world. I'm not sure exactly what she thought was going on, but I didn't think she ever felt threatened by me. This was a very contained intimacy that wouldn't go beyond the combat setting. I never had any intent for it to carry on after that. But I also didn't think that his wife's feelings were any of my responsibility.

When I thought of Tim, however, I did feel a little sorry. But at the same time, I also felt a little pig-headed. Pete and Ricardo made me think that Tim might be too much of a pansy for me. Here I was at war, and he was tucked away in his bed, all safe and sound. I started seeing him as less than a man. I felt sorry for him, but I started to prioritize my needs over any of his. I realized he wasn't going to do it for me.

Tim sent me letters that were mundane: "I went for sushi; I visited my parents; I talked to so and so..." He was a good guy, responsible, nice, good job, stable, but he had nothing exciting going for him. I realized I couldn't be with someone "normal" like that anymore, not after going to war. I started to resent that he wasn't more of a man. Tim came from a military family, but he seemed too lazy, comfortable and scared to join himself, even though he was obsessed with aviation and thought that flying was in his blood. I was OK with observing and tolerating his fears in the past, but now that I was at war, I wanted to scream, *What the fuck am I doing with a guy like that?*

On the other hand, if the situation was reversed, and he had made out with someone in a car for three hours, I knew I would be hurt. But his lack of ambition and bravery prevented me from even imagining him in my place. I was heading back to Baghdad soon, and I wanted to completely change my behavior and be a different person. I bought more sexy clothes. I wanted to be more of a woman, take charge of my sexuality and feel empowered. The entire experience in Kuwait completely opened my eyes. I was ready to embrace the new me.

CHAPTER TWENTY-EIGHT

After flying back to the Baghdad airport in another Black Hawk, I walked around feeling completely different from when I'd left. I also noticed that certain things had changed. For starters, we now had porta-potties instead of slit trenches. Despite this luxury, everyone seemed weary, bored and agitated. They were obviously sick of being there, and there was so much uncertainty about the future.

As I entered the work area, everyone was congregated at the TV, playing Fox News, no doubt. This *Fair and Balanced* broadcast showed President Bush standing on an aircraft carrier (the Abraham Lincoln), declaring victory in front of a "Mission Accomplished" sign.

"Victory!" some of my colleagues sarcastically snickered. I rolled my eyes in agreement. It certainly didn't feel victorious. We were exhausted and bitter from the

~~invasion~~ liberation and had yet to see what good came of it. But at this point, everything was so new to the Iraqis, and they were thrilled to have Americans there, tearing down Saddam and his evil regime. So maybe it was worth it. But we still had no idea when we would get to go home.

Thankfully I missed out on the awards debacle that transpired when I was in Kuwait. The rest of my team handled processing the combat awards in my absence. Colonel Weeds always seemed to stir up anger with deciding who was eligible to receive the higher level awards, and during wartime was no exception.

It is customary to receive an award whenever soldiers leave their unit. The level of responsibility held typically determines the level of the award. For a junior lieutenant as I was, that's usually an ARCOM—Army Commendation Medal. For senior captains and staff majors, the appropriate award is typically a MSM—Meritorious Service Medal. For colonels (both lieutenant and "Full Bird") in charge of battalions and brigades—LOM—Legion of Merit. Someone in the chain of command submits the recipient for that award, and someone else at a higher rank needs to approve the award.

Everyone is also eligible to receive awards for participation in war. There are separate awards for wartime, including the Bronze Star, Air Medal, Silver Star and Purple Heart. Combatants can also receive Valor "V Devices" appended to that award. If someone at war simply does their job, that person typically still receives an award, but it would be an ARCOM or MSM. Regulations dictate the level of bravery or gallantry required to achieve the different war time awards. However, they're rather vague, and discretion is left to the chain of command.

Back in Kuwait, the cavalry staff decided to be proactive and submit their commander's departure award in advance, figuring that war might slow down the process. They recommended that Lieutenant Colonel Victor Yates be honored with a Legion of Merit. I was tasked with processing this award, having Colonel Weeds sign his designated area and then sending it forward to the division staff for a final approval from the General. This was a no brainer, but Weeds wouldn't let it be so.

Colonel Weeds hated Lieutenant Colonel Yates, a larger than life, confident, brilliant tactician and bold leader who was tough on his troops but loved them with all of his heart. Yates was up close and personal on the battlefield, nearly hit by a rocket propelled grenade, and was one of the primary reasons the 3d Infantry Division was able to so swiftly maneuver up to Baghdad. His cavalry squadron ended up taking a lot of fire with both his tank and Kiowa helicopter assets, and there was not a single casualty.

Weeds hated that Yates finally got to report to the ADC-M (Assistant Division Commander for Maneuver) for combat operations and always tried to provoke him. At one point, Yates got so fed up, he called Weeds a "fucking pussy" over the radio, for dozens of people to hear. And he got away with it. Everyone lauded Yates as a hero.

Weeds tried to downgrade Yates's Legion of Merit and subsequently recommended Lieutenant Colonel James Cooper for a Legion of Merit. Weeds and Cooper went way back, having flown Black Hawks together in Hawaii. They weren't shy about their friendship, and Weeds had no problems showing his favoritism. They often left work to grab a Starbucks coffee and could be seen back in the halls, lattes in one hand, with their arms around each other.

Major Putte fed off the drama. He ordered for me to clarify with the division human resources leader that Yates was to get only an MSM and that Cooper get a LOM. There was no way I was going to play this corrupt game. Instead, I informed the cavalry staff of the scandal and subsequently went to the division HR leader and told him everything. He thanked me for being bold and honest and agreed that Yates was deserving of the highest award imaginable. He promised that he would take care of Yates and have the General award him a Legion of Merit.

This wasn't the only time I went behind Weeds and Putte's back to do what I deemed to be the right thing. In another situation back in Kuwait, Weeds had awarded Stephanie Woods, one of the cavalry troop commanders, a "top block" on her annual evaluation. She had a reputation for being an incredible pilot and leader—and graduated from West Point back in 1996. Before the ~~invasion~~ liberation, I mailed Stephanie's evaluation form off to Washington DC for final processing. A week later, Weeds caught wind that she was considering leaving the Army in order to start a civilian career. He told Putte to have me get her eval back so he could change it to a lower rating. Not only did I know this was ethically wrong, it also violated the regulations. I told Putte, "Not over my dead body" and that if he wanted to play that dirty game, he would have to do so himself. Then I made sure to subtly leak that scandal to the cavalry. I figured if I told Hannah, then she would tell her husband, who would tell Stephanie and Yates. I knew my stunt worked when one day Lieutenant Colonel Yates approached me, shook my hand, thanked me for being brave and honest, and promised that he would take care of anything I ever wanted or needed from him. This conversation was one of the proudest moments in my entire Army career. And Stephanie kept her "top block" evaluation rating.

Now there was more awards drama—as Weeds illegally applied his own policy to who was eligible for certain combat awards. When the cavalry submitted valorous awards for many soldiers who were nearly killed and exuded bravery on the battlefield, if they were at the rank of staff sergeant or below, he automatically downgraded them to basic ARCOMS (which ended up being my war award—rightfully so, as I did nothing deemed heroic). Then Weeds decided that anyone at the rank of captain or above could get a Bronze Star, regardless of position, responsibility or combat actions. Furthermore, the air cavalry pilots only received one Air Medal with Valor (AMV) for the entire war, when they were supposed to get individual AMVs for each flight mission. As previously mentioned, Lieutenant Colonel Jeff Radcliffe was recommended (and subsequently awarded) a Bronze Star with Valor for over-torqueing his Apache. But the pièce de résistance was when Weeds asked Cooper to put him in for a Distinguished Flying Cross (the aviation equivalent of a Silver Star). Only the bravest of aviators have ever earned such an honor—and Weeds ensured his place among this elite, distinctive group. *I imagined the awards citation omitted the fact that his heroic efforts occurred while simultaneously noshing on his Pepperidge Farm sausages and sexually harassing Candace.*

I was immensely relieved to have missed out on this complete bullshit. Putte was free to carry out Weeds's corruption without my protests. The awards were all submitted before I landed back in Baghdad. My hands were clean. But in no way did that indicate my problems with Putte were over. At this point, having missed me for so long, he was insanely fanatical about wanting to know my whereabouts at all times. It became so bad, not only were people noticing it, they started approaching me about it.

When I went to our work area in the mornings, Putte would immediately say, "I need you to make a phone call." I knew he had no legitimate work for me to do and was conjuring useless tasks to keep me occupied. Then, not two minutes later, before I even had a chance to boot up my laptop, Putte would ask, "Have you made that phone call yet?" When I said, "Not yet, Sir," he went ballistic.

The company first sergeant told me he suspected Putte became jealous any time I spoke to another man. *Oh great, because avoiding men is really easy in the Army.* He set up an experiment to test his theory. When it was lunchtime and everyone else vacated the work area to eat elsewhere, I remained at my desk, alone, noshing on an MRE. First Sergeant came in to join me, and we started chatting. Putte appeared out of nowhere and started screaming at me to get back to my desk and do some bullshit task for him. He caused such a commotion, Lieutenant Colonel Mike Fuller ran over from his work area and started berating

Putte, telling him to back off, leave me alone and shut up. "You're disrupting all of us; now be quiet." Fuller demanded. I could have hugged him right then and there, but I kept quiet, delighting in my boss getting reprimanded right in front of me.

Major Putte didn't speak to me for the rest of the day. But before I left work, he told he wanted to talk to me later that night. I knew it was under the guise of work, but I suspected it was going to be inappropriate. So, I brought a notebook with me to take meeting minutes.

He ordered me to report to his bedroom, and when I arrived, instructed me to sit down next to him on his cot.

Whenever he spoke, I pretended like I was listening and taking copious notes in order to better my behavior, but I was actually documenting all of the creepy, weird shit coming out of his mouth.

"Laura, what happened to us?" he asked.

"Sir?" I questioned for clarification, deliberately playing dumb.

"We used to get along so well," he continued. "We used to be so close, and now I feel like our relationship has changed." He went on to say that he was worried about me, concerned that other men were having a bad influence on me, changing my character. I wanted to say, "I've just grown up, you creep, and I want to hang out with my friends instead of you." But I didn't say anything, and he just kept going...

I flashed back to my father not being able to handle me becoming a woman, wanting to close me off from the rest of the world, lock me away from men and keep me under his thumb. He, too, would scream any time I asserted my independence. Now it was all playing out again, right here in Baghdad, with someone else who wanted to fill that very role. Interestingly, just recently on Mother's Day, I had received a one-line email from my father—the first communication from him in an entire year. He asked if I ever planned to speak to them again and berated me for breaking my mother's heart. *So much for worrying if your daughter is still alive.* He knew I was in the 3d Infantry Division and had been in the throes of the ~~invasion~~ liberation. Any idiot knew that; it was all over the news. After re-reading his email a few times, I went back to pretending as if my parents didn't exist.

"I'm not like the other guys, Laura," Putte continued. I have some skeletons in my closet, and lately, I haven't been feeling good about us. Do you understand?"

"Yes, I do understand," I said, standing up. "And thank you for sharing your thoughts with me, Sir. Thank you for your time."

Then I walked out of his room and headed straight over to Lieutenant Colonel O'Neil (technically his boss for evaluation purposes, even though Weeds dictated most of his work). "Sir, I would like to report some grossly inappropriate behavior," and I read to him straight from my notes. When I was finished, O'Neil gave his typical shoulder shrug and offered, "Ehh, what's the big deal?"

I stood there in front of him and boldly declared, "No, Sir. You need to do something about this. I can't work with this man ever again." Then I walked away. I felt dirty and violated, and something needed to be done. I wouldn't back down until there was a resolution. But instead of immediately making a bigger stink about it, I decided to allow the chain of command to take course.

I don't know if O'Neil ever reported my complaint. Instead, I think Ricardo interceding on my behalf via email to one of his high-ranking buddies is what got Weeds's attention, because a few days later, Colonel Weeds called an informal meeting with the women of his brigade staff: Candace, Hannah, Sergeant Major Bagley and me. They sat there looking horrified. I was hopeful and glad this awkward gathering was called, and I vowed to not leave the room until my case was heard loud and clear.

"Is there sexual harassment going on here?" Weeds opened the discussion.

Is he kidding, I thought. Just the other day when I greeted him good morning, he asked if I had ever seen his "junk," because people complained that he peed too close to the work area. Only he asked in a way that felt like he was coming on to me. To thwart any possible advances, I retorted by asking if he had ever seen my bare white ass. Ironically, that shut him up, and he seemed to respect me more for holding my own and not allowing him to get under my skin.

Before answering, I wanted to see the reactions from the other women, to give them a chance to voice their complaints. Time after time, they grumbled about the inappropriate treatment that was allowed to go on at work, most of it coming from Weeds himself. They remained frozen with frowns on their faces.

"I think there is, Sir," I said, raising my hand. I couldn't take the silence any longer.

"And what might that be, Laura?" he asked, but I could tell that it was a rhetorical question and that he already knew about my situation and complaint.

"You know, Sir," I said. "Major Putte."

I decided to omit including that Weeds himself was a serious sexual harassment violator. I needed for him to focus on resolving my Putte issue.

"Well, that's a pretty serious accusation, Laura," Weeds continued with our sexual harassment charade. "Are you sure Putte isn't just being a little too friendly?"

"I don't care what he might think it is, Sir. He's wrong. He's gross. He's driving me crazy, and I can't work for him anymore. Everyone notices it. I'm not exaggerating. He's completely out of line."

"But you don't want to make a formal complaint, Laura, do you?" Weeds asked?

"Come again, Sir?"

"If you report this to EO [Equal Opportunity—the formal organization designed to protect officers and soldiers victim to acts of harassment, racism, sexism, etc.], then that formal complaint will tarnish our unit's reputation. We just finished such heroic acts in combat, and now you would ruin that for us."

I knew he was full of shit, and how dare he threaten that I would single-handedly ruin our unit, when I was a victim. But I ascertained that playing his game just might work in my favor and result in a much faster resolution.

"I tell you what, Sir. If you do something to take care of it, then I won't need to make a formal complaint. I will allow you to handle this yourself."

Weeds seemed pleased with my suggestion. I felt hopeful. The other women remained silent.

One thing I knew I had going for me was that Colonel Weeds knew I didn't get offended easily and that I could be one of the guys and handle the dirty jokes that often accompanied Army bonding and camaraderie. I wasn't the kind of woman who needed to be tip-toed around. (These women have every right to be that way; it just wasn't my personality.) If *I* was uncomfortable, shit was definitely out of hand.

Throughout the years, when people have asked if I was sexually harassed in the Army, I've had a difficult time responding. My responses have run the gamut: "Absolutely"; "Yeah, but I think I attracted it"; and "Yeah, but in some cases it was hilarious, and I just brushed it off. That's just the way things were." Only more recently have I been better able to articulate that indeed I was harassed and how unfair it was and how things need to change. Needless to say, the dynamics between men and women in the military are so utterly complicated, and a war environment only compounds that, because emotions become so raw, and it's difficult to contain them, especially because fear and arousal can become so intertwined in the human psyche. However, just because a man may have a difficult time containing his attraction toward a woman on the battlefield in no way should that place the burden on the woman to stop it. Nor does this demonstrate that women don't belong in combat. If that attraction is unwanted, then the man must honor the woman's wishes and keep to himself. (This applies to any gender or dynamic, if attraction is only one-sided.)

I don't have an exact policy plan on how to end the sexual harassment epidemic, but I know that its eradication will require huge cultural changes that I worry the Army isn't willing to embody yet because there are still too many Army leaders who don't truly believe that women belong in their precious boys' club.

There's certainly a distinction between naughty jokes among friends and a woman feeling violated and singled out for her gender. Our brothers in arms better start getting a grasp on the difference between dirty humor and victimizing women. My hope is that when more women are allowed to take coveted leadership positions in the Army, and when the old white male paradigm becomes obsolete, conditions will dramatically improve.

In any case, Colonel Weeds handled the situation in the same way that the Army handles most harassment cases, by removing the victim instead of removing the violator. So while everyone started gearing up to return home, Weeds assigned me to a new task force that was to stay behind indefinitely, comprised of people from our Black Hawk and cavalry forces. I would be the new S1 (Adjutant) of Task Force Knighthawk—summoned to fly daily reconnaissance missions over Fallujah, a predominantly Sunni, pro-Saddam city that was heating up with violence. At first I was pissed, but that quickly subsided when it sunk in that I would never have to see Putte ever again—even if it meant extending my war while he got to go home, back to his comfortable life.

CHAPTER TWENTY-NINE

We started flying reconnaissance missions over Fallujah to keep a military eye on this city that would see some of the worst violence in the entire Iraq war. Upon becoming the S1 of Task Force Knighthawk, I was in charge of administration and accountability for the reconnaissance pilots, their respective supporting elements and our headquarters.

When I reported to the new task force, almost all of my coworkers were new to me, even though I knew of their existence and had seen their names on my daily accountability reports. I also lived and worked in a new area. Instead of the apartment in "Hotel California," I now slept in a cordoned off section of one of the big airplane hangars (still at Baghdad International Airport). The man who showed me to my new sleeping area was the most beautiful man I had ever seen.

His name was Anthony, but everyone called him "Tough Tony." I decided to give him my own private nickname, "Captain Muscles."

Tony was six foot two, with brown hair, light brown eyes, a big smile, straight teeth and a big Italian nose. Never had I ever looked upon such masculinity and beauty wrapped up into one badass uniform. When I first laid eyes upon him, I had to ignore the fact that I was wearing the same damn uniform as him.

His tanned, statuesque body, square jaw, gorgeous white smile and charismatic personality reminded me of the male version of Pete's ideal woman—a very athletic, very tan, All-American beauty.

I never want this war to end, I thought. Tony then informed me that all of the other sleeping spaces in the unit were occupied, except for one empty cot that just so happed to be right next to his.

Oh no, how am I ever going to survive this war, having to wake up next to him each morning, watching him rip off his sleeping clothes, prancing around in his short, white Calvin Klein boxer briefs. Sacrificing for my country is hard work, but I guess I'll take one for the team!

It was the first time I'd felt lust in my life, and I was completely taken aback. I also sensed an innate chemistry between us. Ricardo had left and gone home. Pete too. Now here was Tony.

This is my new buddy, I thought to myself, smiling on the inside. I instantly felt good about things, despite still being stuck in Baghdad.

Tony and I quickly became acquainted with each other. He told me how he had actually auditioned to become a Calvin Klein underwear model, but was rejected because his muscles were too big. Poor guy. Well, his muscles weren't too big for me.

Tony packed a lot of weights to bring with him to war. He was so obsessed with working out and having a perfect body, he basically set up a gym in the hangar. And he seemed eager to have a new workout buddy.

We fell into a routine: wake up around 0700 hours, go for a fast and difficult run, followed by a shower in the co-ed shower station with private stalls. Then we'd head over to our regular 0900 meeting, where we were briefed on flight conditions (i.e. the weather), the current state of the war, what was happening on the ground in Fallujah, and a new threat I'd never heard of: improvised explosive devices, a.k.a. IEDs. Apparently, Iraqi insurgents were starting to make homemade bombs and plant them in unconventional places, most commonly along the roads that our troops used.

After that, we headed to breakfast, and then to work. My new commander, Lieutenant Colonel Joe Nichols, was personable and levelheaded. No longer did I have a micromanaging boss watching over my every move. Nichols was laid back and had common sense. As long as I completed all of my duties, he gave me my freedom (you know, how an adult is supposed to be treated in the workplace). It was such a relief to be rid of the morons from before, and I absolutely loved the people I worked with now. Though it only lasted for two months, from June to August, it was my most rewarding time in the Army.

Lunch was now in an open tent and occasionally included fresh food. And now that the markets were open in Baghdad again, I assumed my combat shopping duties by going into downtown Baghdad a few times a week. Every evening, we received our daily updates right before dinner, and after dinner, Tony, Wilson (his buddy from the ~~invasion~~ liberation) and I lifted weights. Every night we'd focus on a different part of the body. Between the running, weights and abdominal work, I got in the most amazing shape of my life within a matter of weeks. I could actually see my abdominal muscles forming a six-pack.

Working out with Tony every day was also a huge turn on. I knew he was married—he told me that he and his girlfriend had done a justice of the peace deal so she would be covered if anything happened to him in Iraq. But he certainly didn't act like he was married.

One night, I suddenly awoke with him lying on top of me wearing nothing but his gym shorts (and no underwear). Clearly, this was extremely inappropriate in every way. But I was also like, *Wow! When else would I get a chance to make out with a guy this hot?* Tim was nice-looking, but not hot—and definitely not *hot hot* like Tony. Besides, Tony and I were fast friends, and he was so damn sexy, and his bulging muscular body felt so damn good pressing against mine. Was it wrong if I had a huge crush on him and wanted to be engulfed in his muscles?

I gave myself a quick internal pep talk: *Laura, this is likely the only opportunity you will ever have to make out with an insanely beautiful man. Just like you seized Baghdad, you need to seize Captain Muscles too, or you'll regret it later in life. Plus, in war, all is forgiven. Carpe Diem!*

And I knew we wouldn't go all the way. We were both still clothed, and I was still a virgin.

So I wrapped my arms around him, letting him know that it was OK. As we kissed, my fingers traced his bulging chest muscles, savoring each contour and ripple, imprinting them in my memory. It was like making out with a statue from a museum.

Then he said, "Can I hump your leg like a dog until I come?"

I thought, *Whaaaat?* but flatly said, "OK, sure."

Tony started gyrating on my leg, and about sixty seconds later, he came. Then he got up, went over to his cot, changed his shorts and went back to sleep. I remained in bed, frozen. *Did that just happen?*

We never made out like that again, despite how badly I wanted to. I held back when I really just wanted to give all of myself to him and to know what it would feel like to have all of him. But I didn't dare, because I figured we would probably lose complete control—and he couldn't know my dirty secret, the fact that I had never had sex—and Tony wasn't the kind of guy you lose your virginity to. There were a few other times when we kissed a little bit, but mostly, we became close friends.

Later when I saw him flirting with other girls, I realized that Tony was a player. Still, the more we got to know each other, the more I started thinking he was the perfect man in my definition of manhood. Besides being a real-life Adonis, he was an accomplished Army officer and had graduated from West Point after serving as an enlisted Special Forces soldier for a few years. Yes, he was a little cocky, but he treated everyone very well, especially the lower-ranking soldiers, and in return they loved him for it. He was literally the best of the best in the Army: smart, courageous, likeable, physically perfect—an all-around top-notch guy.

When I compared Tony to Tim back at home (which I couldn't help but do), there was really no match. Tim was boring, attached to his parents, too scared to join the military and not gregarious. I knew there had to be other men like Tony out there. And I was attracted to men like Tony. I started thinking that I had to break up with Tim because he was nothing like Tony, the coolest thing since sliced bread.

Tony had no idea I was a virgin. Unlike with Ricardo and Pete, I never wanted him to know. Because I was flirty and had a potty mouth, he was totally fooled. But this new persona actually felt a lot more like me.

On our first shopping trip in Baghdad, some Special Forces soldiers that Tony knew back in the day escorted us, offering extra protection, since we didn't know what kind of danger we would face. But when we got to the main marketplace, we found that the locals were fascinated with the presence of American soldiers, especially an American woman.

As I went from one dilapidated storefront to another, several teenage boys followed, shouting, "American woman! American woman! When we make baby? We make beautiful American babies. I want American wife!"

"Study hard and focus on your grades, boys," I called back while laughing. "An American education is far more valuable than an American wife." This seemed to take the wind out of their sails, and they finally let me be.

After my teenage suitors walked away, we continued searching for the items on our shopping list: air conditioners, USB thumb drives and cleaning supplies. Luckily we found some reputable merchants: Mouyad and his brother Mohammed.

Like their Kuwaiti counterparts, Luai and Shek, Mouyad and Mohammed were a godsend. They could find us everything on our shopping list. And if they didn't have it, or their friends didn't have it, and no one in Iraq had it, they would go on an excursion to the country of Jordan, just to find me the goods. They were just as bored as we were and loved any excuse to go out of their way to help us. I always returned to base with every item on my shopping list crossed off, along with a piece of scrap paper, written in Arabic, serving as my legitimate receipt.

I spent a total of $80,000 in combat. While I didn't come home with any valorous awards or perform any heroic acts, I kicked ass as a combat shopper and came home with rich memories of Baghdad and its wonderful people.

Just when things started to get almost too boring to handle, some of Tony's friends in the Special Forces invited us to hang out with them at "their place"—one of Saddam Hussein's former palaces, complete with a swimming pool. What a coincidence; I had a bikini—one I'd bought back in Kuwait!

These Special Forces soldiers hadn't seen a half-naked American woman in several months, so my bikini and I were enthusiastically welcomed into their community of nightly beer parties. Before the war, I hated the taste of beer, but here in Baghdad, it tasted so good. It was like drinking America in a bottle.

One night, after a particularly boring and scorching day, Tony, Wilson, Desiree (a new friend) and I made our nightly trek over to the Special Forces' occupied palace. It was more empty than usual, probably because a lot of the guys were out on some assassination mission. Only two people occupied the pool, so I immediately ripped off my gym uniform and dove in. When we were all wading around, Tony dared me to take my bikini off.

"Um, there's two guys right over there who don't know us. I don't think that's a good idea." I responded.

"Why not?" Tony egged me on. "You think they would be offended at seeing a naked woman?"

"I don't know. Wilson, what do you think?" Wilson was more the voice of reason, so I would defer to his judgment.

"I think you should do it," he teased with his adorable grin.

"Not only should you do it," Tony interrupted, "You should get up out of the pool and go over to that chair, pretending like you need to grab something."

Before I had another moment to contemplate my next move, Desiree chimed in.

"Here, I'll hold your bikini for you."

There was no turning back. I couldn't disappoint my comrades. They deserved my very best. I deserved to be my very best.

During our conversation the two guys had climbed out of the pool, and one of them started to walk back into the palace. The other one turned away from us, appearing to gather his belongings, so this was my cue to execute my mission. I pushed my naked self up out of the pool and started prancing toward the empty chair. I didn't dare look toward the guy. My heart raced with fear and conquest as I enjoyed being exposed for not just the entertainment of my comrades, but for me. I reveled in the moment as I took off my sports watch, tinkering with it, using it as an excuse for needing to be out of the pool. In slow motion, I removed my watch, placed it on the chair and started walking back toward my friends. They suppressed snickers as I jumped back into the pool. Mission accomplished.

"That was fucking amazing!" Tony high-fived me. He was naked.

"You were awesome!" Wilson congratulated me. He too was naked.

"You are da bomb!" Desiree said as she handed me back my bikini. I placed it within close reach just outside of the pool, beaming with pride. She was also naked. Apparently I inspired everyone to start skinny dipping.

"Did he see me?" I triumphantly, yet nervously asked.

"Yeah, but he quickly turned his head," Tony said. "He looked really confused for a second but then turned in the other direction." Oddly enough I was relieved this guy had some semblance of respect.

Tony started grabbing at Desiree, which I took as my cue to start flirting with Wilson. As we horsed around, I felt an underwater jet shoot water onto my leg and had an idea.

"Hey Wilson, check this out," I said as I led him toward the jet.

"Nice."

"Guess what I want to do with it?" I asked, noticing his burgeoning erection. I wanted him so badly, but with him being married, I knew that would never happen. Plus, there was no way I wanted him to also discover that I was still a virgin. But a little naughty play wouldn't hurt anyone.

"Dirty, dirty Laura," he said as I grabbed the side of the pool, spread my legs, and started bobbing up and down in the water, allowing the jet stream to pleasure me. Just being next to Wilson was practically enough stimulation to orgasm and overcome the awkwardness of needing to hold myself underwater to directly align my body with the jet nozzle. As I delved toward ecstasy, Wilson offered to help.

"Here, let me hold you down," he said when I came up for air.

"Perfect, thank you," I said as he grabbed my head and dunked me underwater. I tried to stay down there as long as possible, letting the jet stream fuck me into pure pleasure. I came up for air one more time and went back down. Wilson then started grabbing my breasts with his free hand, rubbing my nipples, feeling my naked body. I loved feeling his hands all over me, this forbidden lust. Pleasure waves rippled my body and I shook into an intense orgasm. I came up above the water, gasping for air, still shaking.

"Thank you! Thank you! Thank you!" I wanted to wrap my pleasured, naked body around Wilson and kiss him. I wanted to feel his hard penis brushing against my body, but I knew this would make him too uncomfortable. So I pushed him away, instigating a game of chase, only imaging what it would be like to have sex with him. I guess sex would just have to wait. But, hey, I just had an orgasm inside of Saddam Hussein's pool. Not too shabby for another boring day in Baghdad.

The attention from all these of these studs was addictive. Why didn't Tim lust after me like the horny guy who chased me while grunting in the Kuwaiti grocery store, or the Special Forces guy who told me he was a freelance massage therapist and needed to practice his skills on me, or the teenage Iraqi boys who kept asking to marry me?

As I tanned, worked out, shopped and partied nearly every day for the last two months of my deployment, I had ample time to reevaluate my life.

Screw this good Christian girl image and marrying my high school sweetheart. I just lived through a war. And if I go home and settle down, this war might be the last adventure I ever experience. It's time for me to free myself. And man, was I horny.

PART 3

Liberation

CHAPTER THIRTY

My sparkle was holding on for dear life, but I wanted it gone, ASAP. What was once so cherished had become such a burden. I didn't want to be a virgin anymore. My purity and innocence were long gone, left behind at the border of Kuwait and Iraq. So what was the point in keeping it anymore? It was time for this part of me to catch up with the liberated woman I'd become during the war. I was ready.

Imagine if I had been killed in combat. Have any war casualties ever been virgins? What a waste, a tragedy to die never having experienced what is supposed to be life's greatest pleasure. Plus, if I was killed in Iraq, I would qualify to become one of Saddam Hussein's or Osama bin Laden's seventy-two virgins in heaven, and I had no desire to touch either of their nasty penises.

Now my biggest dilemma was where to lose my virginity and with whom. Lord knows there were plenty of candidates who would have gladly conquered this mission. But I needed to carefully weigh my options and conduct a thorough reconnaissance of the greater Baghdad International Airport area, scouting out the ideal location for the sacrificial sparkle ceremony.

I didn't want to end up like Specialist Jones, who conceived her child in a porta potty. Specialist Jones was one of our cooks who greeted us at every meal with her shy smile and polite "Good day, Ma'am." None of us would have ever suspected that she was conducting an extensive array of extracurricular activities that resulted in her having to randomly select the baby daddy when she divulged her new pregnancy. (Hopefully she washed her hands thoroughly before preparing our meals.) Rumor had it she'd hooked up with ten different guys. The one she claimed to be the father was black, so only time would tell if she had selected the correct man. Even though there was no way to prove his guilt, they both received severe punishments for violating General Order #1—a reduction in rank and pay—and Specialist Jones was shipped home immediately, since pregnant women are forbidden from serving in combat zones, as a means to protect the fetus.

To make matters worse for her, Specialist Jones was married, so I couldn't imagine how she was going to explain this to her husband. I also didn't understand why she allowed herself to get pregnant, since birth control was readily available from our unit docs. Thank goodness I had taken my pills every day, just in case I figured out who was going to take my sparkle and decided to act on it. But in a fucking porta-potty! Come on. I didn't care if that was the most private space in all of Iraq. No fucking way.

I shared my dilemma with my friend Amber every morning at the breakfast table. Being bored out of our minds gave us ample time to strategize about the best way for me to lose my virginity. Amber and I had met at a West Point women's Bible study during my plebe year, and since, long traversed the path away from the straight and narrow of our former days. We laughed, saying, "Imagine if they could see us now" and thankful that we had seen the light and stopped trying to be goody-two-shoed ladies for Christ.

We imagined that our old Bible study friends came across as really obnoxious to their fellow soldiers, using every Army leadership opportunity to evangelize the gospel, just as we were taught. Surprisingly, during our two-hour breakfast chats, Amber revealed that she had lost her virginity right after high school because she didn't think it was smart to go away to college as a virgin. I thought that was brilliant and admired how she balanced being a Christian with being smart about her sexuality, although she hadn't had sex in ages. But she was thinking she had a good chance of scoring in Baghdad with Mark, another officer in our unit who was cute and badass, especially since it was known that he was on the prowl. So we planned her conquest while also figuring out mine.

I was certain that Captain Muscles would have sex with me. I could just say the word, and he would be inside of me in a heartbeat. We wouldn't even need to find a private spot, since our shared room was always empty. We could do it in the middle of the night, when everyone was either sleeping or working the night shift, and we could lay a poncho liner on the floor, instead of fornicating on our squeaky cots. I would be proud to have him as my first, even though he was technically married. But I feared that once inside of me, he would be able to feel something that would instantly give me away, an extra tightness that other women didn't have. And what if I started bleeding? He would know. He couldn't know. I needed to save face as his wild and naughty friend.

Mark would be a fun lay. I envied Amber when she reported to me that they had snuck off into a fabric room, tucked away in a corner on the third floor of our airplane hangar, and had their way with each other. She said it was steamy hot, both figuratively and literally, as they thrusted on top of aircraft fabric pieces with the 125-degree sun beating down on them.

Actually, Amber would gladly have shared Mark with me, but I didn't feel the same longing for him that I did for Tony, even though I felt more comfortable with the idea of Mark discovering my secret. So I didn't bother asking her opinion about letting Mark take my virginity. I decided against it on my own.

But then I got desperate. Time was winding down. Our redeployment was drawing nearer, and my libido was about to explode. So I considered my West Point buddy, Eddie, when he emailed me to say that his unit was moving up to the airport and sending him on a reconnaissance mission to find some living space.

Eddie was awkward and unattractive, but I could overlook all of that to get Eddie to take away my sparkle. He deserved it anyway, especially since he helped me get through sophomore physics, tutoring me every night, practicing his destiny of one day becoming a physics professor at Caltech. I could just shut my eyes and pretend he was Tony. And I didn't have to be embarrassed about still being a virgin; I assumed Eddie still was too, since we had both been dedicated to our purity and attended the same Bible study group. Actually, convincing Eddie to lose his own sparkle would probably be my biggest challenge. But I was willing to try.

I emailed my idea to Colleen, since she knew Eddie well from football tailgates and visits to her home in upstate, New York. I could talk to Colleen about anything and diligently kept her updated about my changing views on sex and Christianity in general, so she knew just how horny I was. When I wrote her that I was thinking of giving it away to Eddie, she responded with, "ARE YOU FUCKING NUTS?"

Needless to say, I didn't have her blessing, but that didn't stop me from asking Eddie a million questions about his sexuality when he finally arrived in Baghdad. I didn't think that he could tell I was entertaining the possibility of asking him to take away my virginity. But when I asked him if he thought he wanted to lose it in the near future, he told me that he was still dedicated to saving it until marriage. So Eddie was out.

Discouraged and desperate, I told Amber that I was running out of options. But in some ways, perhaps more than I was willing to admit to myself, I wanted my first time to be a little more meaningful than a dirty romp with a man who was likely in a relationship, someone who actually deserved my twenty-four-year-old sparkle. So we decided that I would give it away to my boyfriend, Tim, after returning home from Baghdad.

Tim had to sense that things weren't right between us. During the last two months of the deployment, I drastically reduced my contact with him. I blamed it on email outages, but the truth was that email was far more reliable than it had been when we first arrived in Baghdad. When I did communicate with Tim, it was hasty and matter-of-fact. He said he completely understood and was happy I was safe. At the beginning of the war, I wrote him long letters, detailing everything about my journey, complaining about everything being bullshit, expressing my longing for his presence and touch, writing how much I looked forward to a future together. But I didn't feel that way about him anymore.

War transformed me, and he was no longer a suitable partner. He had expressed to me his desires to be a pilot like his Top Gun, Naval Academy graduate father, but frankly, he was too much of a wimp to do anything bold with his life. If I kept dating him, I was sealing my fate to a boring man with no sense of adventure. Now that I had a heavy dose of adrenaline and passion flowing through my blood, I needed to be with a real and courageous man. But I couldn't break up with him before returning home. It wasn't the nice thing to do, plus, he was managing all of my finances.

I planned, reluctantly, to use Tim to lose my virginity and practice having sex until I thought it was an appropriate time to end our relationship. I couldn't believe I had become the kind of person who uses another person for sex. I told Amber I felt guilty, but when she detailed my other option—breaking up with him and then meeting someone new to lose my virginity to—I shuddered in disgust, imagining the awkward exchange of telling someone new that I was still a virgin.

I knew I had to inevitably break Tim's heart. Maybe my body would be a consolation prize, I justified to myself. Plus, he really pissed me off when he ignored my last call from Kuwait, two days before the Iraq ~~invasion~~ liberation, because he was chatting with his boss. His boss would have expected him to interrupt their conversation and talk to me; she completely understood that her employee's girlfriend was away at war. But he was too timid to ask to end their conversation. Fucking pussy.

Before coming home, I needed to ensure Tim was onboard with my sex plan. I was afraid that if I came home and out of nowhere demanded sex, he would think I lost my mind, or ask me to take a few days to figure out if that's what I really wanted to do. I wasn't willing to wait, so I sent him an email:

> *Hi Honey,*
>
> *Luckily email is working today. I think things are winding down here and we'll be home in the near future. I don't know the exact day yet, but I will keep you posted. I'm so excited to come home and see you. I also wanted to let you know that I'm ready to lose my virginity. What do you think about us finally having sex? Wouldn't that be awesome? I hope you think so. I'm so horny and want you. I love you oodles and oodles!*

Within 24 hours he replied, ecstatic, and said that he had to go masturbate right after reading my email. Thankfully, that block would be checked. Now I needed to figure out what new car I was going to buy, so that block could also get checked on my long list of redeployment to-do tasks. But before becoming too fixated on what awaited me back home, I needed to capitalize on an opportunity I thought might never come my way again.

"Pull over guys," I said to Tony and Wilson, as we drove on the back roads between the Special Forces palace and airport.

"Right here?" Tony asked.

"Yeah this is fine," I responded. "It's not like anyone is going to see us here. It's pitch black."

Tony stopped the Humvee and turned the engine off. The night sky was tranquil, but my heart was pounding. Not only had I never performed for anyone like this before, it was also dangerous. Saddam Hussein's sons, Uday and Qusay, were recently killed in Mosul, and we were warned there might be retaliations in the form of an increased number of IEDs.

"Stay inside and watch from here," I told the guys.

"Are you gonna be OK?" Tony asked. He seemed to be more comfortable with the idea than Wilson, but it was obvious we were all a little hesitant.

"Of course," I answered, trying to sound confident and not overthink things. I unbuckled my belt and slid my desert camouflage utility pants down toward my tan combat boots. Not removing my pants and boots completely would allow for a quick recovery in case anyone happened to drive by and catch me. I continued undressing, removing my camouflage blouse and brown t-shirt, and placing them on the ground so I wouldn't become completely covered in sand. Then I positioned my butt over the strewn garments, and pulled my underwear down toward my bunched up pants and boots.

As I lay on the ground, only covered in my bra, I began to touch myself. I hoped the movement of my hands would prevent Tony and Wilson from being able to see me entirely.

I rubbed myself back and forth with my right hand for a few minutes. Tony then yelled a few excited hoots, making me laugh and lose focus. I rubbed again and then placed my left index finger inside of me. I tried to let myself enter a state of bliss, but I was distracted, knowing I was on display.

After ten minutes, Tony asked from the Humvee, "Are you close?"

"Not really. Sorry, guys," I was disappointed to be having a difficult time.

"Don't be sorry," Tony yelled. "This is awesome."

"I'm really enjoying it too," I assured him.

As I continued rubbing, Tony and Wilson suddenly exited the Humvee and headed toward me.

"We figured you could use some help," Tony stated as he kneeled down on my left side, and Wilson followed suit by laying on my right.

"Undo your bra," Tony suggested.

I unfastened and removed my bra, then resumed touching myself while Tony and Wilson began stroking my breasts and stomach. As our contact intensified, Tony began kissing me passionately, licking every spot inside and outside of my mouth.

As Tony continued kissing me, Wilson began to gently bite on my nipples. Despite being in the middle of this war zone shithole, I was in heaven. My church friends would be appalled if they knew what I was up to. I wasn't supposed to be doing this with anyone except my future husband, let alone two married men at the same time.

I momentarily thought of the West Point Cadet Chapel congregation I sang to every Sunday, leading their praise and worship. I pictured them shaking their heads in disapproval and threatening to disown me from their Christian family. I knew they would insist on praying for my sinful soul, ordering me to get down *on my knees* and beg God for forgiveness. But I wanted to be down on my knees for other reasons.

Plus, did I really need to ask God to forgive me? Did he care that I was horny and looking to blow off steam? I was in the middle of a war. Isn't this what warriors did in biblical times? Didn't Roman conquerors visit whorehouses? Wouldn't God relax the rules a little for three dutiful, young and willing American soldiers?

I pushed away my guilty thoughts, trying to soak in all of the pleasure coming at me from so many angles. I couldn't believe I was having a threesome, albeit a non-penetrating one. This was the most erotic moment of my entire life. A life with a promising future, especially now that our deployment was nearly finished and we were heading home. But there was a part of it that I knew I would miss and probably never be able to recapture once I was home on safe soil. I needed to make the most of this entire experience, not knowing when I would lie with two men simultaneously again, if ever at all.

Between Tony's mouth consuming mine, Wilson's nipple-play sending shock waves down to my genitals, and my hands writhing back and forth across my most intimate areas, I should have exploded into an orgasm right then and there. But it wasn't happening. My body was failing me. I began losing faith.

"Guys, I know I'm not finishing, but I want you to know, I'm in complete bliss right now."

"It's OK," Tony reassured me, "as long as you feel good. Because I'm having a fantastic time."

"Me too," Wilson said.

It was getting late, and we really needed to head back, so I soaked in one last grope before putting an end to the fun.

"Well, maybe we should head back," I suggested.

"Only if you're ready to," Tony insisted.

"Yeah," Wilson responded.

"I'm ready. Thank you for such an incredible experience. You guys are amazing."

"So are you," they both high-fived me.

We donned our clothes, climbed back into the vehicle and giggled hysterically, replaying the night's event as we rode in a Humvee all together for the very last time.

CHAPTER THIRTY-ONE

For the entire deployment, we had no idea how long we would be gone. Back when Donald Rumsfeld came to speak to us, he was a super cocky prick. At the end of his speech, he asked if there were any questions. Someone raised his hand and asked, "Sir, when do we get to go home?" A completely valid question—the number one thing on all of our weary, battle-ridden minds. Instead of exuding empathy or appreciation for our efforts, Rumsfeld laughed an evil laugh, reminiscent of the Wicked Witch of the West and said, "You'll go home when I say you can go home!" What a fucking asshole.

We wished to be home for July 4, but the holiday passed with still no indication of when we could go. (At least the Special Forces guys hosted a barbeque with a legit Iraqi belly dancer to celebrate.) After the launch of our task-force, there was talk of staying indefinitely, and people were really bummed out. Just about everyone ached to go home to their families, but all I had to go home to was Tim. I wasn't in a rush to return home anymore, especially since I was enjoying my new persona and the adventure of exploring the new me. I was OK with having to stay in Iraq for however long it would take. It was like my personal incubation period to figure out life and how I wanted it to play out once I returned home.

Toward the end of July, we unexpectedly got notice. "We're leaving in a week," my commander announced that morning. We were stunned. Some of us were in disbelief. Cheers filled the headquarters area, but a big part of me strangely felt sad. This was the end of being surrounded by my combat family. My band of brothers. I knew I would never feel the intensity of this bond ever again, and I wasn't ready for it to be over. But it was time to turn to the future and embark on an exciting journey, full of new opportunities, not knowing the final destination, and having the freedom to be exactly who I wanted to be. Butterflies filled my stomach. We were getting the hell out of Iraq.

We all packed the Humvees with our gear. Right before leaving Iraq, I snapped photos of my living area and bid adieu to the porta-potties. I noticed that the Halliburton oil field services company moved in and was starting to build more permanent structures, starting with a fancy dining facility that was going right on top of our old shit hole slit trenches. *Thank God I won't ever have to eat there,* I thought as I got into my Humvee bound for Kuwait. We needed to go back to Kuwait in order to load all of our Humvees, helicopters and equipment onto ships before flying back to Savannah. Unlike during the ~~invasion~~ liberation, when we spent three weeks navigating the bomb-infested 500 miles between the Kuwait-Iraq border and Baghdad, we drove for fifteen hours straight in the desolate desert, with the only noise coming from our helicopters overhead and Avril Lavigne, Dave Matthews, Coldplay and Michelle Branch blasting from the speakers in my portable, battery-operated CD player.

On our last fuel stop just before the Kuwait border, it was time for a breather. I set my pistol down on my seat and removed my helmet and vest to get some air flowing to my head and body. Then I grabbed a fuel can and poured the fuel into my Humvee and shot the shit with my Humvee mates, Wilson and Desiree. Suddenly, we heard gunfire. *FUCK!*

The three of us quickly ducked behind the front passenger side of our Humvee and did a rapid sanity check. Desiree, struggling with heat exhaustion, was almost completely undressed, and her rifle was strewn across the back seat. I yelled at her to switch weapons with me, while she got dressed, so I could cover us with the superior firepower afforded by her M16. Wilson pointed his pistol toward what we believed to be the source of the gunfire, about 250 meters away. We both broke out into hysterics, knowing that the 9mm pistol was worthless in this effort.

I zeroed in on the source, ready to kill if necessary. This was the closest visible danger I encountered in the entire war. *I will not die. My comrades will not die. Not now. We're too damn close to safety.*

More gunfire. I quickly assessed the scenario to decide if I needed to move the rifle's safety switch to fire, in order to pull the trigger. AK-47s were pointed in the air, spewing bullets. But they weren't aimed at us. I kept the safety on and resisted the urge to shoot.

Then I saw a group of Iraqi men standing outside of a shack, drinking what appeared to be beer out of cans, laughing and shooting AK-47s in the air. Phew. They weren't trying to kill us. They didn't even notice our presence. Apparently shooting rifles into the air is simply one of the ways that Iraqis celebrate happy hour.

"All clear!" I yelled at my mates. We raced back into our Humvee and got the fuck out of there, stat. *Thank God I won't die a virgin after all.*

We were in Kuwait for about a week before heading back, mostly packing stuff up at the port of Kuwait City. Then everyone left except for eleven other people and me, because there wasn't enough room on the flight home to fit our entire taskforce. Since I was in charge of admin, my commander asked me to wait with the others for an extra five days, before there was another flight home. I used this brief window of opportunity to take my friend Sam and a few others out on the town in Kuwait City, shopping and eating, blasting the radio in the SUV. To the tune of Kool & The Gang's "Celebrate," Sam shouted out of the window, "Burn your burqas!"

Finally, after the five days were up, the twelve of us boarded a flight headed for home on August 6, 2003. Two weeks later, a suicide bomber blew up the United Nations compound in Baghdad, killing seventeen people, including Sérgio Vieira de Mello, the UN Secretary General's special representative in Iraq. Thank God we weren't there anymore.

I decided I wouldn't have Tim pick me up when I landed because I knew I was going to break up with him and wasn't ready to see him just yet. I needed to recalibrate my bearings. A part of me worried that he wouldn't show up, regardless. I actually felt that I wasn't important enough to anyone, so I didn't bother asking for someone to meet me upon returning. Instead, I coordinated with Tim's co-workers to surprise him with my arrival when I was ready to go down to Tampa.

I stepped off the plane in Savannah and followed the others into an airplane hangar on Hunter Army Airfield—where it all began seven months ago. Colonel Weeds stood in front of a small group of family members who cheered as we approached them. A large US flag was hanging, and the "Star-Spangled Banner" began to play on the sound system. I fought back tears as I saluted the American flag. It was so surreal and emotional. *But nothing made me cry more tears of joy than the first time I heard the sound of an actual flushing toilet.* I was home. But I didn't know exactly what that meant. I didn't have a home; everything I owned was in storage, and my family was nowhere in sight.

Ricardo was there to welcome me home. He said he wouldn't miss it for the world. And Sam's mom brought me flowers, making me feel a little special and girly. When our formal welcome concluded, Ricardo ran over and greeted me with a giggly, warm embrace and donned me with a welcome back gift he told me to open once we were in private—my very first vibrator. Then he brought me back to a hotel room he had reserved and watched me use the vibrator for the first time. Nothing else happened between us. We simply hugged and cuddled and caught up on life.

The next day, Ricardo drove me to Tampa, where I spent the night with his very loving, boisterous, festive family. They were so kind to take me out to dinner and made me feel very welcome. His wife didn't seem the least bit intimidated by my presence and the chemistry and bond I had with her husband. Instead, she appeared to be genuinely happy to help welcome me home.

In the morning, as Ricardo drove me to Beef O' Brady's, where Tim was having lunch with his coworkers, he gave me a pep talk. It almost felt like he was my father giving me away at my wedding, preparing me for this new journey. I wanted to cry as he dropped me off. This was the last time he would ever see me as a virgin, and he had played such an integral part in my liberation.

My heart pounded as I tip-toed into the restaurant and made my way over to Tim's group, already seated at a long table. I nervously inhaled a deep breath as I stood behind him, placed my hands over his eyes and announced with a smile, "Guess who?" He spun around and froze. Then he crinkled his face, staring at me, processing what had just happened.

"What are you doing here?" he asked, less enthused than I would expect from a man who was seeing his girlfriend for the first time since leaving for war.

"I'm home!" I replied. "I arranged this with Sharon so I could surprise you."

"Wow," he said, still seated.

"Are you glad to see me?" I asked, opening my arms for a hug.

He awkwardly stood up and limply hugged me, still stunned. Sharon broke the tension with a hearty laugh and invited me to sit down and order my lunch. For the rest of the meal, Tim periodically patted my leg and back, as if I was only a phantom and not actually present.

Tim's boss, who was also seated at the table, told him to take the rest of the afternoon off, and we went to the Toyota dealership so I could buy my new 4Runner. After exhausting back and forth negotiations, during which I instructed Tim to keep his mouth shut, I bought my dream car for $5,000 less than the sticker price. I was proud of my negotiation skills. Then we grabbed a quick dinner at Hooters and headed to his apartment. It was finally time.

It was obvious we were both nervous, the way we walked around the apartment, reacquainting ourselves with each other after seven months apart, prolonging the inevitable. A part of me was surprised that he wasn't compelled to rip my clothes off right then and there, especially as I was now twelve pounds lighter and tan and buff from my three-hour-per-day workouts with Tony. Finally, we walked into the bedroom and started discussing the logistics of our first sexual encounter.

"I bought condoms," Tim said, grabbing a few out of his nightstand drawer.

"Oh good. Thank you," I said, relieved that he was still onboard and committed to doing the deed. The war made me forget about things that normal people do, like buy condoms. "Are you ready?" I asked.

"Yeah, are you?"

"Absolutely. It's only been twenty-four years for me, and you've been waiting seven years to sleep with me!" I laughed.

We stared at each other for a bit, both unsure how to get started. Then we simultaneously started removing our own clothing. I threw mine on the floor, but Tim neatly folded his into a pile, so I followed suit, knowing how tidy and orderly he liked things. When I stood naked before him, he didn't seem to notice the dramatic changes to my body, so I took it upon myself to ask if he liked what he saw.

"Of course," he flatly tried to assure me, "you look great."

I wasn't convinced that he cared or was turned on.

"Do you want to get up on the bed?" he asked.

"Sure," I said, disappointed that I had to do this with Tim, despite him being the most deserving and ideal candidate.

In bed, we lay side by side, and he put a condom on. (Unfortunately, he didn't think to buy lube, as I was bone dry.) Then he rolled on his side and went to insert himself into me. I panicked.

"Just a minute!"

"What is it? Are you OK?"

"Do you think we can try something different? I don't know… maybe some foreplay?" I suggested, hoping it would improve my mood.

"Huh? What do you mean?" he responded, puzzled, like I had just asked him to recite the Arabic alphabet.

I silently thanked myself for making the decision to eventually break up with him. There was no way I could ever tolerate such ignorance and un-sexiness in my man. Especially not when there were plenty of others who would gladly satisfy me into bliss. But I had to stay in the game. So I explained what I thought would help.

"Let's kiss for a while, to stir things up. Make us hornier."

"Um, OK." He started slobbering in a way that showed he was making an attempt, but failing miserably.

Before Iraq, I never gave much thought to whether or not he was a good kisser, but after having three different tongues in my mouth, I realized that he just plain sucked. I closed my eyes and visualized myself back in Baghdad, surrounded by my sexy and lustful war buddies. I returned Tim's kisses, but the imagery wasn't enough to conquer my repulsion. I instantly regretted not losing my virginity back in Iraq and wanted to simultaneously cry and punch Tim in the face. After a few minutes, I couldn't take it anymore.

"Stop it!" I begged.

"What, are you OK?" he asked again, backing off. I feigned fatigue in an attempt to be polite.

"I'm just really tired. I can't get into it. I'm so sorry. Let's just try again in the morning."

He must have been relieved, because he instantly agreed, turned out the lights, and rolled over, falling fast asleep. I curled up into the fetal position, dejected, with my sparkle *still* holding on for dear life.

The next morning, we woke up famished.

"I want to lose my virginity before breakfast," I announced. There was no way I could spend another hour with this burden weighing me down.

"OK," he acquiesced, donning a condom once more.

"Don't even bother with the foreplay," I instructed. "Just ram it in there."

He obeyed, and a few moments later, I screamed in agony, feeling the most excruciating pain I ever felt in my entire life. Half of Tim's penis was inside of me.

Instead of crying, I celebrated my victory, declaring a triumphant, "THANK GOD I'M NOT A VIRGIN ANYMORE!" Then I told Tim to immediately remove his penis and gasped a sigh of relief. Twenty minutes later, we were eating bagels at Atlanta Bread Company—my first meal without my sparkle. It felt so uneventful, and I thought—*Imagine if people knew what just happened to me.*

A week later Tim came up to Savannah, where I was once again stationed. The first night we had fun drinking and getting tipsy. But he fucked me so hard and fast, like a jackhammer, our encounter ended with me screaming. When I sat on the toilet afterward, I bled profusely.

We tried to do it again later (with lube this time), but he was so aggressive about it, I was disgusted. Tim wasn't trying to hurt me—he just had no idea what he was doing.

He even had the audacity to tell me that I had to do all of the work because he couldn't "see my hole." Obviously we were never going to last as a couple.

The third day, Sunday, he went limp, and I lost my temper, breaking up with him on the spot. Tim cried and then left to go back to Tampa. We briefly spoke a few days after, but I never saw him again.

CHAPTER THIRTY-TWO

With my sparkle gone and no one to hold me back, I felt completely free to experience an entirely different world with endless possibilities. I bought myself a new, slutty wardrobe to reflect how I felt on the inside, wanting to attract sexy men who could take me to new levels of passion. But I was terrified that I had no sexual skills in my repertoire. How could I possibly reciprocate a hot man's advances when I was still clueless on how to have good sex? And would it always hurt so badly? Would it ever actually feel good? How could I be confident in my ability to please a man if there was the risk of needing to beg him to stop?

I figured Ricardo would come up with a good solution. He was spending his last two weeks of Army service in an extended stay hotel just outside of our military post, eagerly waiting for his retirement to begin. I finally settled back into a routine, renting a room from a friend whose home was close to work.

Appalled by my tales of how Tim treated me in the bedroom, Ricardo was more than happy to help. One night, after going out to dinner, he brought me back to his room for some role-playing exercises, but only after I made him swear that he wasn't trying to have sex with me. A part of me worried he may think it was OK to bone me now that my sparkle was gone.

"Just come over here, my dear, onto the bed."

"Wait, what are you trying to do to me?"

"Nothing, I promise."

"Well I'm not taking my clothes off."

"Of course not, my dear, now just get into this position," he said as he guided me down onto my hands and feet. "I will lie down on my back, facing you," he explained as he got into position. "Now you can put your weight on your hands and feet and pretend like you're sliding up and down my penis."

"Like this?" I asked, feeling like I projected a horny gorilla more than a knowledgeable, sexy woman. Despite feeling utterly silly, I was also thankful for this teaching demonstration and appreciated Ricardo's creativity. *How else are people supposed to learn how to have sex?*

"Very good, my dear," Ricardo applauded me. "Let's try some other ones now."

He went through the basic sex positions that a couple could do on a bed. I knew there were other ways to have sex because Tony bragged about holding women up against a wall. I wanted a strong man to throw me up against a wall and have his way with me, but I knew I needed to master the basics first.

"This is all nice and good," I said, "but how do I get it to not hurt?" I asked at the end of my sex lesson. The next time we went out to dinner and went back to his room, Ricardo answered me with a Publix shopping bag.

"What's this?"

"Open it and find out!" he said, excited.

"A cucumber? What? Wait a minute…"

"Yes, my dear. This is going to help you so much."

"Dude, I'm not going to put a cucumber inside of me, that's disgusting."

"No I swear it's not. Look, I picked you out a really nice one."

"A massive one at that!" I said, studying its texture. It really was a nice and smooth cucumber. But I wasn't about to start fucking produce. I had to draw the line somewhere. But Ricardo convinced me that it was necessary for my future pleasure. (Ironically, the Publix slogan just so happens to be, "Publix: Where shopping is a pleasure.")

I assumed I would just take the cucumber home and experiment with it in private, but Ricardo begged me to let him handle it.

"I really don't feel comfortable with you doing this to me," I explained.

"Honey, it's not like I'm having sex with you. I promise I just want to help you."

I believed him, so I lay on the bed, removed my bottoms and let him begin my next sex lesson.

"First you need some lube," Ricardo said as he applied some K-Y jelly to the cucumber. I put some on myself to prepare for the insertion. I anticipated intense pain, but Ricardo was very gentle, taking plenty of time to gradually ease the cucumber inside of me, inch by inch.

"It's very important for the guy to take his time with you," Ricardo explained. "I'm so angry at Tim for pounding you the way he did. He didn't deserve you, and I want to make it right."

My relief and confidence grew the more the cucumber disappeared inside of me. *I can do this! I can handle a penis!*

It was almost as exciting as meeting President Bush when he came to Fort Stewart the next day to award the 3d Infantry Division with a Presidential Unit Citation, a very rare award and huge deal... but not as huge as being able to handle a penis for the first time.

A month later, Sam asked to set me up with a pilot named Chad. After explaining a few details about him, I realized that he and I technically met in the back of the Black Hawk that flew me to Baghdad after my shopping trip in Kuwait. (He had gone to Kuwait to obtain some helicopter parts for his air cavalry unit.) It also dawned on me that he was going through a divorce because I had processed the paperwork allowing him to return home early in order to deal with his "family emergency." His wife was leaving him.

"I don't want to deal with that kind of baggage," I explained.

"Don't worry about it. He's totally over it and is looking to have a lot of fun."

"Alright," I agreed, barely believing I had quickly gone from losing my virginity to my high school boyfriend to entertaining the idea of hooking up with a divorced guy. *Hopefully he has some experience under his belt.*

I donned a tiny orange tank, khaki miniskirt and the rhinestone stilettos that my Iraqi friend Mouyad gave me to meet Chad and his group of friends. We set out to a festive drag show. Two of the other guys were also hitting on me, but since they were from out of town, I decided to pay the most attention to Chad. He was cute with blond hair and blue eyes and looked much younger than his thirty years. He was lean and on the small side, standing at five feet ten, but I could tell that he was ripped after grabbing his leg on the dance floor. *I guess this is who I will probably end up sleeping with next,* I thought as we gyrated against each other to the fast beat.

At the end of the night, we pecked on the cheek, and our lips slightly grazed each other. We said our goodbyes and planned to go out again with the group the very next night. Having fun was on the top of everyone's agenda; we had to make up for lost time.

The group decided that our next adventure would be a strip club. I admitted that I had never been to one before (my brief stop at Café Risqué didn't count), so Chad immediately asked me to point out my favorite stripper and bought me a private lap dance with her.

I pushed my uneasiness aside. *I'm the new Laura. The new Laura is liberated and is totally cool with strip clubs and lap dances,* I told myself. *The new Laura likes wild and adventurous guys; I can do this.*

I followed the stripper into a private room fully enclosed with floor to ceiling windows. I liked how she was big boned with little makeup and a cute Catholic schoolgirl skirt. She almost looked out of place, youthful and innocent compared to the other strippers who had more sultry looks to them. She started dancing on me and chatting away, as if we were hanging out at a Starbucks. I tried to ignore the group looking at me, especially Chad. His eager glares made me self-conscious. So I asked the stripper about her life and her career ambitions. She loved telling me about the more famous clubs that she hoped to dance in one day. I wished her luck as she took off her bra and started slapping my face with her boobs. When she was finished, we hugged goodbye.

"That was so hot!" Chad chimed.

I silently congratulated myself for turning him on, not to mention the other guys in the group.

Later we made out for three hours in my car. He invited me inside his house, but I resisted. We joked that we looked like high schoolers, but remaining in the car was really exciting for me, like playing with forbidden fruit. After kissing my mouth hard for the first two hours, Chad began moving the zipper of my pants up and down with his mouth and promised to one day show me more tricks with his "talented mouth."

The next day Chad called and told me he was interested in seeing me again. "I don't play games," he said, "so I'm not going to avoid calling you and make you guess if I like you." I appreciated his candor and finally had the opportunity to learn a little more about the real Chad.

Even though our first encounters were all about partying, he let me in on a deeper side. He sounded intellectual and philosophical, with an impressive vocabulary. Chad also explained that he was emerging from a religiously repressed marriage, so he could relate to some of my experiences, or more accurately, my lack thereof. (Sam had let him in on some of my background.) I was impressed that he was a military badass with an education and had started taking online graduate courses. He also kept a journal during the war and hoped to write a book one day. *He's different from the other guys. Maybe this is a good idea,* I thought, as I agreed to come over in a few days and let him make me dinner.

I appreciated the romantic effort as I watched Chad stirring the pasta at his stove. I stared at him when he had his back turned to me, so I could better remember his features. Some of his appearance had eluded me since the night at the strip club. *He's cute, but that outfit has to go.*

After dinner Chad played a Damien Rice soundtrack and we danced. He started taking my clothes off, and we continued dancing, topless. Then he led me outside. He had a nice four-bedroom home that had no trace of his ex-wife. Since he had a privacy fence, we dared each other to get naked and giggled as we revealed ourselves to each other. Liberation felt amazing.

Then Chad led me to the bedroom where he continued the soundtrack and lit some candles. After more making out, he moved his head down between my legs. Within a few minutes I exploded into an intense orgasm. He repeated this pleasure three more times throughout the night.

I figured I should return the favor so I grabbed his penis in my hand. Fully erect, it was massive.

"This is going to hurt so badly!" I said, making him laugh. I knew we weren't going to have sex that night, but my statement made it known that this was the direction in which we would eventually head.

I proceeded to give Chad the best blowjob possible, marveling at his penis size. *It's amazing how much smaller he is than Tony, yet so much bigger,* I thought as I could only fit three quarters of it in my mouth. When he came I gently allowed his semen to fall onto his leg. *I should probably learn how to swallow if I'm going to be the very best.*

About a month later, when I told Chad that I wanted to learn how to give amazing head, he bought me flavored lube to camouflage the taste of his semen. He also started drinking pineapple juice, which seemed to make it less pungent. Between that, him coaching my technique, and my determination to become a sex goddess, in no time I was giving him the best blowjobs of his life, even better than his college girlfriend, Katarina! I felt proud.

Chad and I ended up having sex just six days after our very first night out. I begged him for it, and he made me assure him that I was ready. With lots of lube, he gingerly placed himself inside of me and slowly thrusted. It hurt, but only a little. He used extreme caution as he went a little deeper and faster. In the middle of the dull pain, I could actually feel a little pleasure. This gave me hope that sex would feel amazing one day. There was no way I was going to have an orgasm, so after fifteen minutes together, Chad asked if it would be OK for him to finish. I appreciated him placing my comfort above everything else and thanked him when we were done. Soon enough, I got the hang of sex.

A few months after we started dating, Chad's mother woke us up with a phone call at 6:00 a.m. on Sunday morning, December 13, 2003. "They got Saddam," she said so loudly, I could hear her heavy southern accent through the receiver Chad was holding. We turned on the news to watch the story unfold. It was surreal learning that he had been caught at all, but in a foxhole looking like a grimy, disheveled homeless man? I felt detached from the entire situation and almost felt sorry for him.

On the other hand, I was glad he was caught, because it might bring some closure to those who lost loved ones in the war. Saddam was an awful human being who deserved his fate. He would be executed on December 20, 2006, six months after I left the Army for good.

CHAPTER THIRTY-THREE

Chad and I continued dating and falling in love. It took a good year before sex stopped hurting altogether. Luckily my determination and focus seemed to pay off because Chad said I became the best he'd ever had. College was fun and wild for him, typical of most American guys, so I felt marvelous about my accomplishment.

Chad capitalized on my open-mindedness. His previous lovers were more reluctant and sometimes critical of his fantasies. Not me. I did everything I could to be the opposite of any repression in his past. I marveled at how quickly I went from an inexperienced virgin to a confident sexual woman. But when a West Pointer puts their mind to something, amazing feats can be accomplished!

Even though our Army assignments were taking us to different places (me to Tampa and Chad to Alabama), we were determined to stay together and make it work. I figured if we survived the distance, then we belonged together for good. So for a year, we saw each other every other weekend, making the six-hour drive for two nights of pure bliss, until the Army agreed to let me move to Alabama. Finally, we could start building a real future for us, with no more threats of geographic separation, as long as we didn't stay in the Army. But neither of us wanted that. The freedom of civilian life was too alluring.

Settling into domestic bliss was a little shaky, as our wild dynamic began to wear on my nerves. Among our friends, Chad and I were always known as the fun, adventurous, crazy and horny couple. It was obvious that our sex life dominated our identities, and we were proud. But at times it got out of hand for my comfort, especially when other couples wanted in on the fun.

Apparently swinging was a favorite pastime among a lot of military personnel, and I was missing out on all of the festivities. I first learned about this from Tony, who told me his wife, Amanda, was bisexual and that they liked to couple swap.

"She would be so attracted to you, Laura," he had said in Baghdad, trying to convince me that I needed to meet her. "I think you'll like her too. You're both really muscular and fun. Plus, she's in the Army too, so she totally gets you."

Tony extended the invitation again around the same time that Chad's friend, Bob, told him he and his wife were starting to dabble in couple swapping. Chad seemed intrigued and asked if I would be interested in experimenting with some of our more open friends. While it seemed intriguing and maybe a little exciting, something didn't sit right with me. But I didn't want to disappoint him by being too prude. I was liberated, after all. So after several conversations and deliberating, I agreed, but with one stipulation—absolutely no penetration.

Messing around with our friends sounded better in theory than it actually panned out in reality. I never knew when it would happen and seemed unable to shake a nervous sensation in the pit of my stomach. Every encounter started with awkward stares and gestures that even copious amounts of alcohol couldn't assuage. *When is the party really going to get started?* I worried. But I couldn't allow my true feelings to show.

In the midst of kissing and touching other people, I pushed aside guilt and tried to concentrate on making Chad happy and proud. This guilt had nothing to do religion or rules. I felt adequately removed from the shackles of Christian purity. But it still didn't feel right—every act felt forced and absent of the thrills of being at war. Instead of connecting, I was merely performing. I could fake a good performance, but soon I felt drained, and even bored with these acts that didn't stem from genuine desire and attraction. Sometimes when I looked over at Chad, I swore he seemed really out of his element, and perhaps a little sad. I hoped he would eventually tire of these charades, and instead, solely focus on me.

Outside of work, partying and our sexual escapades, Chad and I fell into a harmonious dynamic domestically. He cooked most of our meals; I managed our joint finances, including the mortgage of our new town house, and we both shared laundry and cleaning chores. He was still messier than my preference, but he explained that he would never be able to live up to my standards of cleanliness, and that our home didn't need to be West Point inspection ready. So we reached a compromise.

Sometimes I felt judged for cohabitating in Alabama without being married. I felt it the most when we met with a financial planner. He never came out and said anything against our union, and he had to give us credit for attempting to be a fiscally responsible couple, but I could feel the judgment seeping from his pores as he stared down at us through his beady reading glasses. He was old school Alabama, and in old school Alabama, couples get married before they live together.

It became increasingly difficult to live as a couple without being married. We feared our mortality most, suffering from hyper-vigilance about death. Chad and I worried what might happen to each other if one of us died, and we wanted to make sure that we were protected financially and legally. Even though we both had life insurance policies and wills with each other as the beneficiaries, we still didn't feel 100 percent protected. We also worried what might happen if only one of us found a civilian job and the other wouldn't be able to get health insurance if we weren't married.

"Maybe we should just get married," I suggested one Sunday night at the dinner table.

"OK," Chad agreed.

"We could elope in New York City," I offered, "since the diamond district has a ton of nice jewelry at wholesale prices." I had clearly thought this through, explaining that I wanted a wedding band with diamonds in it, since I wasn't interested in having an engagement ring.

"OK," Chad agreed again.

"I know," I said excitedly. "Wouldn't it be awesome if we could get tickets to see *The Daily Show with Jon Stewart* on the day we get married?"

"That would fucking kick ass!" Chad yelled.

"But if we're going to do it," I warned, "no more fooling around with our friends. I don't think a married couple should be doing that. We need to focus on just each other." I felt a weight lift off my chest expressing my wishes, but I worried he might think I was attempting to cut off his manhood. But we had recently witnessed the rapid deterioration of both Bob and his wife and Tony and Amanda, so we were seeing that swinging just wasn't conducive to a happily functioning marriage.

"OK, that's probably a good idea," Chad agreed, yet again.

Five days before we were scheduled to fly to New York, a health scare confirmed that we should be legally married. A while back, my Army doctor changed my birth control to the IUD, even though the manufacturer recommended against it for people who have never been pregnant. It never felt quite right; Chad could feel the strings (even though he wasn't supposed to), and I had developed an unusual pain in my left side whenever we had sex. So I had the IUD removed. Chad delighted in this being gone and had his way with me right after my doctor's appointment.

After one powerful thrust, I screamed in excruciating pain. It felt like something burst.

I took 800 mg of Ibuprofen and napped for three hours. A half hour after waking and still in pain, I fainted and then vomited. I rarely vomit and never faint, so Chad knew this was serious and took me to the emergency room. It took two days and a follow up doctor's visit to receive a diagnosis. At that point, my stomach had distended, and I was seven pounds heavier.

"I believe you had an ovarian cyst rupture," the doctor explained. "And based on your red blood cell count, you're hemorrhaging into your abdomen. I want to admit you to the hospital right away for emergency surgery."

Just before wheeling me into the operating room, the doctor handed me a clipboard.

"I need you to sign this disclosure, in case I have to remove your ovary."

I laughed at the irony. Chad had just gotten a vasectomy a few weeks prior. Neither of us wanted children.

"You can have it," I said. But the doctor was able to save it.

That night the charge nurse allowed Chad to spend the night with me, and I was released the next day.

"You're lucky I'm one of the cool nurses and am letting him stay with you tonight. Some of the other nurses here are really traditional, and they would only let him stay if he was your husband."

One week later, we stood before a justice of the peace in New York City's City Hall, saying our "I dos" in a ceremony that lasted forty-five seconds. Woody and Colleen were our witnesses. We just had sex earlier that morning. After a week of doctor-ordered abstinence post-surgery, Chad couldn't hold out any longer.

We ate our first meal as a married couple—a late lunch at a trendy Thai restaurant and then waited in line for *The Daily Show*. Stephen Colbert had recently launched his new show, and I was also able to score some tickets to *The Colbert Report*, so we would be seeing the live recordings of both shows back-to-back. Chad wore a nice suit, and I wore a beautiful floor length white satin dress with black lace overlay. It was December in New York, so we both had snazzy overcoats, and I wore black knee-high boots. Underneath, I had a desert camouflage garter on one leg and a penis garter on the other.

Jon Stewart conducted a meet and greet with the audience prior to the show's start. I raised my hand and announced that we had just gotten married. Jon took one long look at us.

"And you're here?" he asked, puzzled.

"Yes!" I answered. "We didn't want to be anywhere else."

"Interesting," he said. "When you're divorced twelve years from now and wondering what went wrong, remember this day, here with me," he joked. The audience erupted into laughter. I was beside myself in stitches. *Jon Stewart made fun of me on my wedding day. I will remember this blissful moment forever,* I imprinted into my memory. He was also predicting my divorce, but I knew in my heart that Chad and I would beat the odds. We had a bond unlike most others—our unique version of a family, in which we didn't take ourselves, or life, too seriously. "We're best friends who love each other's genitals!" Chad described us. And as best friends and lovers, we promised to fill the rest of our days with fun adventures because we lived in fear that those lives could easily be cut short by tragedy, something we were all too familiar with.

Little did we know that life was about to bring us some completely unexpected challenges, ones far more confusing to navigate than war, especially in transitioning to civilian life without any built-in support system. Chad was just days away from his official Army separation date, and I had just six months left on my obligation. But our future difficulties were far from our minds. It was time to celebrate newlywed bliss.

At the end of *The Daily Show* recording, when Jon Stewart bantered with Stephen Colbert, he gave us the best wedding gift imaginable. Jon announced to Stephen that he had a couple in the audience who had just gotten married three hours prior.

"So Stephen, I guess that makes me their foreplay!" Jon chimed.

As we all sat there, dying with laughter, Stephen chimed in, right on cue:

"Well, Jon, I guess that makes me their birth control!"

CHAPTER THIRTY-FOUR

November 2013
Newton, Massachusetts

"Laura, can you call me when you get a chance?" my Aunt Betsy texts me. I don't think much of it and wait until the next day to call her back. As soon as I call, she puts my Uncle Dominick (my mother's brother) on the phone.

"Have you heard anything?" he asks.

"No, what do you mean?"

"I spoke with your mother," he says. I freeze. He tries to avoid speaking with her at all costs and is well aware of my estrangement with her. *This can't be good*, I think.

"What's going on?" I reluctantly ask.

"It's your father."

I know what he is about to say.

"Your mother said she thinks he's dying."

In my mind, I have played out this scenario at least a thousand times, my father's last days on Earth. I have questioned whether or not I would even bother to attend his funeral. I fantasized about attending and approaching the podium at the front of the church, incognito in a wig, and unleashing diatribes about the monstrosities of his evil soul, allowing everyone he's ever conned to know the truth once and for all. But as eleven and a half years of our estrangement have passed, I am apathetic toward any semblance of revenge and simply assume I won't bother. *His death will just be another day crossed off on my calendar.*

But now it's here. Completely unexpected. And despite all of the daddy issues I have worked on with my therapist, Jack, over the past three years, my father isn't on the forefront of my mind. It's been a hell of a year, and I'm in the midst of dealing with a lot of other shit.

I have been divorced for five months. Chad and I separated a year before that but waited a year before making it official to avoid acting impulsively. Despite us expressing the desire to remain friends when we initially split, since we felt more like siblings than lovers after six years of marriage, we are completely out of each other's lives. He quickly found love again, and I remain single (but not celibate) after extricating myself from the world's shortest-lived, yet still tragic affair (the sordid details of which you can perhaps read about in future writings). Suffice it to say Rielle Hunter and I have a few things in common.

I also feel like I'm hanging on by a thread in my new job as a technology platform architect in clinical research. The bureaucratic work dynamics lend to messy technologies and processes, and I practically kill myself trying to fix shit and prove I deserve my nice salary. I must prevail. I have fought so hard to make it this far in the corporate world after a less-than-stellar transition from military life, seven years prior. Most of my previous employers didn't give a shit that I went to West Point or earned my MBA while simultaneously surviving a war, and they made me prove myself all over again. I have to make this job work. I need to stick around a company for at least a little while before giving up on it, in the hopes of finding something better. *Maybe it's me*, I realize, accepting that perhaps I'm not cut out for corporate life.

And I crashed my new BMW just last week. It barely had any miles since I have spent a majority of the past few months working in Europe, seizing any opportunity to personally connect with my French and British colleagues. I miss them dearly and hate being back in the U.S. My gorgeous new condo in Newton is of no comfort either, as I've barely unpacked and settled in. The neighborhood feels more foreign than where I stayed in France for two months. I'm anything but grounded. And now Daddy is dying.

I wonder if it's fate that my friend Jane is getting promoted to lieutenant colonel at MacDill Air Force Base in Tampa, and I have a plane ticket to go see her in a week and a half. I'll be so close to my parents, but will I bother to go see them?

"What are you going to do?" my uncle asks me.

"I have no idea," I respond. I need to talk to my therapist.

I love therapy. I've always regretted not having the opportunity to become a psychologist myself, but at the very least, my fascination and appreciation of psychology allow me to benefit tremendously from therapy. It also helps that I now see a psychotherapist in private practice, and I've been able to see him every week for the past three years. In the four years prior to that, I only dabbled in therapy provided by the VA because just as soon as I started to make progress, the VA would assign that therapist to another position, or they would leave the VA system altogether. But now I don't have to worry about starting over again. Luckily I have private insurance. The co-pay is steep, but it's a necessary investment. Jack is worth every penny.

Naturally any skilled therapist should be able to relate to any of his patients, but I feel as if Jack is perfect for me. I'm grateful that another therapist who the VA assigned to evaluate me when I moved to Boston suggested I see Jack, and that Jack accepted me as a patient. But I feel more like a valued friend than a clinical patient. And that's what I've needed more than anything. Someone who genuinely cares about my well-being and who also isn't afraid to call me a knucklehead when I'm screwing up.

I love that Jack calls me out on my shit when I need it. He's not like those notorious therapists who answer questions by asking another question. He gives it to me straight, and he's not afraid to use swear words. One of the most therapeutic things to ever come out of his mouth was, "Laura, your family is fucking crazy!" I can almost guarantee he's taught case studies about me and that my family history is floating around in papers distributed among students at The Boston Psychoanalytic Society and Institute, where he teaches.

Jack is brilliant and intellectual, financially successful and highly regarded in his field. He's on faculty at Harvard Medical School. He also loves BMWs and good wine. What impresses me most is that he's married to a psychiatrist who also practices out of their home. *Any male psychologist who is married to a female psychiatrist gets extra bonus points in my book!*

Pouring my heart out to Jack every week has been my lifeline. I don't make any major decisions without discussing them with him first. I marvel at how he's able to keep track of the cast of characters who enter (and sometimes exit) my life. Lately I feel like a soap opera, and he remembers every episode. He's the only person whose opinion I truly trust and cherish, so I update him on the sudden news about my father.

We agree I need more data before coming to any conclusions. That's a huge thing I've learned from Jack—to allow things to evolve organically before making any rash decisions—and to pay attention to my feelings and how they may change during that process.

I don't exactly know what my father's diagnosis is. My uncle has only spoken to my mother once. It sounds terminal; he used the word myeloma. But we have yet to know his exact condition or how much time he has left. And how can I be sure that my mother isn't being melodramatic? In the years leading up to our estrangement, my father often acted as if he was going to die. Is this another false alarm? I need to dig around and get some answers first-hand, but I know this will be impossible if I still want to avoid speaking to my parents. Maybe there's some way I can call the hospital and pretend as if I have authorization to access his medical records. I work in this field, though, so I know the chances are slim. But I have to try.

Before I do anything else, I need to tell my Aunt Irene (my father's sister) what's going on. She doesn't have a cell phone, and no one picks up her home line, so I send her a Facebook message to call me, explaining that it's urgent. She hasn't seen her brother in seven years, not since he physically assaulted her badly enough to land her in the emergency room. All because he wanted *all* of their childhood photos and didn't want to share.

Aunt Irene isn't sure how she wants to proceed after learning about my father's condition. She knows my mother doesn't like her and that her presence is the last thing my mother would want at this point. So that helps her to decide she will momentarily lay low and not try to make contact. She's happy I'm coming to Florida soon, and we agree to meet up. I also promise to keep her posted on everything I learn.

I Google the number to my father's hospital and take several deep breaths before picking up my phone. I try to imagine how the conversation will play out. I accept that my attempt at obtaining information will probably be rejected, and I will likely hang up, no more informed than I already am. I am prepared to have to make a decision without more data. My fingers shake as I tap the numbers to make the call.

"Good afternoon, operator, how may I direct your call?"

"Yes, my father is a patient, in oncology, I believe, and I'm trying to get some information," I quickly respond, hoping I've guessed the correct department.

"I'll connect you now. One moment please."

"Nurse's desk," the next person on the line says.

"Um, yes," I pause, "my name is Laura Westley, and I'm trying to get some information on my father, William." I say. "I live in Boston and am trying to figure out when I need to come to Florida. Is there someone I could talk to about his condition?"

"Hold one moment please."

I'm surprised by this response, that I'm not immediately dismissed. *Who are they getting?* I wonder. I remain on hold for several minutes. It's torturous. I go through the next lines in my head, imaging myself pleading with a doctor to get his formal diagnosis. I still remain on hold. I want to fucking yell.

"We'll get your mother right now," the same voice comes back on the line.

FUCK! This is not supposed to happen. "No—wait!" I say, but it's too late. They reroute my call before ever hearing my response.

I could hang up. I need to hang up. But something stops me from hanging up. Before I can consider my next move, another voice comes on the line.

"Hello, this is Phyllis."

I hear my mother's voice for the first time in eleven and a half years.

"Hi Phyllis, this is your daughter, Laura Westley." I sound a little silly, purposely formal, but I can't think of anything else to say.

"Hi Laura!" my mother responds, sounding tired, but very happy to hear my voice.

I keep it professional. I just need answers, not reconciliation. So I let her know I want details and answers. She complies without hesitation. She gives me an account of everything that has happened since my father first went into the hospital a week prior. I tell her I'm taking notes, and she slows down a little to make sure I've captured everything. My father has both leukemia and multiple myeloma. Not only is he too sick for chemo, they've just decided to stop his dialysis treatments. Now it's all about comfort and quality of life. It almost sounds like my mother wants reassurance, that she's making the right decisions, that it's OK to stop fighting. This is his third bout with cancer (the colon cancer from years earlier later metastasized to his lungs). I've always expected my father to die young, so I tell my mother I agree with her choices. She sounds grateful, and I let her know that I appreciate her candor.

"Of course, Laura. I love you."

Shocked, I can only think of one response. "Thank you," I quietly muster.

I can tell she understands my subtext—*I'm still very angry, and don't think for a second that I'm going to let you sweep the past under the rug.*

"Do you want me to wake up your father so you can speak to him?"

"No, please don't," I implore.

"So what about you?" she asks.

I tell her I live in Boston. In that moment, I realize that I do want to see her when I'm in Florida. But I don't say anything. Not yet. I don't want to get her hopes up. I could still change my mind. So I let her know I'll be in touch. She sounds relieved, knowing that she will hear my voice again.

A few days later I spend Thanksgiving in New York with Colleen, Woody, Uncle Dominick and Aunt Betsy. I call my mother and learn that my father has rapidly deteriorated in the past few days. Luckily her friend Dawn is at the hospital. I've known Dawn since I was a baby. She's been a loyal friend to my mother all of these years, despite witnessing her submission to my father's abuse. I know I could never remain friends with someone who refuses to walk away from that kind of situation and am in awe of Dawn's tolerance. Dawn, very sensitive about our family dynamic, respected my decision to leave my parents, and she had me visit her before I left for Iraq, so she could wish me well. I know she won't bullshit me just so I come and see my parents. Plus, she's a nurse, so I want to hear what she has to say.

Unfortunately, or fortunately, however one would look at it, I'm stoned out of my mind. After drinking some delicious wine (Uncle Dominick spoils me with the nice stuff), he shared his bowl with me—and he smokes some strong shit! I only had two puffs, but I am completely out of it when I call. I wonder what Dawn is thinking, as I ask pointed questions in a much slower cadence than how I usually speak.

Dawn tells me my father is being transported to hospice.

"How much time do you think he has?" I ask.

"It's hard to say. But not much at all."

"Are we talking weeks, or days?"

"Definitely days."

"I'm supposed to be in Florida on Thursday. Is that soon enough?"

"I don't think so. If you want to see him, you should come as soon as you can."

I decide to change my plane ticket to Sunday. *I'll call JetBlue first thing tomorrow, when I'm not completely fucked up.*

Suddenly Dawn announces that she's handing the phone over—to my father. With reflexes operating in slow motion, I don't have a chance to protest.

"Hello?" my father asks, in a foggy, medicated voice.

We're both drugged up. This should be interesting, I think, my stomach in knots.

"Hello!" I fake enthusiasm, made easier by the marijuana. And the only thing I can think of next, is to rely on my sense of humor and deliver him the very comedy routine I created in his honor.

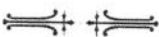

When I first started writing *War Virgin* in 2009, it read like a cross between an angry Alanis Morissette rant and a psychology doctoral dissertation on how my father, West Point and the Army fucked up my life. But whenever I gathered with friends and shared stories of my past, I had them in stitches. I knew my life had been absurd, and I had a natural, entertaining way of regaling people with my stories.

"You need to do this on a stage with a microphone!" my friend Josh told me.

"What do you mean? How would I do that?"

A year later, I enrolled in a comedy-writing class in an attempt to learn how to make my stories on the page match the way they were told in conjunction with a glass of Cabernet or bourbon in my hand. The scrawny hipster instructor criticized me for being a storyteller in lieu of a stand-up comedian, and I told him that was exactly the point. So instead of signing up for his intermediate class, I Googled "Boston storytelling" and stumbled on a workshop given by a lady who would become one of my dearest friends, supporters and fans.

As soon as I met Andrea in a downtown Boston bar, I knew she saw something special in me, and I wanted to become a part of her life. In her mid-fifties and standing at just five feet tall, Andrea's bubbling personality and knack for telling funny stories in her thick Boston accent gave me a sense of coming home. She immediately gravitated to my mission of sharing the raw, unadulterated and often naughty truth about my family, West Point and Army life.

Besides teaching me how to tell a good five-minute story for the sake of her story slam competitions, Andrea insisted that I piece them all together to create a one-woman show. She helped put *War Virgin* on the Boston comedy map and even hooked me up with mentions in *The Boston Globe*. Her support has been essential to me discovering and developing my creative and artistic side.

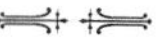

"I'm a recovered Jesus addict!" I declare to my father.

"You are?" he asks, intrigued?

"Yes," I continue. "When I say Jesus addict, I mean pure and innocent virgin, but when I say I'm recovered, it means all of my Christian friends now think that I'm a dirty whore!"

He laughs. His sense of humor hasn't changed one bit.

"Do you remember what you told me about my sparkle?"

"Yes!" he answers, in hysterics.

I'm in disbelief the phone conversation is going so well.

"Well, according to what I learned in church, sex means penile penetration. So I was perfectly justified dry-humping Tim Morgan in the front seat of his mother's Buick!"

His roaring laughter continues. "Why are you admitting this to me Laura?"

"It's hilarious, isn't it?"

"Yes!"

"And remember what you told me about birth control? The only thing I need is an aspirin. Stick it between my legs and don't let it drop!"

"You're so funny!" he slurs.

I'm not sure what else to say, so I start singing "Time to Say Goodbye," my favorite opera song. I begin bawling in the middle of it. It doesn't seem like he can tell. Aunt Betsy stands nearby, making sure I'm OK. She knows I'm stoned, but I also sense a lot of sympathy coming from her.

I regain my composure and tell my father it's been fun chatting with him. He sounds tired and ready for a nap, so this is a good point to ask him to pass the phone to my mom.

"I love you, Laura," he says.

"Thank you," is all I'm willing to say back.

I now have the data I need. I'm going to see my parents in two days.

CHAPTER THIRTY-FIVE

December 2013
New Port Richey, Florida

When I walk through the doors of the hospice center and lock eyes with my parents, my outfit will need to make a statement. Several statements actually: success, confidence, strength and beauty. But most of all, I want it to make them feel intense regret. Regret for missing out on the life of such a capable, fascinating daughter. Regret for never loving me enough, but despite this neglect, I still turned out pretty amazing (even if I don't feel amazing at the moment). So I select a clingy, colorful animal print Max and Cleo brand sundress (which works perfectly for this warm December) and sparkly silver Michael Kors high-heel sandals. I'm not just going to walk into hospice. I'm going to make a grand entrance.

After arriving in Tampa and renting a car, I pull into an empty parking lot to change into my getup and apply more makeup. I think I look stunning but am still anxious. I can't believe this is happening. It feels more like I'm watching a fictitious movie instead of experiencing my real life. I continue driving toward my home town, a place I've managed to avoid almost completely since I graduated from high school, even though I have been back near the area multiple times to visit my aunt and cousins.

I drive up to the hospice center, relieved it's a nice-looking building with pretty landscaping. Despite any hatred I've ever felt toward my father, it would make me really sad to watch him die in a dump. Even though my parents made me suffer more than anyone should have to endure, I don't want them to suffer. Many times before drifting off to sleep, I've imagined how poor they were when I left them and hoped they figured out a way to make ends meet a little better. Uncle Dominick told me they were able to purchase a home with some inherited money from Italy, and that made me feel better. I guess this shows there's still some love for my parents buried deep beneath the layers of stone walls surrounding my heart.

I park the car and feel intense dread and anxiety, but also a twinge of curiosity. I text my friend, Claire, "I'm here, waiting in the parking lot, but I don't want to go inside." She reassures me that I got this. She's right. If there's anyone who can rise to any occasion, it's certainly me. No more fucking around. It's time to conquer these demons and put them to rest (literally and figuratively).

I call my father's room to let my mom know I'm outside. She says she will meet me out front. I walk toward the building, faking confidence, and she's already there, sitting on a bench next to the entrance. She looks older and puffier, like she's been crying and not sleeping. She's definitely gained weight, but she doesn't look overweight, especially for fifty-nine years old. She's just not skinny as she used to be. Her clothes are frumpy and faded. She used to be fashionable in my youth but started to let herself go when we ran out of money. It seems this hasn't changed.

"Oh my God, you're all grown up!" my mom says when I approach her.

"Yeah, I'm in my mid-thirties," I respond, sitting down next to her.

We sit in silence for a moment, and I take it all in. Thankfully it's a gorgeous, sunny day, and the warmth is a nice reprieve from the frigid Boston air I just left. I always feel more alive in the sunshine, and right now, more than ever, I need all the help I can get. It's just so weird to be sitting here with my mom, like nothing ever happened. I don't think she's going to acknowledge the elephant in the room, so to speak, so I just go along with whatever she says. My mom explains that these are my father's last days. He's definitely dying. I accept her words, and she seems calmer, happier to have me there.

"Let's go in to see your father."

I practically tiptoe into his room, my heart pounding louder than my footsteps. Immediately I am relieved to find him fast asleep in a blue recliner, hooked up to an IV. It's like nothing has changed. He always slept in a blue recliner at home, head canted to the side. Granted, he looks a bit older and more discolored, with just a little less hair, but he doesn't look any closer to death than he did eleven and a half years ago. My mom and I sit on the couch, staring at him. I'm no longer afraid. He's helpless, and I know he can't hurt me. Plus, I can easily escape in my rental car if need be. In uncomfortable situations, I always have an escape route planned, just in case.

My father wakes up about thirty minutes later but doesn't notice me. My mom explains that sometimes he's pretty out of it, so she asks if I'll walk up to him with her.

"Billy, this is Laura," my mom says gently.

It takes him a minute to register her words. He stares at me, and then suddenly realizes who I am.

"Damn, you look great!" is the first thing out of his mouth.

Oh my God. I think my father thinks I'm hot, is my first thought. *I'll need to text that to my friends.* I want to laugh.

"Wow, you look incredible!" he repeats.

"Thank you."

"Look at your arms! Do you work out?"

I laugh. "I do get a lot of comments about my arms. I actually don't work out as much as I used to," I explain. "I run and do yoga, but I look like I'm in better shape than I'm in because I'm on a really strict diet, and it makes my muscles stick out more. I can't eat gluten or lactose." I refrain from explaining that this is most likely from getting dysentery in Baghdad.

A singing chorus of elderly Salvation Army volunteers enters the room. They sing, "Hark the Herald Angels Sing" in high shrills, attempting to spread some Christmas cheer. The way my parents seem to get into it makes me realize they are still devout Christians. After they finish the song, the chorus leader asks my father if he has any requests.

"Do you have any Jewish songs?" I blurt out. I can't miss this opportunity to fuck with my father and his denial of how Jewish he is.

"Um, probably not," the choir director answers politely.

"Well my dad's half Jewish, so if you could sing "Dreidel, Dreidel, Dreidel," I think he would love that."

"Laura!" my mom half yells, half laughs, feigning embarrassment. My dad is laughing right along with me. I know my mom thinks my request is hilarious, even though my father has always downplayed how Jewish he is. Growing up, he always told me he was a quarter Jewish and that I was an eighth Jewish, but my Aunt Irene swears that she and my dad are half Jewish. She also set the record straight on a lot of other family lore, including the fact that my parents were "doing it like rabbits" before they got married and that my father was married once before marrying my mother.

"I'm sorry, but I'm afraid we don't know that song," the choir director informs me.

"Ah, that's too bad," I say with a big smile on my face.

"But we can sing something else," he offers, and my father asks for "Amazing Grace."

I decide to sing along, and everyone is blown away by how good I sound. So far, I'm nailing this reconciliation with my parents. Then I decide to throw myself into full entertainment mode. Hospice is boring, and I don't know what else to do.

"I have more songs I can sing for you," I announce when the choir leaves the room.

"Oh yeah?" my dad asks.

"Yeah, in fact, I didn't want to say this right off the bat, but I'm actually Lady Gaga."

"Huh?"

"No you're not!" my mom interjects.

"Yeah I am!" I insist.

At this point we're all laughing again.

"OK maybe not, but I still have a Lady Gaga song that I want to sing for you."

I cue up my laptop to play the karaoke sound track of "You and I" and do Lady Gaga proud, modifying a few of the phrases to reflect our personal story.

It's been a long time since I came around
Been a long time but I'm back in town
This time I'm not leaving without you.
You taste like whiskey when you kiss me, oh
I'd give anything again to be your baby doll
This time I'm not leaving without you.

Somethin', somethin' about this place
Somethin' 'bout lonely nights and my kisses on your face.
Somethin', somethin' about my New Port Richey dad
Yeah something about, Daddy, you and I.

"Laura, that was incredible!" my dad tells me when I'm finished. "I should have been your talent manager!"

Ah, *there's* the regret I wanted from him.

Each night, I stay with my cousin Jason (Aunt Irene's son) and his wife, Annie. They provide me with a safe sanctuary where I update them on the day's events over glasses of wine. Their sarcasm and understanding of the situation keep me sane and laughing.

I return to hospice the next morning and find several people visiting. Shockingly, my parents have a lot of friends, especially my mother. *When did she become so popular?* I wonder. Many of them are from the elementary school I attended—her place of employment for the past eighteen years. They're funny and cool, which is even more difficult to fathom. Based on some of their conversations, jokes and gossip, it seems as if maybe my parents have mellowed out a bit in their older age.

My father seems more out of it than yesterday. He's sleeping more. Now that the initial shock of reconciliation is over, I become a little bored. I volunteer to make a grocery run and bring back to my mother delicious food that she appreciates. I know she hasn't been eating much since my father's diagnosis a few weeks ago, and she refuses to leave his side. She's made her bed on the couch in his room. It's like a cute studio apartment, adorned with a Christmas tree and several poinsettias.

The following day is more of the same, only even more sleeping. We're waiting for him to die, but there's no guessing when this will happen. The doctor explains he will die of renal failure, and that it will most likely be sudden. "He could be talking to you, and out of nowhere, his kidneys will stop, and he will be gone."

That evening, in a subconscious way, I try to help speed along the process. When my mom and I are in front of his recliner, watching him sleep, I whip out my laptop and play the instrumental version of "Time to Say Goodbye." *It will be nice to sing this to him when I'm not completely stoned*, I think. I actually have been smoking a little weed with Aunt Irene in the parking lot, in an attempt to chill the fuck out and also be a little rebellious. Earlier I did it outside, right on the bench by the entrance.

"Be careful, they're not pot-friendly here like they are in Boston!" my mom warns. "The Pasco County police could arrest you!"

I laugh, almost wishing they would try to arrest me, but more so, because I can't believe this conversation is transpiring with my mother. She doesn't care that I smoke weed. Only that I don't get caught.

I sing the "Time to Say Goodbye" opera, hoping its words resonate with my father, willing him to let go of his life on Earth and die to beautiful Italian music, Italy being his mother's homeland. My mom seems convinced it's his time to go. Tears are flowing down her face. She kneels before him and prays. I keep singing. It's the only thing I know how to do. I haven't prayed in years, and I don't feel like starting now. He still hangs on, so I guess I'll try again tomorrow.

On Wednesday, he seems really uncomfortable, almost in agony. He's starting to have repetitive tremors, and he's even more out of it than before. I can tell he's still fighting to hold on. I'm prompted to get serious with him.

I place a chair next to his recliner and sit down. I reach over and start rubbing his arm, hoping that my touch will help ease some of his pain. When he shakes, I calmly rest my hand over his arm, hoping he feels some semblance of stability.

"Listen, you don't have to fight this anymore. I know you're trying to fight this. You can let go now."

My mother inconspicuously watches me from the couch with her friend, Barbara. They're curious but don't want to interrupt me.

"I'm here. You don't have to worry about anything anymore. I've got your back." I repeat myself a few times, hoping the message resonates with him. I continue stroking his arm. It feels cold and hard, and it's yellow. *I hope he goes soon,* I think to myself. *He's suffering too much.*

"Trust me, your legacy will live on," I assure him. *Yeah will it ever!* I think, picturing my website and YouTube channel, where he's the source of much of its comedic content. Since he laughed at all of the jokes I made about him, I assume his laughter connotes some kind of retroactive blessing. He doesn't need to know about my public platform and social media outlets, plus he's too far gone now. Still, if he were conscious enough for me to show him, I know he would initially be mortified, but then would think *War Virgin* is ingenious, brilliant and hilarious.

"And you don't need to worry about Mommy," I tell him. "I make a shit ton of money! So I can take care of her," I joke, which ignites raucous laughter from both my mom and Barbara.

"In all seriousness, though, please know that you can stop fighting this. Nod your head if you can hear me and understand me."

My father becomes more alert than he's been in the past several hours and nods his head. We have an understanding. I don't have anything else to say except one thing.

"I love you, Daddy." I kiss his cheek.

I get up and tell my mom that I really want to go have dinner with my friend Jane and her family. I've already missed some of her pre-promotion festivities the past few nights, and I'm ready to go see her.

"But you know, Laura, this could be it. Are you sure you want to go?" my mom urges me.

"Yes, I'm aware that this could be it. But I'm OK with that. I'm ready."

"OK, if you say so."

I give her a hug and kiss and say goodbye, then walk over to my father for one more kiss.

"I love you Daddy," I say again. Then I whisper the infamous memoriam of West Point, "Be thou at peace."

On my way to dinner I stop at the local CVS to fill a Valium prescription. When I get back to my car, Katy Perry's "Roar" is playing on the radio, and I get a text from my mom's friend, Barbara.

"Your father just died."

I immediately head back to Hospice.

The chaplain's room, located right next to my father's room, is swarming with all of my mom's friends. The scene reminds me of an Army emergency alert roster activation. He only died fifteen minutes ago, and they're all congregated here, full of love, comfort and support. I realize this won't be the case when I return to Boston.

I crave some alone time with my father, before he's cleaned up and taken away to a funeral home to be cremated. I return to his room and find him in his usual reclined position, with his head canted to the side. He looks so peaceful. I can't believe he's dead. I want to soak it all in. It's so tragic and glorious, all at once. I climb onto the hospital bed and rest in a meditative state. I feel more connected to him now more than ever. I snap a selfie of us. I want to remember this profoundly complicated moment forever.

A nurse comes in to let me know they need to get him ready for transport soon. Some of my mom's friends come in to say their final goodbyes. Then I ask for one last moment alone. Now is the time to say what I really need to say. I couldn't say it before; he was too drugged up to understand. The previous night, before singing the Italian opera, I asked him if he had anything he needed forgiveness for, and he merely slurred a confused, "Why? Did I do anything wrong?" I realized his mind was too far gone to discuss the past and get an apology that's been years overdue. I would just have to accept letting things be. But now is a perfect time to say what's on my heart, and I would be remiss if I keep my mouth shut.

I go into drill sergeant mode and start hazing my father's spirit, like he's a bad private in basic training.

"If reincarnation is real, then you need to listen very carefully to me!" I picture his spirit floating just above our physical heads and coming to attention.

"You're dead now, and someone is going to be waiting for you. Maybe it's Nana. And I'm sure she has a lot to say. You will probably go over what you did in this lifetime, and a lot of it wasn't good. You were a bad soul. But you can fix that. You need to fix that. You must fix it. You better not come back on this earth again until you do. Listen to what Nana or your other guardian angels have to say." I choke on my words, tears streaming down my face. I breathe through the sobs, knowing this is the last mission I need to do to right all of the wrong he ever caused. Relief begins to wash over me.

A nurse peeks her head in, ready to prepare him for transport. I'm ready to let go. I step out of the room until he's on a gurney and cleaned up, and then I return, capturing one last glance of my father. My mother sobs over his body as he's wheeled away. Wednesday, December 4, 2013.

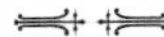

I describe my father's death to my energy healer, Maura. Maura is a gentle, yet powerful spirit who I've been seeing near my home in Newton for the past year. I tell her how it felt as if I granted my father permission to die and then how I hazed his soul right after he died. I consider Maura my spiritual guru, and she's expanding my faith, giving me hope to believe in something again. She gives intuitive readings, tuning in to energy fields and listening for angelic guidance. She also helps to balance the chakras through Reiki. Some may consider this bullshit, but I feel comforted, enlightened and inspired whenever I receive one of Maura's energy healings. She explains that archangels are entities that comfort the dying and help them pass into the afterlife. Maura believes I've just essentially served as my father's archangel, and it's a beautiful gift that only the strongest of souls can provide someone. She tells me if I want to learn more about this, I can start reading "The Tibetan Book of Living and Dying."

Several months later I'm in Florida again, and I have a session with Raine, a psychic reader. In the middle of my reading, she suddenly stops, sensing a disruptive spirit. Raine then tells me she's also a medium, and someone wants our attention.

"Did you have someone close to you die recently?" Raine asks.

"Yes, my father."

"He's apologizing."

"What?"

"He's terribly sorry for everything he ever did to hurt you. Not only that, but he's here to thank you for what you did. And he wants to let you know that he's transitioned on into the afterlife. He's doing well and is comfortable, and he really appreciates you."

I want to believe that it's really him, but I also know this could be a generic message, and I imagine that many mediums have relayed similar sentiments to their clients. But the next thing she says can't be made up.

"Well this is strange. He keeps saying, 'That's my boy!' Does that make any sense to you?"

"Oh—that is 100 percent my father!"

In uncanny timing, I'm still able to attend Jane's promotion ceremony, the original reason for my Florida trip, just two days after my father dies. Seeing her and all of her family who flew in from San Francisco (my adopted family when I lived in San Francisco from 2006 to 2008) is exactly what I need at this moment. They are supportive, loving and fun. I'm able to take my mind off everything for 24 hours, and my Lady Gaga song makes a reemergence at the karaoke party after her formal ceremony.

The funeral home won't cremate my father until my mother comes up with the cash in full. My father has left her with hefty credit card debt and no savings. Luckily there's a small amount of life insurance she will receive, but not for a few weeks. She's facing a dilemma that I quickly solve. My mother won't accept my cash as a gift, but instead, as a loan, and she immediately pays me back when she receives his life insurance settlement. I'm impressed my mother is proud and autonomous and independent and doesn't want my money. She's determined to fight her financial woes on her own.

My mother says she wants to wait for a memorial service: "Maybe in the spring, after the dust has settled." My cousin, Jason, and Annie host a family barbeque that Saturday, which ends up being the only gathering we ever really have. The memorial service never happens. And my father's remains won't be available until well after I'm back in Boston. There's not enough closure.

It's strange visiting my parents' home. It's not the same one I grew up in, but it's a close resemblance, with the same furniture and voluminous shelves containing books on subjects my father loved reading: astronomy, literature, psychology, Christianity and the dangers of Satanism. In his bedroom I find a large box with at least forty different prescription pill bottles, including Oxycodone, Methadone, Ambien and Testosterone. There are also some needles in there. My mother is embarrassed at my discovery and quickly dismisses my confirmation of his drug problem.

On Sunday, the day before I head back to Boston, Jason takes me to a Buccaneers game. It's my first wedding anniversary, post-divorce. The killer seats he scores, the radiant sunshine, the cheering crowd and winning score, not to mention the three Crown and Cokes I drink, take my mind off of this tremendous year of loss after loss.

Luckily I leave my mom in good hands. Her friends are committed to rallying around her. She's figuring out her finances. In many ways, I think she's relieved to not have to stand vigil as a result of my father's frail health anymore. I'm relieved that she has a strong, supportive community; it's something I know will be painfully absent when I return to Boston. Before I leave Florida, as I'm driving my mom home from an outing, she begs me to never leave her ever again.

"I'll follow any of your rules, Laura. Just tell me what I need to do."

"You don't need to do anything," I explain. "Life and relationships aren't about rules."

"OK, whatever you say."

I realize it will take a while to decondition her from living under my father's rule.

"Well, there is one thing you could do," I suggest.

"OK, yes, anything!"

I pull into a CVS parking lot, the same one I was at when I learned of my father's death, and ask my mom to do me just one favor.

"If you really want me back in your life for good, you'll go inside of this CVS and buy me a box of condoms."

"Laura!"

"You heard me. Here's a twenty-dollar bill." I start laughing.

"Anything but that," my mom pleads and then joins in on the laughter when she calls my bluff, although I wouldn't have stopped her from buying the condoms if she went in.

In the week that I've been on bereavement leave, my job assignment and manager change. With this change, there's no more need to make a presence at the office, so I start working from home every day. While my mom has been able to throw herself back into work, I'm not even sure what I'm supposed to be doing. When I log back into my work computer, there are only two emails from colleagues expressing their condolences. And only two friends text to make plans to see me in the near future. I start to think that if I were to die, no one would notice.

CHAPTER THIRTY-SIX

Super Bowl Sunday, 2014, will always be a day of infamy for me.

I wake in my Newton condo on this morning after vividly dreaming about the helicopter crash in Iraq. In the dream, I'm trying to honor the memories of the six fallen soldiers. I'm begging people to remember them, to talk about them, to extract something meaningful from their deaths.

I'm frozen in my bed, much like the blistering winter ground outside. It's a position I've become familiar with. Numb. Unable to move. I spend many days like this, even doing my conference calls and emails from the confines of my bed, a place that keeps me safe from external sources of pain, but not a place that shields me from the unbearable pain that permeates my mind and heart.

My brain plays the narrative of my life like a movie reel. I review my childhood. I see myself at war again. I watch my divorce. It concludes with me seeing myself in this bed, with no one around, no one aware of how much I yearn for human contact, for someone to care enough to be here and make the pain go away, just by a comforting hug, a sympathetic understanding that no one should have to live the life I've been forced to live. I crave a life do-over. I've written this in my journal numerous times. I even recently texted it to a friend, but she didn't respond. I don't think she understood, and I didn't have the energy to explain it.

I want to go to yoga. I should go to yoga. The instructor gives such joyful hugs. I could use one of her hugs right now. But a part of me is insanely jealous of how happy she is. How she has a loving husband and family and friends all around her, and she gets to work in a career that she loves. She's happy, and I want to be happy like her, but I don't think it's in my life cards for me to ever really be happy.

I continue lying in bed.

If I want to put myself out of my misery, I know I must do something. I think about my friend, Christine, who tried to end her life with carbon monoxide poisoning in her car. But I can't do that. The garage next to my condo is actually deeded to my upstairs neighbor, and I lease a space from her. It would be horrible to put her in that predicament, to make her be the one to find me in the first place. I need to do something less intrusive and messy.

I don't want to swallow a bunch of pills. I don't really have anything besides ibuprofen and birth control pills. I only have a few Valium, not enough to do any damage. I also don't want to do irreversible damage to my organs if I live, and chances are I would live. My digestive system is bad enough from the Army; I can't afford for it to be any worse. So pills are out of the question.

I Google "best methods for suicide" and suicide hotline numbers appear at the top of my search list. I scroll down and find an intriguing article that matter-of-factly details the various methods people might choose to end their lives. I read about asphyxiation. Between Christine's attempt and the fact that I tied a shoelace around my neck when I was thirteen, asphyxiation resonates with me. Effective. No mess. But I have to get out of bed to get a bag.

I muster just enough energy to go to the hall closet and retrieve a plastic shopping bag. It's from City Sports of Boston. I bought a few sports bras here just the week prior. If only this bag knew how it would be repurposed…

I come back to bed, lie back down, get comfortable, clutch my favorite childhood doll (which I sleep with most nights post-divorce) and apologize to her for what I'm about to do and what she is about to witness. I place the bag over my head.

I try to hold out for as long as I can, but I remove the bag and catch my breath when it becomes too much to bear. So I try again. When I run out of breath again, I allow myself shallow breaths inside of the bag. *Holy shit, my breath fucking reeks,* I think. I can't handle it. I remove the bag.

Three more times I try to run out of breath and let myself drift off into nothingness, but I fail. Maybe I don't want to actually die, and my body is preventing me from carrying out this mission that's not meant to be. But this feels better than nothing. There's something a little fascinating about toying with death, and it certainly beats just lying in bed frozen.

I realize that one of two things could happen. One, I could die. I think of who would be impacted by my loss. I know my therapist Jack would be devastated. I think my mother would be heartbroken, but I've only been back in her life for two months, so that doesn't really seem significant enough to keep me alive. I know there are many others who would be saddened to learn of my death, but I don't play a big enough role in their lives for their sadness to linger and for their lives to be impacted enough.

I'm not a priority to anyone, I think and believe wholeheartedly, as I place the bag over my head again. Once more, I need to catch my breath right away, and my breath disgusts me. So I remove the bag, failing again.

Something needs to change. I know I can't do this all day. It's completely unproductive and ineffective. Again I imagine Jack getting the news that I'm dead. I picture him crying in his overstuffed leather chair at the time that I'm supposed to show up for my weekly appointment; he's mourning the person who is supposed to be sitting in the empty overstuffed leather chair across from him, tears streaming down his face. Worse, I imagine Jack finding out that I tried to kill myself without seeking his help first. I can see him unleashing every swear word in his vocabulary, not just out of anger, but also out of love and frustration that I didn't come to him when I needed him most. This prompts me to text him.

"I think I'm in trouble."

I feel bad for disturbing him on a Sunday morning. I imagine myself ruining his family day. But I know this is what he would want me to do. I'm honoring our relationship by reaching out to him.

Only a few minutes later Jack calls me. This alone lets me know that I will be OK. It won't be easy. But now he knows I've hit rock bottom, that what he calls my "trap door" has opened and led me completely into the deepest layers of my abyss. We can only go up from here.

Jack tells me to go to the local emergency room and wants to know how I can get there. I run an inventory of the friends who live in close proximity to me and tell him that I will take a taxi. I ask if I can eat breakfast first. He agrees, but only if I promise to text him when I leave for the hospital. "And if you don't listen to me," he warns, "you're on my shit list!" I crack the first smile of the day and chuckle.

Before heading out I email my relatively new boss that I don't feel well and am heading to the emergency room. Then I leave an out-of-office auto reply on my email and text my main client that I'm sick and heading to the hospital. (She immediately writes back and asks if I'm OK, and I tell her that I had an ovarian cyst rupture. She wishes me well and says to text her if I need anything.) Then I grab a change of clothes, kind of expecting to be admitted at least overnight, and I pack my personal laptop, a book and my doll.

When the taxi drops me off at the Newton-Wellesley Hospital emergency room, I check in and am handed a buzzer, just like the ones that restaurants give out when waiting for a table to open up. Because I'm not in cardiac arrest, I assume I will wait here for several hours. On the TVs set to CNN in the lobby, I see that Philip Seymour Hoffman died earlier this morning. I'm saddened by the loss of such a brilliant and talented artist that has departed the Earth years before his time. I hope that isn't the case with *War Virgin* and that I'm given my chance to contribute my very best to this world. *Which means I need to figure out how I'm going to stay alive.*

My name is called in less than an hour, and I'm taken to the examining room, where a friendly security guard sits outside, ensuring that I don't leave. But I don't feel trapped. This is for my safety, the ER tech explains to me. I'm comforted that people are watching out for me, even if it's simply due to hospital protocol.

A cheerful nurse and then a young, sweet physician examine me. They are kind and treat me with utmost respect. We have intelligible conversations about how I'm feeling, my pertinent medical history and what I'm hoping to gain by being here. We have collaborative interactions. They trust my input, and I trust their guidance. They recommend I admit myself to the psychiatric ward and ask if I'm OK with this. They explain that I will most likely be there for four days, enough time to get acute help and be set up with outpatient resources upon my departure. I agree and sign the papers, legally giving my rights over to them, kind of like the Army, only I know this institution really does have my best interest at heart.

The psychiatric ward reminds me of the West Point barracks. Both places must have hired the same interior designer. Before I'm taken to my room, I hand over my phone, computer, purse and doll. I'm allowed to have some comfort items, but only ones that don't pose a threat to my safety. Chewing gum is allowed, but apparently the Altoids tin can somehow be manipulated into a sharp edge that I could use to cut myself. The staff nurse also asks for my shoelaces. When I answered questions about any previous attempts to hurt myself, I disclosed having tied a shoelace around my neck when I was thirteen. Just in case I'm propelled to do it again, the hospital needs to ensure I don't have the means to do so. But she lets me keep the string in my hoodie, after I promise to not manipulate it. I like my nurse. She's nurturing, rational, funny and doesn't treat me like an idiot.

I'm given a tour of the common areas—the break room with the TV, the nurse's station, the community phones, the art room and library. The nurse tells me I'm welcome to catch the tail end of the Super Bowl if I'd like. Most of the other patients are sleeping in their rooms (I will later learn they are on much stronger medications than I am), but a few are watching the Seattle Seahawks hand the Denver Broncos their asses. I decide to join them before venturing into my room.

When the game is over, I settle in. I have a roommate, someone who appears slightly agitated that she has to share her space. I keep to myself, not wanting to set off someone who is probably dealing with enough mental distress as it is, but I offer her a warm smile. As I'm making my bed with the clean linens I retrieve from the linen closet, she introduces herself and apologizes for being rude initially.

"You don't feel good. No need to apologize." I offer. She appreciates my kindness and explains that she's been here for two weeks, has had a slew of roommates and is supposed to be discharged the next day. I assume she's a lot sicker than I am. My heart aches for her, as I feel her pain.

I climb into bed and under the covers. The plastic mattress and linen thread count of what must be negative 350 are nothing compared to my own grand bed and fancy sheets, but I feel safe. This timeout from life is exactly what I need.

The next morning I meet my assigned inpatient psychiatrist—Dr. Schmidt, who appears to be in his mid-sixties and highly intelligent. He asks if I'm OK with having a medical student from Tufts University shadow him, and I cheerfully agree, saying that I am in full support of learning this way. Dr. Schmidt asks questions similar to that of my initial intake, and I answer them thoroughly and succinctly.

For starters, Dr. Schmidt tells me I've isolated myself too much. He's stating the obvious. I explain that I know this already, I've tried reaching out to friends for help, but no one is ever available or wants to be available. Ever since my divorce, I've stopped hosting parties and initiating get-togethers, and no one wants to pick up the slack, so to speak. Then Dr. Schmidt says something that catches me off guard.

"That's because you're a great actress, Laura."

I'm stunned. He's totally right.

"Laura, you have superior social skills. You're highly intelligent and articulate. Just look at the way you're explaining your medical history and current status with me. You're eloquent. You're engaging. No one would ever think you tried to hurt yourself just yesterday or that you're hurting at all. I wish I could hire you on the spot to run my program at this hospital, I'm so impressed with you."

Suddenly I realize that I've been acting most of my entire life. Even the CEO of my previous job at a consulting firm taught me that consulting is mainly just acting. And while this acting ability has helped me accomplish some impressive feats, maybe they're not the actual feats I should have been yearning for in the first place.

"Wow, you're spot on," I tell him.

"It's time for you to stop acting and start being real. If you want help, you need to genuinely ask for it. I'm also going to prescribe you an antidepressant."

"OK, I'm going to start being more authentic, I promise," I assure him. When he nods, pleased with our progress, I ask which drug he thinks would be best for me.

"I'm leaning toward Celexa."

"Is there a reason for that one specifically? Like why not Prozac?"

"We want a drug that's flexible to work with. Sometimes it's a trial-and-error process, figuring out which one you respond to best. Something like Prozac can take up to six weeks to leave your system, so that's not ideal. We want something that would leave your system the moment you stop taking it. Only Lexapro and Celexa are like that. They're essentially the same. So I just say let's pick Celexa."

"His explanation makes sense to me. It's worth a try. I'm not thrilled I have to go on an SSRI because I worry about weight gain and the loss of sexual functioning. But right now staying alive trumps any ability to have an orgasm.

"We'll start with a low dose and slowly increase it until you're comfortable and functioning well."

Even though I only start with a 5-mg dose, I swear it makes me a little sleepy and feel like I'm mildly stoned. I continue my day, how most days are in the psych ward—attending group sessions where we talk about our emotions, going to lunch, napping, writing, attending more group sessions, having dinner, then sharing movie time. Surprisingly the food is pretty good; there's even gluten free bread so I can eat sandwiches! Groups seem like a waste. Most of the other people are pretty sick and drugged up and not engaging at the same level I want to engage in. A lot of them ask if I'm on faculty and are surprised to learn that I'm a fellow patient. "You seem so happy!" many of them comment.

I start writing an essay I title "Emergency Point of Contact." It makes me realize that for all of my life, despite what difficult circumstances I faced, someone always had my back. The Army does a phenomenal job of generating alert rosters and creating accountability, so whenever you're in trouble, it's someone's duty to make sure you're OK, even if that person's an asshole to you. But now that I'm on my own, divorced in a city without any family, I don't feel like anyone has my back. It's not safe to live this way anymore. At some point, I know I should leave Boston.

That evening my friends Sandra, Kelly and Christine come for a visit and bring me clean clothes. Throughout the day, my friend Sam has been calling me on the community phone. I have barely told anyone about my hospital visit, but I felt it was important to at least let these friends know. The human contact feels incredible. I'm glad the hospital confiscated my phone, so no one can text me. Talking keeps my spirits up, and it's a more authentic way of engaging in a friendship.

Jack visits me the next evening. I feel elated and sad simultaneously, but he assures me that he's not disappointed in me. He's just glad I'm in a safe place and that I am getting better. He says we have our work cut out for us, and I'm comforted knowing he has a plan. I never shy away from work. At our next therapy session, just a few days later, I explain that the thought of devastating him with my death gave me the will to live. I see him holding back tears as I'm sobbing, and he says that he would grieve my loss for years. I know he loves me more than just a patient; I'm a cherished friend. That bond is how his therapy has been so healing for me.

The next morning, I really want to shave my legs. In order to do so, I have to ask a nurse's permission to use a razor, and I need to sign it out on an accountability sheet at the nurse's station. Then I must return it immediately after my shower and sign that it's no longer in my possession. I feel like Piper in *Orange is the New Black*, when she's assigned to the electric shop and needs a screwdriver to complete her work, but must sign for it, for fear that she may use it to escape prison.

I'm ready to leave on my final day. But a part of me will miss being cared for. I meet with a social worker who isn't much help to me. I've asked her to find me a good support group for highly functional people suffering from depression, but she comes up short. I also want her to find some kind of dog agency that can provide me with a cute therapy dog, something I've started to hear more buzz about, but she can't find that either. I feel that I'll be able to accomplish more that she can in her job once I have access to a Google search engine. At least she helps me realize that my canine clock is ticking. I commit to finding a dog shortly after settling back home.

I walk out of the locked ward, through the hospital, to my taxi and head home. I'm out in the land of freedom, and it's surreal. I'm not ready to face the world, my responsibilities and my demons on my own just yet. I check my phone and see that I don't have very many emails or texts from the past four days. Only Colleen was able to guess that something was wrong when I didn't respond to a text, and she called me back in the psych ward.

My mother is en route to Boston. Initially I didn't want to tell her what was going on, but she has made it a habit of Facebook messaging me every day after my father died. My lack of response would freak her out. I can tell that she's happy to have me back in her life, and she wants to do whatever it takes to make it work. So I let her know that I was being hospitalized, but I didn't tell her any details. She was able to ascertain enough.

When she visits, I won't be able to put up a front anymore. I won't be able to pretend like nothing is wrong, like nothing bad ever happened in my childhood, like she can just sweep eleven and a half years of estrangement under the rug. I need for her to acknowledge how bad it was for me growing up. If she doesn't, I'm afraid I can never truly heal.

Prior to my hospitalization, I had sent my mother a Facebook message asking what she thought about my childhood and why she thinks we stopped speaking for all of those years. In her response she said she thought that I had a good and happy childhood, and that our estrangement happened because of misunderstandings, probably because my father lost a lot of money and couldn't afford nice things anymore. I wrote back, saying this was completely inaccurate, and apparently she had a lot to learn. We both agreed it would be best to resolve it later, face-to-face.

I assume she won't want to upset me and bring this up right after leaving the hospital, but a few days into our visit, over breakfast, my mother asks, "So what do we need to talk about?" I'm surprised, but admire her candor.

"Well," I begin, "I know you miss Bill (I'm not ready to refer to him as Daddy), but you need to know how he really was. It's not pretty."

I can tell that my words sting by the way she moves her lips, but doesn't say anything.

"Just tell me, Laura. I want to know." She braces for what I have to say.

"He abused me. He was a horrible father. He didn't respect me or teach me how to respect myself. Most of all, he never loved me unconditionally. His love was based on how perfect I was, and in his eyes, I was never good enough. I'm surprised you don't know this, because he would abuse me right in front of you." I give her a few examples, ones that I've recited to my therapists throughout the years, ones that I've written about in journals and memoir drafts. "I don't want to bombard you with too much." But this is a start.

"I'm so sorry, Laura. I'm so sorry. May God forgive him."

I'm going to need more from my mom for things to be right. But with this initial apology, perhaps my healing can now begin.

CHAPTER THIRTY-SEVEN

In order to properly heal, I realize I should probably overhaul my sex life. I slept with many guys after leaving my husband. I sowed wild oats that I intended to sow after losing my virginity, but didn't because I fell in love with my husband so quickly thereafter. I was chasing a thrill, longing to connect again. I also needed a distraction from my loneliness and heartache. Plus, how can I have the validity to write about love and sex if I've only slept with two men in my life? My number should be much higher. So I launched a quest to increase that number.

My plan didn't go as expected. Most of my sexual encounters have been utterly disappointing. (*For starters, I think we need to start adding Viagra to our water supply and ship some to France, especially for that guy who was supposed to give me a passionate "Eat Pray Love" experience, but instead went limp.*) Besides that, I seem to attract crazy, suffocating men who cling to me out of a need to fulfill their loneliness instead of wanting to authentically connect with me. I'm sick of getting marriage proposals after knowing them for just one week. Being the bad guy and breaking their hearts have taken a heavy toll on my already fragile state. So taking a break from sex isn't actually that big of a deal. Plus, Celexa has destroyed my libido.

While Celexa prevents me from descending into the abyss, it also numbs me. I miss feeling. It also stifles my productivity. My brain doesn't fire as rapidly as it's accustomed to. This is evident in how long it takes me to comprehend anything I read and the loss of my ability to multitask. I can't function as Laura in this state, so I must figure out a way to heal without medication.

I rally my platoon of healers. In Boston, the epicenter of top-notch healthcare providers, it's relatively easy, especially with private insurance and disposable income. I'm grateful I don't have to rely on the VA, and instead, can request specialized doctor's appointments with the ease of an email, portal message or even, in some cases, a text. But before I dive head-first into healing boot camp, it's time to start a family.

The only thing that gets me to smile lately is perusing the Cove Angels breeding website and looking at photos of their doodle puppies. They look like little stuffed animals, and it melts my heart. I'm so ready to bring this ridiculous cuteness and joy into my home. My friend Rhonda, a trained psychiatrist in New York City who knows about my mental health struggles, has an adorable Goldendoodle named Penelope. I fell in love watching Penelope grow up through many Facebook photos. Rhonda recommends the doodle breed for many reasons, especially considering my health and lifestyle. They make ideal emotional support animals, given their temperament and friendliness, and I decide that my new dog will become my service dog in this capacity. I make an appointment to visit the breeder and learn more about a potential adoption. I feel excited and a little nervous.

I'm not sure how the adoption process works and when a new puppy will become available, so I have no idea how this visit will go. While I'm there, Kerry the breeder is doing a training demonstration with a group of puppies that are seven weeks old. She invites me over to the circle and hands me a white ball of fluff. It fidgets in my arms until Kerry teaches me how to hold it firmly to my chest, so it relaxes and simultaneously learns that I'm the leader.

After I get the puppy to settle, it falls asleep, and I start studying it. It has a ridiculously cute round face with a big, black button nose. It feels like I'm holding a favorite childhood toy, and I'm immediately comforted. I picture myself becoming a mother to this precious little creature, and I ask Kerry if this particular puppy is available.

"Yup, no one has claimed her yet."

"Oh good, she's a girl. I thought so but wanted to make sure," I laugh. "Can I play with her for a while?"

"Sure, why don't we all go outside," Kerry suggests to the group.

I watch all of the puppies run around the yard and am overwhelmed by the cuteness overload. I stay close to mine, observing how she interacts with her world. While the other puppies stay close together in a pack, mine is off sniffing nooks and crannies. *She's independent and adventurous, like me.* I keep my eyes glued to her, not wanting to confuse her with any of the other puppies, since they look so similar. I already feel a sense of attachment and responsibility for her. Kerry offers to take pictures of us, and I hold her, kiss her and proudly display her. I imagine us as a family. I want her. My heart is pounding.

"I'm going to ask you what you've decided," Kerry says, "but I think I know the answer."

"Yes, and I want to name her Savannah!"

On March 29, 2014, Savannah—who is actually a Double Doodle (Labradoodle/Goldendoodle mix)—and I begin our lives together. She's twelve weeks old, born the day before my birthday. Two Capricorn soulmates. In our first year together, she amasses more frequent flier miles than most people, accompanying me on trips to St. Thomas, Montreal, San Francisco, Denver, and back and forth between Boston and Tampa multiple times. She's also been to West Point twice and heard President Obama speak at the 2014 graduation. Savannah is such a loving, sweet, fun, fearless, social and sometimes sassy companion. I feel complete with her. I just wish she wasn't so enamored with eating poop. Dog parks with negligent owners can end up serving as an all-you-can-eat buffet. But we're getting it under control. Now we just need to work on her not being so inclined to walk up to strange men in airports and start sniffing their crotches—or at least be more selective and only dive into the testicles of attractive men.

Shortly after becoming a new "mom," I invite my mother to stay with me for the summer, since she's off work then. Initially Jack thinks I should reconsider, but he understands my motivation. I still have a long way to go in my recovery, and I'm sick of being by myself. I also think it would be an ample opportunity for my mother to come to therapy with me. Now that she's back in my life, I need to figure out how to make things work between us. And my way of doing that involves tackling our issues head on. No fooling around and pretending like everything is OK. We need to dredge up the past and work through the most painful parts of my childhood, and it's best to do this with an experienced, professional therapist who can moderate our discussions and facilitate our resolutions. Jack knows my entire story. No one knows me better. Thankfully my mother agrees to start "couple's therapy" with me.

I'm proud of her for exhibiting the courage to come to therapy, but she's nervous as hell. I assure her that she will be in good hands with Jack, but I suggest she pop a Xanax before our first session. I also offer her a glass of wine, but she declines. When we enter Jack's office, he has an extra-overstuffed leather chair ready for her. I can tell he's ecstatic, though he hides it well. After initial introductions, we all sit in our respective chairs, and I announce, "Guess who didn't wait for marriage, and instead, lost their virginity when she was sixteen!"

"LAURA!" my mom yells, mortified but chuckling.

"Well, I think it's an important fact for him to know!" I declare, proud of myself for starting the conversation on my terms.

"Laura always has a flair for the dramatic, doesn't she?" Jack laughs, accustomed to my theatrics.

I start our session by explaining that my mother has already apologized for the past, but she doesn't really know what that past entailed. Jack asks what that means, and my mother says she can't remember anything that happened before 1997, the year I graduated from high school. Not as in amnesia, but her mind was focused elsewhere. She feels bad that my childhood has resulted in my developing PTSD and that my mental health has been so impacted, but in apologizing, she's been going off my word in lieu of being able to draw her own conclusions. I appreciate that, but it's not enough. What's fascinating is that when Jack asks my mom to try and remember anything from my childhood, she lists in fine detail all of my father's illnesses, doctors and prescription medications.

Jack teaches both of us the importance of understanding each other's perspective. He gives us a safe space for me to list some of the most egregious ways my father hurt me, while my mother is able to listen, comprehend and accept. Then Jack allows my mother to talk about how for her entire married life, she lived in fear of my father dying. I understand how manipulative my father was about his health, and that even when he wasn't on his deathbed, he controlled not just my mother's actions, but her thoughts as well.

"But it's still not enough!" I plead. "There are plenty of mothers who witness their husbands abusing and harming their children, and they choose to leave their husbands for the sake of the children. Why couldn't you do that?"

In reality, I know that my mother wasn't capable of being on her own. That she was too brainwashed to even comprehend the existence of abuse, so there is no point in holding her accountable for this negligence. But getting it off my chest and throwing it in her face bring me relief. I know she's sorry, and she's here now to try to make it better. I need to credit her with this milestone.

For the rest of the summer we continue to talk about the past and also seek guidance on how to get along in the present. My mother eases into our weekly therapy routine and actually begins to dominate some of our sessions. Some sessions are joyful. Others are agonizing. Living together in a small space for two months takes its toll on both of us, especially since I work from home, and my mother doesn't venture outside of the house without me. We agree that we need boundaries and a lot more square footage if we want to better enjoy each other's company in the future, but at the very least, it's been a productive summer for resolution and healing. Jack calls us battle buddies. We're proud of ourselves.

Right before returning to Florida, my mother turns sixty. I throw her a birthday party at a Mexican restaurant, where the margaritas flow a plenty. She's a fun drinking buddy. We dance to the Latin band. She's having the time of her life. She's finally free to really start living.

I still need to make more sense of everything, and while Jack's psychoanalytic approach to treatment has helped me understand and accept so much about my life, I yearn for more. Like—WHY? Why did this life happen to me? What's the purpose of suffering so much? How can I be genuinely happy, despite radical external factors that threaten the existence of my happiness? Even the best of theories can't answer these existential questions. Perhaps the answers can only be derived from the supernatural.

I gave up on organized religions, and discriminating philosophies, rules and mandates years ago. I allowed this to pollute my belief in God. But living as an atheist left me hopeless and in too much despair. I think losing faith altogether deteriorated not just my character, but that of my ex-husband too. I don't want to live without believing in anything anymore.

Maura, my energy healer, teaches me about karma. At the beginning of our first visit, before sharing my background with her, Maura closes her eyes and uses her intuitive gifts and ability to read my energy fields and hear angelic guidance to see beyond that of the naked eye. The most prevalent theme that emerges is my "warrior epic."

"You've lived many lives as a warrior," Maura tells me as goose bumps appear on my arms. "You're a very wise old soul who has purposely chosen a difficult life of suffering. But there's a reason for that. Your suffering makes you human and vulnerable and able to empathize with other humans who have suffered. And you take that suffering and transform it into valuable lessons that you use to help heal others. You're very powerful."

I can't help but cry.

"But you're not meant to suffer anymore. It's time to stop sacrificing and start living joyfully."

I feel a pang of hope and a desire for faith. Maura's insight makes sense. But the analytical part of me wants more data, so I venture off to two other energy healers / intuitive readers, and they all see the same thing.

"It's only natural that you would go to war in this life," they all express in their own words.

They also explain that I'm a pioneer who is on a mission to speak the truth, and humor is one of my main tools. "You're like the Chelsea Handler of abuse support groups," a healer named Julie says. I'm blown away. She knows nothing about *War Virgin* when she says this.

Maura and Julie also teach me how to hone in to my own intuition. I have the power within me to connect to the divine, to feel that ultimate source of love and comfort and guidance. I start praying again and attempt to draw from this higher power. I think it's working. I am hopeful. At the same time, I'm comfortable with ambiguity, with not having all of the answers. What's important is that I believe I'm living purposefully and contributing to making the world a better place by being on a path that's uniquely designed for me. And the more I stay connected to this higher power, the more I will attract other souls who are committed to living in the same manner and who will enhance my life with love, support and happiness.

I pray, or more accurately, beg the universe to send me people to help me expand my *War Virgin* platform. I'm more passionate about *War Virgin* than anything else, and I have so many dreams about what I hope to accomplish with it. But I know I can't do this alone. With the right souls, I know that our synergy will take it to the next level.

At a veteran songwriting retreat outside of Albany, I meet a freelance journalist and writer, named Niva. She's there to write a story about the retreat, and I'm impressed with her interest in the veteran narrative. I barely give her a chance to get to know me before I announce, "I'm hiring you to help me finish my book!"

A few months before meeting Niva, I took an advanced memoir-writing class and received valuable feedback on how to expand my manuscript, go deeper and not just be funny and sarcastic. I finished the class knowing that I still had months of work ahead of me and decided that I was sick of going at it alone. Between working from home and still living somewhat isolated in Boston, I don't want to write in solitude anymore. Thankfully Niva agrees to my proposal.

Writing and sharing my story with Niva, who I believe is the world's best listener, has been the bonding experience I've been yearning for. I love hard work. Being able to work with a vested partner is a bonus, especially with someone who is supporting and cheering me on, helping to make the result of that work far better than what I can achieve on my own. My soul is filling with gratitude.

On the same day I meet Niva, my new friend, Lil, tells me that a big venue in Florida has accepted *War Virgin* to perform there. Lil owns a nonprofit theater company in Dunedin, Florida, a progressive, artsy town I can see myself settling in one day. I met Lil after another new friend recommended that we unite our creative forces to augment *War Virgin* and her theater company. Lil has me transform *War Virgin* from a one-woman show into a full-fledged musical play, and she serves as the show director and co-producer. She hasn't asked for a dime and works tirelessly to put *War Virgin* on the Tampa Bay theater map.

(She's a fellow Capricorn with a similar work ethic.) Lil believes in me. My soul fills even more. With Niva and Lil entering my life, I'm finding my new tribe.

Armed with more hope, confidence and life satisfaction, I realize I have a lot at stake to protect. Not just the fruits of my labor and potential for more success, but my very heart and soul. Ever since I returned from Iraq, I identified as a sexually liberated woman, meaning that I can sleep with whoever I want, regardless of what society or religion may say. And while this definition is still valid, I begin to think that sexual liberation means so much more than that.

I've learned to cherish myself as a sacred entity that deserves the very best. I know my background didn't teach me to cherish myself, but my healing journey is repairing that. And now I want to preserve my heart and body for someone who is of like mind, body and soul. I have yet to find that, so I've gone into protective mode. I don't have sex for the sake of having sex anymore. I don't need it. I don't search for it. Now I yearn for intimacy. But until I find someone suited for me with that capacity, I say "No."

In the past, saying, "No" meant repression, and in my attempt to be more liberated, I said, "Yes," even when my heart wasn't truly into it. I am finally learning to say and do what I truly want for myself, and right now, that means saying, "No," and when I say, "No," I feel truly liberated. Ironically I've been celibate for the longest amount of time since losing my virginity.

As for finding someone to share my life with in the future, I accept whatever is in the stars. If I'm meant to be partnered, then I'm going to be really fucking picky and exercise extremely high standards. I deserve that. We all do. And if I'm meant to be single, then I'll just get a new puppy for every year that I'm celibate. With how long I've been holding out—it's almost time to expand my family again! So I'll either have a life full of deep intimacy with another human being or a menagerie of Doodles. You can't go wrong either way. Both paths lead to happy, fulfilling and meaningful lives.

I hope my fellow sister (and brother) warriors also feel liberated and empowered to accept and love themselves for who they are. I hope they feel comfortable in their own skin. I hope they are able to move past the pressure to be perfect, especially the pressures that stemmed from West Point and being in the military.

Currently West Point is making strides with gender equality and integration, and the percentage of women cadets increases every year. But in order to truly offer women (and even men) the ability to reach their fullest potential, it has a long way to go. Success is still portrayed with masculine perfection, calculated behavior, rigid emotions and following a prescribed path that's become obsolete and stifles creativity. Leaders are reluctant to share their most difficult lessons and be authentically vulnerable, fearing that their true selves will be discovered. Impressionable cadets who are coming of age at a crucial time are left to believe they must maintain an unrealistic professional decorum throughout their West Point and Army careers. Denying the essence of their human selves results in long-term psychological damage that they may never be able to overcome.

There are still men who don't want women (or any kind of minority) at West Point. Some of these men are older graduates who make their voices heard via social media or in nasty letters to the academy, threatening to withdraw their financial donations any time progressive, positive change occurs. It's unfortunate that these men have their heads buried back in the olden days, and I feel sorry for their wives and children who have to live amid their prejudice and discrimination. But there is no excuse for the young men who harbor these sentiments. In this day and age, they should know better. Shame on them!

West Point could also improve in other ways to better prepare cadets for the *real* Army, especially in its very definition of success. In the Army, there is no class rank. There is no simple formula or GPA that determines if an Army officer is doing a good job. Often times, it's simply sheer luck that yields a successful Army career. Your boss could be a caring mentor or an insecure narcissist. You have no control over that. The former could make you a shining star; the latter can destroy your life. Until the Army comes up with a better way to prevent the abuse of power and not make success so subjective, West Point needs to be more candid about the real Army and stop sheltering cadets from the very lifestyle in which they will live and lead.

The Army and military at large are trying, though. There are some dramatic improvements in equality for women, racial minorities and the LGBT population, but it's not enough. Even Gloria Steinem agreed to this sentiment when I serendipitously met her in the lobby of a New York City theater and shared a few details about my *War Virgin* platform with her. While I applaud the fact that "Don't Ask, Don't Tell" was *finally* repealed, transgender service members are receiving more support (but sadly still run the risk of a service discharge), women can now serve in combat arms roles, and women are fighting to graduate from Ranger School, I believe the Army has a very flawed approach to equality, especially with women.

The Army's answer to gender integration is to masculinize women. The starkest example that comes to mind is the fact that women candidates at Ranger School must shave their heads. I must ask, "Why?" Why does the successful integration of women into this long-held masculine institution mandate that women must look exactly like men? Sure, it's one thing if the women opt to cut their hair for convenience issues, as regular showers are absent from Ranger School. But why can't women make that decision for themselves? Based on my own experiences with the often chauvinistic men that lead our military, femininity just seems too damn uncomfortable for them. They can't handle serving with women. They declare that femininity has no place in the military and assume it detracts from strength. As a result, most women have felt the need to apologize for our gender at some point in our military careers. Until that stops, gender inequality will prevail.

I believe inequality will prevail with respect to not just gender, but also race, sexual orientation, creed, political affiliation, body size, how masculine or feminine someone is, and even their degree of extroversion or introversion—if the military continues to emphasize uniformity above all else. It's simply asinine to expect over a million officers and soldiers to look and act according to one standard—the white, heterosexual, extroverted, macho, musclebound, conservative Christian, gun-loving man.

Perhaps I knew my days in the Army were numbered because I realized I didn't want to change who I am for an arbitrary standard that simply makes no sense. We don't need this standard to effectively fight wars or protect our country. But many try to change and fit into this standard. Many torture themselves with eating disorders, altering their appearance, pretending to love the opposite sex, and hiding their true selves in futile attempts to have the military love and accept them. Some even commit suicide when that torture becomes too painful to bear.

Hate and abuse will continue to flourish in the military as long as uniformity prevails above respect. The military needs to realize that women (and even men) can simultaneously be feminine and strong. Being an effective warrior does not mean leaving one's God-given characteristics behind. Perhaps when more women and other minorities are genuinely welcomed into the top tiers of military leadership, a paradigm shift can occur, one in which we might exhaust more diplomatic solutions instead of defaulting to war. I don't know about you, but frankly I'm sick of being at war. Killing people and destroying civilizations never resolve anything and only ensure that war is perpetuated in a vicious, never-ending cycle. Many people believe that war is a necessary evil, but if we as a nation and military want to truly establish ourselves as a world leader, then we should strive for peace, and make it our top goal to eradicate war.

I think the best way to sum up my journey of healing is that I've finally allowed my heart to catch up with my head. I have learned how to listen to my heart. I now make decisions based on what my heart wants. I've also learned to truly love myself.

I can't ascribe to the notion of self-sacrifice anymore. It contradicts my ability to love and value myself. I won't allow anyone or anything—family, institutions such as the military, society, religion and government—to make me believe that I need to sacrifice my rights and happiness in order to live a worthy life. I won't allow anyone to make me feel inferior anymore. And I will never let any man dictate how I should look, act, speak, think, behave or regard my place in the world, even if he claims to love me and have my best interest at heart. I love me more!

Genuinely loving myself is the key ingredient to my personal liberation. My own love has set me free. This freedom has nothing to do with notions like celebrating the Fourth of July or fighting terrorism or being the most powerful military in the world. It's simply just being me, and there's no greater feeling. Ironically, it took being at war, under the guise of liberating another country, in order for me to begin the process of liberating myself.

I will never take my newfound freedom for granted. I am compelled to share it with whoever will receive it. Dear readers, my number one wish in sharing my *War Virgin* journey with you is that you'll also learn to love yourself and set yourself free.

EPILOGUE

April 2015
New Port Richey, Florida

"Laura's New York cousins just arrived. Show starts in three minutes!" my stage director, Lil, announces to our cast. We're backstage, tucked away in the break room of the New Port Richey Public Library, next to the large room that's used for plays and other events. It's surreal, being in my hometown, where it all started. I used to do everything possible to avoid this town, but now I don't want to be anywhere else.

There's a packed house waiting to watch my new *War Virgin* musical play. Half of the audience members are related to me. I'm dressed in a flashy costume with heavy stage makeup. In a lot of ways, it feels like the wedding I never had. But when I consciously associate significant events, it feels so much more important. The hospice center where my father died is just a mile and a half down the road. He's one of the main characters in my show. It's evident in today's front-page *Tampa Tribune* article that features a photo from rehearsal—a photo in which my actors are portraying his death scene. My mother is here, armed with a box of tissues.

My condo in Newton is close to being sold. I'm real-estate shopping in Dunedin, my dream utopia town that's coincidentally just thirty minutes south of where I grew up. I've been obsessed with the prospect of moving here for a year, and it's finally coming together. In essence, I'm coming home, but I get to craft what "home" means in my own unique way.

"Oh Say Can You See!" my actress and I belt out, commencing the show with the National Anthem. We're holding the huge American flag that the hospice center presented to my mother when my father died. The audience rises to their feet, hands over hearts and joins us in song. The energy propels me to deliver an incredible show as I take the audience on the journey of my life, narrating and singing, while my cast members act out my favorite scenes. They're praying and dry-humping and marching and fighting and shooting and pondering dilemmas, such as how they're going to go to the bathroom while in combat. There are props of toy rifles, Barbie and Ken, toilet plungers and a bulletproof penis plate. We're all singing and dancing. We exude love and hate and courage and fear and heartbreak and reconciliation and ultimately, forgiveness, all within the span of the ninety-minute performance. Just when the audience thinks they can't laugh any harder, a drag queen emerges… (But you're going to have to watch the show for yourself to find out what they do.)

There's a standing ovation. I ask veterans in attendance to stand and be recognized for their service. Even though I may mock a lot of what I was asked to do in the military, I'm still proud, and I'm proud of them too, and I want to revel in our special bond.

Everyone individually congratulates me and then thanks me for being brave enough to tell the truth. They all find a way that they can personally connect to my story. They are inspired to be true to themselves. They implore me to keep going. I know this is my calling. I am happy and fulfilled traveling this path. My unique path.

My family gathers on stage for a photo, including my beautiful Savannah. *I just nailed my father's memorial service!* I think and laugh to myself. At some point I have openly struggled with most of the family members on stage here, demanding more effort from them in our relationships. I've taken many temporary hiatuses from them. Thankfully now it's improved so much, not because they changed—because I changed. I learned to love and appreciate each of them for who they are and how they impact my life, and to accept them for being human. Even if I'm not a top priority in their lives, that doesn't define me or my importance in the world. I feel supported and grateful to be moving back near them, and I see clearly that they love and cherish me dearly. With this support, I know I will be able to fly higher than I ever could on my own.

When people ask me—knowing what I know now, would I do it all over again; would I go to West Point? Would I serve in the Army? My immediate answer is "FUCK NO!" But the longer answer is that this is my life. This is my story. It is what it is, and I can't change that. But I can take charge of what I do with it. And my God, if someone was meant to have their life portrayed in a crazy musical comedy show—it might as well be me!

AFTERWORD

August 20, 2015
Fort Benning, Georgia

In reference to the West Point Women celebration honoring the first two women Ranger School graduates:

Dear Sisterhood of the Traveling Trou,

As we congregate tomorrow to celebrate this historic win in our decades-long battle for gender equality, I want to caution you of one thing—the tendency for us to worry that we don't measure up. To compare our lives with those of others, and to feel that somehow we just aren't good enough. Whether you make $0 a year or $1,000,000 a year, whether you can still max a PT test or suffer from crippling pain, whether you have a combat patch or never deployed, whether you're happily married with your own squad of offspring or divorced with no kids other than the dog you wish you could claim as a dependent on your tax returns (*me*)—we are all incredibly special and badass. Think about the population of our country. Then think about how many women have graduated from West Point. My math skills took a deep dive in the shitter after being subjected to Plebe Discrete Dynamical Systems, but according to my rough calculations, we are the 0.001258 percent!

We all have our own unique warrior epic. And no matter how different our lives may look than they did when we first began our warrior journeys, we will always be warriors and pioneers and strong and beautiful women who have accomplished feats that most people could never imagine possible.

Clearly we all had to be badasses in high school in order to even want to apply to West Point. Unfortunately, the South Hudson Institute of Technology beat many of us down. The infrastructure that exists to compare us to our classmates, rank us against one another, pigeonhole us into roles outside of our control detracts from the very teamwork, selfless service and camaraderie that we all value. And it made many of us feel like worthless pieces of shit. And many of us still harbor that worry. I know I felt it at my ten-year reunion. I worried I didn't measure up. That I didn't make enough money and that my career was stupid compared to everyone else's. (So I dressed like a total hoochie mama to compensate—but damn I looked good!)

If you're still harboring any resentment regarding any of these sentiments—IT'S TIME TO LET THEM GO! Do whatever you need to do to let it go. If it's therapy—go to therapy. If it's writing a book about your story—write a book. If it's writing a musical comedy show featuring drag queens—bring on the drag queens. If it's getting a service dog—get a service dog! I have employed all of these tactics in my journey toward healing.

But you know what—our sisterhood can and should be our number one source of inspiration, support and healing. And our new Ranger sisters have given us this gift—this amazing opportunity to congregate and celebrate and share and love each other. So accept who you are—because we honor you!

Cheers to you my sisters—the most badass, nurturing leaders I'm so privileged to know and be a part of!

And if any of you indeed make $1,000,000 a year—you better pick up our lunch tab tomorrow! ;-)

I love you all,
Laura, a.k.a. War Virgin

ACKNOWLEDGEMENTS

It takes a village.

As already mentioned in my manuscript, I especially thank Jack Foehl, PhD. for his commitment to my healing. Your friendship helped save my life; you taught me to follow my heart, and the therapeutic work we endured enriched the way my journey unfolded in this very book. My story undoubtedly continues because of you.

Thank you Niva Dorell for helping me to not only complete this book, but also elevate it to a level beyond my imagination. To sum up our collaboration, you helped me birth the representation of my heart and soul. You're not just an editor and cherished friend; you're my doula! I implore others who are compelled to share their stories to reach out to you for guidance and birthing support. I'm eternally grateful that our souls get to navigate the rest of our lives together.

Thank you Andrea Lovett for helping to bring my stories to life on stage. You brought me back to the performing arts and taught me a gratifying and entertaining way to connect with the general public. The show fed the book, which fed the show. I can't imagine one existing without the other.

Thank you Lil Barcaski for making me become a playwright and helping to transform *War Virgin* into the theatrical "experience" it is today. Your tireless devotion to directing and producing our show has been life-changing. I can't even contemplate the trajectory of my life without you in it.

Thank you to everyone who has played a part in performing, hosting and supporting my show in its past, present and future forms. A special thank you to Ann Scott of the New Port Richey Public Library for hosting my show's homecoming, John Robinson and Sharon Robinson for making key connections, and singer/songwriter Wendy Barmore for our beautiful original song.

Thank you to my Boston GrubStreet writing clan for your insight and challenge to dig deeper.

Thank you to all of my business vendors for your extraordinary talents and work, especially my logo graphic designer, Nicolle Renick; copy editor, Valerie Berrios; and photographer, Angel Callahan, who captured the map at the beginning of the book.

Thank you to every reporter and media person who has ever written or produced a story about *War Virgin*. Thank you to my fans. Thank you to my team of healers; keeping me healthy certainly takes a village! Thank you to everyone who has ever believed in me and encouraged me to keep going.

Thank you, Mom, and my four-legged baby Savannah for our unique family of Westley women. Our shopping excursions are among my favorite ways to bond and enjoy life's simple pleasures.

Finally, thank you to my special community in Dunedin for helping me to find and experience what Dorothy taught us in *The Wizard of Oz*: “There’s no place like home.”

CRISIS INFORMATION

War Virgin has the potential to evoke a lot of emotions within you, especially if you can relate to its themes of abuse and oppression. If reading my story has caused you to experience any pain that may be too overwhelming to process on your own, I implore you to find a trustworthy person with whom you can share your feelings.

If at any time you feel that you can benefit from the help of a mental health professional, I encourage you to find one in your area. You can start this process with a simple Google search.

However, if you're undergoing unbearable and debilitating pain that you fear won't end, please seek immediate help. On March 1, 2015, my dear friend Lieutenant Christine Michelle Crocker tragically lost her life to suicide. Every day, twenty-two veterans commit suicide. My wish is that no one else ever attempts to end her or his own life. There are organizations dedicated to protecting our lives and well-being. Please reach out to them if you need or want help.

National Suicide Prevention Lifeline
Call 1-800-273-8255
Available 24 hours, every day

Veteran Crisis Line
Call 1-800-273-8255 and press 1, or
Chat online at VeteransCrisisLine.net, or
Text 838255
Available 24 hours, every day
(Anyone can call on behalf of the veteran.)

AFSP – American Foundation for Suicide Prevention
Afsp.org

You can join a local chapter, donate locally or donate to the national organization. This is a wonderful organization for families who have experienced a suicidal loss or for suicide attempt survivors.

Finally, if you are in a relationship that feels violent or unsafe, I encourage you to use this resource for immediate assistance:

The National Domestic Violence Hotline
Call 1-800-799-SAFE (7233), or
Chat online at TheHotline.org

We are all interconnected as spiritual beings, experiencing the journey of life. Sometimes that journey can be more challenging than what we might be able to bear. Thankfully there are human angels who make it their life's mission to help those in need. Please reach out to one who wants to help you in your time of need. You are loved and supported; you simply need to allow that love and support to enter into your life. I promise it gets better if you believe that it will.

ABOUT THE AUTHOR

Laura Westley is a West Point graduate, former US Army Captain and Iraq War veteran. She is the playwright and lead performer in her musical comedy show, also titled *War Virgin*. Laura's show has been featured in *The Boston Globe* and *The Tampa Tribune*, and she has been published in *The Washington Post* and *The Hill*. Laura is also a veteran mental health advocate who speaks up for veterans and their unique mental health challenges by giving frequent speeches and making radio and television appearances. For more information, please visit WarVirgin.com.

Made in the USA
Columbia, SC
25 April 2018